Get Your A Out of College

Mastering the Hidden Rules of the Game

Revised Edition

Clark McKowen

CRISP PUBLICATIONS, INC.
Menlo Park, California

GET YOUR A OUT OF COLLEGE

Clark McKowen

CREDITS
Managing Editor: **Kathleen Barcos**
Editor: **Carol Henry**
Designer: **ExecuStaff**
Typesetting: **ExecuStaff**
Cover Design: **Carol Harris**

Printed in the United States of America by Bawden Printing Company.

Distribution to the U.S. Trade:

National Book Network, Inc.
4720 Boston Way
Lanham, MD 20706
1-800-462-6420

Library of Congress Catalog
Card Number 95-83229
McKowen, Clark
Get Your A Out of College
ISBN 1-56052-389-1

This book is printed on recyclable paper with soy ink.

For
Kathleen, Tony, Andy, Emily and Patrick
and
their mommies, Patty and Kate

To remind them of the difference between
schooling and education

Contents

CHAPTER 4

Reading Textbooks

CHAPTER 5
Taking Classes and Doing Assignments
203

CHAPTER 6
Controlling School Anxiety
239

CHAPTER 7
Writing for First-Year English
265

Appendices
289

How to Use This Book

Browse ⇨ Focus ⇨ Absorb ⇨ Reinforce

Stress-Free Learning

No ideas in this book will work if approached when you are stressed, anxious, or fearful. See Chapter 6 on Controlling School Anxiety, particularly the section on "Treating Fear as an Ally," for lots of ideas. Some of them can be initiated at the beginning of every learning session, in or out of class.

1. Browse

Approach this book as if it were a love letter, which you

skip, skim and scan

until you get the essentials, right? Do the same with this book. That will get you *formatted*. You have a definite purpose in picking up a book on college skills, so do whatever it takes—and no more—to satisfy that purpose.

Or treat it like your favorite magazine. **Leaf through it** and see if there is anything you want to come back to later on. If you are looking for a particular topic, you might **check the table of contents or the index.** But most good readers of a good magazine (or this book) won't do any concentrated or prolonged reading the first time through—except perhaps a juicy sentence or two that won't wait.

So, the first time through, just mess around for 15 minutes or so. Don't push it. Your intelligent mind knows how to do this. Trust it. Then put the book down and go do something else. Without any conscious effort on your part your brain will be setting up a little *Get-Your-A-Out-of-College program.* Your next encounter will be amazingly easy and ten times more meaningful. Your mind will make sense out of it effortlessly.

2. *Focus*

For immediate information, browse again.

If messing around unearthed something you would like to get to right away—maybe some tips for taking a biology test—go directly to that part of the book and repeat Step 1, but **Browse** only the section you turned to. Remember, treat it like a love letter.

Your mind automatically starts setting up a subprogram for just this material. It seeks out the structure and begins to **Focus**, just like a telescope when you adjust the focal length.

As you **Focus** in on your topic, you will know without effort what has become clear and what needs further tinkering.

For the time being, this session with *Get Your A Out of College* is finished.

3. *Absorb*

For mastery and absorption, browse again.

You will find that **Browsing** and **Focusing** have brought you to the threshold of mastery and absorption already. But check it out:

- See if you can put it in your own words.
- Tell someone else or write it down.

If you can, that means you have *interfaced* between your language and the author's. You have successfully programmed your mental computer.

If anything is still fuzzy, go back and fiddle with that part a while. Look for words in italic, headings, and boxed text.

When you **Browse, Browse, Browse** and **Focus** in, you can feel your mind **Absorb.**

You haven't had to pound anything into your head. The learning atmosphere is *pleasant, productive* and *efficient.* You are using powerful natural learning strategies. They work well for you outside of school; they can work in school just as well.

This procedure works for a whole chapter or a whole book. Just **Browse** the whole thing first and break it into work sessions: what you want to master in one sitting. Then **Browse, Focus, Absorb**. It is painless and even fun, and you will cut down your study time by two-thirds or more.

4. *Reinforce*

Save or lose it all.

Check your results before you shut off your mental computer. This will ensure that *imprinting* does take place. Don't lose it: Without imprinting, nine-tenths of your work is likely to disappear. It is a matter of biology.

But each pass through the target material sets up stronger traces on the brain's neurons. **Reinforcing** saves your work on your internal hard disk.

To **Reinforce,** put the general idea and any important details into your own words. Once it is in your own language, it is *yours*. That is what makes it stick. Go back and touch up anything vague or elusive.

Reinforce or lose it. Most students skip this step and lose most of their work. A minute or two of **Reinforcing** will save nine-tenths of your work.

Browse. Focus. Absorb. Reinforce.

BFAR.

This process works for anything printed or for just about any other human task.

A Look at the School Game

Getting Formatted

The test and commentary in this section will *format* your mind for the philosophy of this book. If you have the time, thinking through these ideas will give you a point of view, or framework, for storing powerful learning strategies.

If you are in a hurry, skip this part. *Browse, Focus, Absorb* and *Reinforce* the rest of the book for what you do want.

But in self-defense, have a look at this section *sometime.*

Taking Tests Without Knowing Anything

Skilled test-takers might get a perfect score on this "test." But test anxiety could interfere. Almost anyone who has been subjected to schooling gets a physical reaction to the word *test,* no matter how insignificant—even a drivers' test, which you always pass and which has been deliberately designed so that even idiots can succeed. Is test anxiety deliberately induced? Consider the following:

> "And you will be tested on this."
>
> "All right, since you won't settle down, get out pencils and paper and we'll have a test."
>
> "Get ready for a spot quiz on your assignment."
>
> > *Fear makes us perform worse, not better. But "catching on" to testing improves scores and turns taking tests into a game.*

Thus, if you already understood this book, you could get a perfect score on this "test" (if *perfect score* means marking it the way the test maker would). You would have browsed already and would know the

The School Game: A Test

Mark only the ideas you agree with. Then read the commentary that follows.

☐ **1.** We learn what is taught.

☐ **2.** Classrooms are good places to learn. Traditional classrooms are the best places to learn.

☐ **3.** Education involves lesson plans, grades, curriculum materials, textbooks, assignments, group-paced activities, prerequisites, competition.

☐ **4.** Knowing a subject well ensures high grades.

☐ **5.** High-school grades, college grades and scores on the SAT are good indicators of adult success as measured by satisfaction in life, leadership, self-acceptance, mention in *Who's Who*.

☐ **6.** A teacher is someone who knows.

☐ **7.** Learning is logical. Learning is sequential.

☐ **8.** More than one person can be taught the same thing at the same time.

☐ **9.** Learning is gathering and storing information.

☐ **10.** Lectures and textbooks are the best means of transmitting information.

☐ **11.** Schools provide tools for school success.

☐ **12.** Schools provide tools for life success.

author's point of view. You would know the *wanted* answers, even if you don't agree with them. Indeed, reflection on just the title of the test would be a tip-off on answers that would please the test maker. If you are test-wise, a preview of the test is a dead giveaway. The statements form a pattern, an atmosphere.

Once you guessed at several answers, you would notice quite a few of the statements are false—from the test maker's point of view. (In the test-taking game, it doesn't matter what your answer would be. If you want a high score, give the answer the test maker would give.)

You might guess that we think all of the statements are false. You would be right—read on.

See Chapter 3 of this book, "Raising Test Scores," for more eye-openers.

Commentary: Myths About Learning

1. We learn what is taught?

There is no guaranteed connection between a teacher's mind and 30 other minds in the same room. Check your own behavior. A serious student with the best intentions finds it impossible to tune in and track incoming information 100 percent of the time. Furthermore, what someone thinks he or she is saying and what a listener hears are never identical.

Consider 30 differently formatted information-processing minds and see the wonderful diversity that must be recognized and welcomed by any good message sender—including teachers.

What is taught is not what is learned. We learn what we do.

Learning is change. When an organism changes, when it can do something it couldn't do before, that is learning. Even if the mind recorded every word uttered in a lecture, unless there is growth and change, nothing whatever has been *learned.*

But we *do* learn *some* things in classrooms: We learn to sit in rows or circles (or learn to rebel against this). We learn punctuality, respect for authority (or to rebel), passivity, inattentiveness, self-doubt, fear, boredom. You can make your own list.

2. *Classrooms are good places to learn things?*

Margaret Mead said her grandmother wanted her to have an education, so she kept her out of school.

From the time you were conceived, how much of your learning has occurred in school? Each of us has learned billions of things: Where and when the sun comes up and what it feels like, the feeling of love, how to walk on two legs, how to tie shoes, what eating is, what excreting is. Of all the infinite numbers of things perfectly embedded in each nervous system, how many of them were learned in school?

Before we were allowed into a classroom, we had already accomplished our most amazing feat: We learned to talk. If learning to talk or to walk required schooling, most of us would still be in remedial classes.

Classrooms are inefficient places to learn, and traditional classrooms are the worst. They ignore and interfere with the natural learning processes we all use instinctively. Many teachers think learning is hard, even painful. It is not.

> *If we are not interfered with, we learn effortlessly. So to master a school subject, find out how you really learn. Then do it on purpose.*

3. *Education involves lesson plans, grades, curriculum materials, textbooks, assignments, group-paced activities, prerequisites, competition?*

Actually, there is no connection between these things and learning. In fact, they are counterproductive. Look at how you did learn all those wonderful things you know and can do, and you will see how stifling school is. The mind hates such straitjackets and refuses to respond.

No two minds can learn at the same time, at the same pace, in the same manner.

Regimented curricula make school subjects needlessly difficult.

4. *Knowing a subject well ensures high grades?*

If two people understand a subject well but only one knows the school game well, you know who will get the higher grade.

Knowing the school game is much better insurance.

Understanding, seeing, growing, changing are a joy. But grades are not awarded for them. Grades are a separate matter with their own rules and must never be confused with education.

What Grading Really Shows

Is grading for the benefit of students? Does it show them what they can do and how well?

There is no connection. The only thing grades show is skill at getting grades. An A student may *also* be good at whatever he or she has been studying, but the two are independent of each other. Having been a student yourself for a number of years, you already know that.

5. *High school grades, college grades, and scores on SAT are good indicators of adult success as measured by satisfaction in life, leadership, self-acceptance, mention in* Who's Who?

Grades do reveal grade-getting skills, and scholastic tests call for similar skills. So SATs and grades do have a connection. But their meaning remains within the closed network of schools.

Grades and tests have no significance once we step outside.

But you already knew that.

6. *A teacher is someone who knows?*

A teacher is someone who knows how to learn and is willing to do it in public.

Students hang around teacher models until they get the knack themselves. Once they can direct their own learning in math, physics, English, painting, *the teacher becomes simply someone who started before they did.* In the midst of an information explosion, it is inappropriate to use teachers as fact pushers.

7. *Learning is logical? Learning is sequential?*

Logic and sequence come *after* we have learned something. A part of the brain, most likely the right hemisphere, is capable of making sense out of information that comes in haphazardly. The information doesn't have to be received logically nor in any systematic sequence. Since there is no conscious way to witness this kind of mental activity, most school systems act as if the major part of our thinking doesn't exist. But the nonconscious processing is tremendously powerful. Only a small part of understanding is stored in linguistic data banks—and if you observe your own thinking, you will see that you use language to nail down and file things you have already discovered.

When the whole brain is allowed to function, schooling is easy.

8. *More than one person can be taught the same thing at the same time?*

Many people can learn at the same time. In fact, we are all learning all the time—but we learn different things. Not even one listener will be learning just what the teacher thinks is being taught. That is the biological nature of unique organisms.

Each mind contains a unique program that picks and chooses among available data and puts bits and pieces together in its own way.

If teachers understood this obvious fact, schooling would be more comfortable for all concerned.

9. *Learning is gathering and storing information?*

Gathering and storing are what reference librarians do—or squirrels. Reference librarians are skilled at both storing and retrieving. But people who squirrel away lots and lots of facts will soon forget where they put 90 percent of them.

Information is learned when it is processed, when it is chewed and digested. We know this has happened when we have grown and changed.

Schools devote most of their time to gathering and storing. Hardly any time is spent on getting new ideas onto the nerve endings.

10. *Lectures and textbooks are the best means of transmitting information?*

If so, then why do most students find them so dull? And if the mind finds the environment stultifying, will it bother to retain what it hears or reads? The mind cannot learn (process) while it is being talked at, and it will not tolerate insipid textbooks. It simply turns off.

Lectures are the least effective teaching devices. Indeed, lecturing and teaching are separate activities.

It is true that some lectures are beautiful and brilliant. Some lectures may be horrible but presented by poetic and brilliant people. I would go out of my way to hear either kind of speech. But the learning would have to be done afterward—by me. When a student makes the mistake of trying to process a lecture while it is going on, it drives the speaker nuts.

"Mr. Johnson, why are you staring off into space?" It is bad etiquette to try to learn while being spoken to.

11. Schools provide tools for school success?

School success depends on memorizing, taking tests, plowing through textbooks efficiently, doing assignments, taking classes, and so on. *In most schools little attention is given to these skills.*

12. Schools provide tools for life success?

There is no relation between schooling and living a successful life. The kid who manages his or her own paper route, lawn mowing, or housecleaning service or becomes absorbed in a meaningful hobby is much more likely to lead a fulfilling adult life than the competitive grade-getter.

> *Even sitting down to dinner with one's family has more correlation with a rich, full adulthood than does anything that happens in schools.*

Introduction

Don't let your school work interfere with your education.

Remarkable Results

Students who use the ideas in *Get Your A Out of College* have remarkable results. Try them. They will work for you, too. Getting high grades is easy and fun. You can really enjoy being in school and you won't waste any time. With the spare time gained, you may even decide to educate yourself—since no one else can do that for you.

In a nurturing environment, all humans seek to clarify the meaning of their experience.

School is a wonderful place for getting an education. Somebody ought to try it sometime. I have spent my life around schools and have had a thoroughly good time. I have met thousands of students brimming with curiosity, enthusiasm, and a love of thinking. And everything one needs is right there: A library, an audio-visual center, peers, mentors, an intellectual environment.

But to use the facilities, one has to set one's own agenda. Rarely is the drive for education allowed expression in classrooms or in student work. For most students, school builds in so many distractions that there is never time to think things through.

Schooling Is Not Education

The problem is that *school* and *education* are not the same thing, although they do sometimes coincide. Education, as every human being knows, throbs in the veins, sets the nerves tingling, peels the eyeballs, sears the intellect and makes the hair stand up on the neck. It is thrilling, frightening and alive. It can happen anywhere.

But, too often, school is plodding through assignments and following rules. It is proper behavior, multiple-guess tests, 500-word themes, teacher monologues, GPAs, padded and poorly written texts, competition.

One hurdle is your grade-point average. Your college knows what this is when you enter, and what it will likely be throughout your stay.[1] A grade-point label is a self-fulfilling prophecy. Most students actually accept someone else's judgment of their abilities and cooperate with the verdict. Anyone who gets less than an A feels like a bit of a failure, not quite good enough. Since most schools allow only about five A's in 100 grades, think of the huge gray cloud of failure hanging over almost every campus. But that judgment is arbitrary. No one can *ever* know enough about you to say what you are or what you may become. That knowledge is inside you, and you have to sit still long enough to discover it. *No one is ever unhappy with his or her own true self.*

It is even more ironic that school is a game you are expected to play without knowing the rules and goals. It preys on unwitting, innocent students who assume the goal is mastery or understanding. But clearly, what is really going on is sorting, ranking, grading and labeling.[2] What else is the massive record-keeping in the registrar's office all about? (An Irish college once answered our registrar's request for a transcript with the apology that it didn't keep such records: it spent all its money on education.)

This labeling can be devastating to students' self-esteem and performance. Nevertheless, everyone goes along with the ranking: friends, parents, graduate schools and employers. Sadly, even the victim goes along. "Oh, I was always a C student." Try to unleash the joy of learning under that burden! No wonder so many adults need therapy.

The rule makers and even most of the players consider this arrangement reasonable and normal. Remember, the school game calls for the failure of 95 percent of the players. Only those testing in the top five percent are considered to have succeeded. The rest to some degree

---

[1] Jennings, Wayne and Nathan, Joe, "Startling/Disturbing Research on School Program Effectiveness," *Phi Delta Kappan*, March 1977.

[2] Ruth, Leo, "Standardized Testing: How to Read the Results," SLATE Steering Committee Newsletter, NCTE/SLATE, Urbana, Illinois.

have not. This arrangement has been accepted decade after decade. The result is that in far too many instances, schools themselves actually cause poor performance.[3] Many peoples of the planet find such abuse of young people barbaric.

Not only do schools build in excessive failure, they don't even expect much will be learned or retained, even by A students. Most teachers know that

> *Ninety percent of what is taught will not be retained beyond the final exam.*

To verify this outrageous face, examine the residue in your own mind. Schools accept these depressing results as part of the game. Most teachers are happy if occasionally they can reach three or four students in a class. How much business would an animal trainer do who had such results?

Reversing the Trend

But surprise, surprise: It is quite possible for 95% of an average group of college students to succeed. Benjamin Bloom and his colleagues at the University of Chicago, for example, designed a game in which 95% did indeed achieve the goals specified.[4] They did it not by watering down the expectations but *by changing the learning atmosphere.* These experiments expect long-term retention not of a mere 10% but of 80% or better.

> *Ninety-five percent of any class can master the subject, with 80% achieving long-term retention.*

Imagine a game in which almost all of the students of French can count on mastering it, students of auto mechanics can become fully capable, and students of calculus have every right to expect proficiency. On

---

3 Cross, K. Patricia, *Beyond the Open Door,* Jossey-Bass, 1971.
4 Bloom, Benjamin, "Learning for Mastery," UCLA-CSEJP, Evaluation Comment, 1, no. 2, 1968.

reflection, it is not at all unreasonable. As John Carroll points out, it is not even necessary to have talent in a field to master it.[5] You don't even have to like it.[6] Anyone who is mentally and physically okay—not great, just okay—can master anything he or she feels like trying, be it painting, music, gymnastics, whatever.

Why haven't schools rushed to adopt these practices? Because *mastery and achievement simply are not the purposes of schooling.* It is abundantly evident that sorting and ranking *are* the purpose. How could we tell a B student from a D student? What would employers and graduate schools think of us if we sent them nothing but A students?

You yourself may be so used to ranking and competition that a school in which everyone is successful is hard to envision. Even though that is quite possible, it is not likely to happen. It would take a miracle for these massive institutions to change their ways. Meanwhile, if you know how the school game really works, you have an inside track. Once you know the hidden goals and learn to play the real game, getting A's will be far easier than you might think.

Although you may not now be aware of them,

You already have all the skills it takes to get A's.

But schooling is a game; education is not. And the school game, like any other, has boundaries, scoring systems, penalties, and performance rewards. To try to participate in a poker game year after year without being conscious of how to play it is touchingly naive—and expensive.

School is a game, education is not. Understanding that simple distinction can profoundly affect school success—and affect it immediately. This book will show you how to apply your natural intelligence to school. You will use what you already know and perform brilliantly on tests, cut through textbook slush, memorize, and keep the knots out of your stomach. If you have already caught on, this book will help you refine your skills.

---

[5] Carroll, John B., "A Model of School Learning," *Teachers College Record*, 64, 1963.

[6] Carroll, John B., "Problems of Measurement Related to the Concept of Learning for Mastery," *Educational Horizons*, 48, no. 3, 1970.

What every student needs to learn is how to learn.

School is a wonderful place to get an education. By getting familiar with the ideas of this book, you will gain the time and peace of mind to start.

Dancing
particles of light
disguised
as
dust motes

CHAPTER

1

The Tao: Trying Without Trying

The Art of Effortless and Delightful Learning

"To know plum blossoms,
one's own nose
and heart."
—Onitsura

Do You Have What It Takes?

Mark only the statements you agree with. Then read the commentary.

- ☐ **1.** It takes brains to get high grades in college.
- ☐ **2.** Learning skills are developed through rigorous discipline.
- ☐ **3.** Some subjects are just plain difficult.
- ☐ **4.** Students who study hard get the best grades.
- ☐ **5.** Being told exactly what to do makes learning exciting.
- ☐ **6.** Learning is an orderly, sequential process.
- ☐ **7.** We can't change how we feel about a school subject.
- ☐ **8.** We learn better when we are tested regularly.
- ☐ **9.** We learn better when there is competition.
- ☐ **10.** Rewards from teachers are the best incentives for learning.

Commentary: You're In Charge

In Wonderland everything is upside-down. So in most schools the statements in the preceding test seem perfectly reasonable. But only a masochist would set sail under *that* charter. The truth is that you have all the brains you need to get top grades. You don't have to be tricked into using them, nor threatened or shamed. You have already used your brains to do things far more difficult than anything schools have ever dreamed up.

> *You are in charge of your own schooling. You already know how to set up your learning so that it will be effortless and efficient.*

This chapter will remind you of how you *do* learn and of how *well* you learn, and of how effortless and delightful it feels when you put yourself in charge of your own learning.

> ### *Looks Who's in Charge*
>
> - **You are an expert learner already.**
> - **You can take charge of your own learning.**
> - **You know how to learn effortlessly and efficiently.**
> - **You can make your learning pleasant and free of stress.**

You will know all you need from this chapter when you realize *you are in charge* and when you are conscious of your own way of learning. If somewhere along the way you misplaced your trust and confidence in your learning ability, take the first steps now toward recovering them.

It doesn't take brains to get high grades in college. It isn't low brain power that holds people back; it is the lack of self-esteem to kick into gear. Your brain works just fine, and this subject wouldn't even come up if someone hadn't persuaded you to doubt your abilities. Even with brain damage, you would probably have more grey cells than you would ever need to perform brilliantly in college. Congratulations.

A Most Extraordinary Learning Machine

You *are* an expert learner. Lots of people may have tried to convince you that you are not. But look at the evidence. Look at what you have accomplished since you emerged from your mother's womb. For one thing, you figured out your native language. You did it all by yourself. You internalized a program of such complexity that *no one* knows consciously just how it works. Even though they already used language fluently, your parents could not have taught it to you even if they had tried. They wouldn't have known where to start. Nor would anyone else. Schools won't even let kids into kindergarten until they have already mastered language and can go to the toilet by themselves.

By age two, you broke the code of language, a feat far more demanding than any rinky-dink school puzzle.

Make yourself feel great; make a list of all the things you programmed into yourself outside of classrooms. How many subprograms do you suppose you had to figure out just to put one foot in front of the other? Or even to pick up a fork?

You have about three pounds of greyish-yellow wetware in your skull that make you the most extraordinary learning machine we have been able to discover anywhere in our solar system. We do not know how or why. From one point of view it is a miracle. From another, it is just natural. This is certain: You have it and you know perfectly well how to use it. Your dog has its own computer, too—a different brand from yours, but equally miraculous. Then there are whales, spiders, viruses, and algae. Every living thing comes equipped with a genetic code that enables it to fulfill its own nature.

You have more brains than you know what to do with.

Your Wetware

Here is what you have going for you. You came equipped with three computers inside your head.

The Hind Brain

Your most primitive computer sits atop your spinal column. It takes care of self-preservation and survival and probably stores material from forgotten ancestors, tribal lore, and so on. This computer is always on, and you can turn your whole organism over to its care anytime it is necessary.

The Midbrain

This computer caps the hind brain like a toadstool. It is the brain that generates, among other things, feelings and emotions: fighting, feeding, fleeing and sexual activity. It is also called the *old mammal brain* since it works similarly to the computer in most of the other breast-feeding, warm-blooded animals. It is your black-and-white TV. When you need to, you can turn everything over to this computer, as when a 98 pound mother can lift a car off her child, moving directly from *feeling* to *action.*

The New Brain

This is the part with all the wrinkles, the outer layer or cortex. The spread-out surface would fill a three-foot square. Actually, it functions more like *two* computers. It is split fore and aft but has a network of more than 20 million paths connecting the two sides. The left side in most humans is our color TV, but the right, ah, the right. We don't have any man-made computer like that yet! It works more like laser holography. It is tremendously swift and powerful, but most of us don't even suspect its existence—and for a good reason. It has its own way of communicating, and *not* in words.

The left brain has a wetware chip that comes formatted for language, and babies program into it whatever language is being used around them. Since almost all the thinking we are aware of is closely linked with language, people think that part of the mind is all there is.[1] But it is just the tip of the iceberg. Only in the past few decades have we begun to fathom how this supercomputer works.

Nevertheless, if we keep in mind that research on the wiring is in its infancy, we *can* make a model for the functions of each hemisphere. We can surmise the necessary commands for mastering the school game.

---

[1] *Brain* is the physical machine, and *mind* is the nonphysical thing it is doing. In Washington D.C., if you look for the government, you won't be able to see it—even though it is going on all over the place.

The Order-Seeking Left Hemisphere

We know that the left hemisphere in most people has that small computer chip that encodes thoughts in electrochemical patterns, which in turn stand for the sequential sound patterns of speech. In other words, it contains our *language program* (with plenty of feedback from our other computers).[2]

Some of this activity we can bring up on our mental screen, enabling us to do some deliberate adjusting at the keyboard. By means of our conscious minds,

> *We can format the computer(s) for whatever new program we need.*

This "logical" side of our new brain is *systematic,* conscious of time and sequence. One thing leads to another. It *analyzes* step by step, part by part. It draws conclusions based on facts. It describes, defines, counts.

The Structure-Seeking Right Hemisphere

Even though it is the most advanced, this is the computer that is virtually ignored in schools. The left brain takes things one at a time. The right brain takes things in as a bunch. That is, it sees overall patterns and thus appears to solve problems all at once—if not all at once, certainly with lightning speed, making leaps of insight. It's the "Aha!" illumination we all know. This computer gets on perfectly with sloppy, incomplete, or even "wrong" data, and it works happily with *hunches* and *feelings.*

The right brain also uses words, but much differently from our language computer, and words are only part of its raw material. It has almost no use for sentence structure or sequential thought. It is not "reasonable" at all. It works *holistically* (as a whole, all at once).

---

[2] To disallow or ignore the input of messages from other areas of the brain—survival, emotive, and metaphoric—would severely limit the smooth functioning of the left hemisphere. They all contribute to what ultimately prints out as "logical."

This right hemisphere operates metaphorically, as well. It sees one thing as if it were another—or lots of others. For the word *mother* it has immediate access to all the associations you ever made or could make, consciously or nonconsciously, with that concept. The conscious part is sometimes shocked or delighted at the connections the right hemisphere hands over. This nonconscious brain can take a new image (say, a chemistry concept) and scan the data bank for a similar pattern, even though "logically" the two might come from quite separate realms of experience.

This holographic computer is also *visual* and *spatial*. It has no sense of time; everything is *now*. It is nonjudging and amoral. It has no sense of decency. It is play oriented rather than work oriented, and *it has no use for external rules of order.*

> *We must allow our nonconscious right brain to operate according to its nature, or we will frustrate a powerful part of our learning machine.*

Acting Stupid

Attempting to think with only the conscious, logical mind is self-abuse.

The Wiring

These three, actually four, computers are designed to work together. Just how they interface is not well understood. By they are not isolated from one another, and in the new brain one hemisphere has sometimes been found to compensate for a damaged chip in the other. In some people the functions of the hemispheres are reversed. The point is this:

There is a harmonious network of brain cells clustered behind your eyes. The network has done wonderful things for you already. In your studies it can perform remarkable feats of learning for you—if you give it permission. We don't know really how all this works, but we do know if we give this awesome computer network a few simple commands, it will do the job cheerfully and effortlessly. In fact, after a good session, you will feel refreshed rather than fatigued.

Your mental computers have their specialties, and once upon a time you shifted confidently among them as naturally as a tree grows leaves.

Of Discipline, Difficult Subjects, and Hard Work

Conventional wisdom, as usual, is dead wrong about discipline.

> *Discipline, true discipline, the only kind that really works, is internal and does not feel like discipline at all.* Intense play *is a more apt description.*

Nor is it true that some subjects, by their very nature, are difficult. If you are motivated and lucky enough to be in a nurturing environment, you are perfectly capable of learning anything any human being ever thought. There is always a way to connect the programs in your head with those in any other head. It is simply a matter of *interfacing.*

Studying hard does not do it, either. It simply makes you tired, fuzzy, and grouchy. To get your operating system *formatted* and ready to *interface, mess around.* The puritan work ethic might get one to heaven but it will feel like hell. Messing around may seem frivolous, but it is the most direct route to understanding.

To experience the joy of learning, mess around.

The Way: Natural Learning

If you *go with nature* instead of fighting it, you can get all your computers on line and freely receiving data. The following pages describe this natural process.

1. *Format*

For any new task, your mind is going to set up a new program, but it will not do that until you give it a chance to create a structure, or *format,* to store it in. First the mind has to look things over. We don't usually create the structure consciously—the brain is designed to do that for us. After the mind has played with the new task for a while (with the left brain's blessings), we realize a suitable framework for the new program, be it physics, soccer, or philosophy. So,

First, look the job over.

The more we relax and let what needs to be done *come to us,* the better. The logical conscious mind can weed out unproductive messages cluttering the program. The left hemisphere can monitor the process and make sure the hind brain, midbrain and right hemisphere are heeded. The mind is most efficient when all are in harmony.

If we get serious, the right hemisphere will not cooperate. When the conscious mind gets the message that it is time to be playful, it has to know messing around is "reasonable" behavior. The rational mind is puritanical, but if it knows there will be a chance to put the messiness in order later it will be willing to wait.

It is natural to look things over at first in a relaxed way—without forcing any predetermined structure onto the task. Just run your mental hands over the task and trust the mind to deliver a suitable format. The mind will always do this if you treat it with respect. When we try pushing the nonconscious mind around, we are in trouble. Most problems in school come from trying to force the powerful hidden mind to obey the "will" of the limited left hemisphere. When each is allowed to do what it does best, harmony will prevail.

The first run-through will not be straightforward or systematic and may seem haphazard. But you will find that your next pass through the task is ten times clearer, and there will be no laborious huffing and puffing. Observe any good mechanic or musician and you will see the same effortless process.

Think of this first step as an *advanced organizer* or *formatting* or *getting ready* or *laying out the work* or *previewing.* Pick your own term. The key is the manner in which you go about it.

The first step must be playful and stress free.

It doesn't have to be done in one sitting. It can be, and likely will be, a series of swoops and passes.

2. *Interface*

Any truly new task, skill or understanding will not make sense at first.

Learning is translating the target material into your own frame of reference.

Learning is finding a bridge between some other program and one's own. But it is the nature of the mind to know exactly how to go about it. Once we have made a couple of passes through the target material, we have a pretty good idea of what we are getting into and of what translates fast and what needs more attention. In other words, we have laid out the job. Realization of this process leads to effortless *translating* or *interfacing.*

In the conscious mind is a partial picture of the new task or concept. Some of it is filled in, some not.

Put the fuzzy section on your mental screen and tinker with it until it comes into focus.

You will feel your computer searching your data bank for something similar. You will be offered a selection of possibilities. One of them will click, or none will. If nothing really fits, that just means another file will have to be searched. It is certain that no human program is so remote or different that a bridge cannot be found to your own mind. That may be true of whales, maybe, but not humans.

All human wetware is compatible. So if the fuzzy section of the target material remains obscure, it is time to back off and play around with some other part. The strategy is like filling in a crossword puzzle. Sometimes we review what we have already figured out and sometimes we go on to new material. Meanwhile, the right brain hasn't forgotten the obscure screen. The nonconscious mind continues searching the files for a match, but we are not conscious of this activity. In fact, the right brain would rather you did something else. It doesn't like being watched.

After some time elsewhere, have another look at the trouble spot. *You will be delighted at how often the problem solves itself.* If the problem doesn't clear up on its own, it may be time to go play baseball or go to bed. Such apparent nonchalance will not be a waste of time. Your mind will still be working on the problem. More often than not, when you look again, you will say, "Oh, so that's it!"

This is the natural way of learning, and you've done it innumerable times already as you grew and changed. Remember learning to swim or ride a bike, how hard it *seemed,* how easy it *was*? Learning a new language, driving a car, tying your shoes, typing, using a computer, frying eggs—remember the formatting, the final effortless ease?

Learning does not begin at the beginning. Learning can start anywhere and can go in any direction, back and forth, in short spurts or in long periods of effortless concentration. The orderly, sequential descriptions of chemistry or math concepts, of economics or art history, are constructed by thinkers *after* they have gone through the messy but delightful process described above.

The Joy of Learning

Turn on your computer.

In most schooling, a missing ingredient is what the whole process is about: JOY, the pleasure of finding things out. Mammal "computers" are turned on by feelings. There has to be strong feeling or desire and the promise of a payoff of pleasure.

Interfacing with a new concept has to be something you want to do. The conscious mind cannot force you to be fascinated. Beating yourself will not help. And fear of low grades just leads to neurosis. But if the desire is already there, then the process will be automatic. You will feel great.

If the curiosity isn't there to begin with—and with assignments from other people this is usually the case—you can deliberately set the stage by *going through the formatting and interfacing process anyway.* In other words, *imitate the natural learning approach.* At some point the midbrain will boot up the system, the computer will take over on its own, and you can relax and enjoy the ride.

In order to use this artificial approach, it helps to know how trying without trying can get the machine going. Our instincts tells us that real learning will not start until the mind is working on its own without prompting. So in this case, the fooling around is to

Find an angle that is naturally intriguing to the mind.

There is a vital connection between what is in your own data bank and everything else in the universe. From some point of view one can be fascinated by *anything.* Remind yourself of that when you start any study session. Your mind will be looking for a way to have fun with the material. At some point you will feel the whole organism come together as one thinking machine. That is the state of mind to cultivate. Once the computer is "on," the learning will take care of itself.

One sure way to know the right hemisphere is turned on is that *time seems suspended.* You can sit for hours and it seems like an instant. When you do stop, you do not feel tired. In fact, you feel refreshed. We all know this feeling. You had this experience as a preschool child. Perhaps you have been lucky enough to enjoy it as an adult. If you know what it feels like to think automatically, you can simulate the proper conditions.

That is what is meant by *trying without trying.* We cannot force the brain to gear up to this level of thinking, but we can set the stage.

Once the process becomes a habit, the mind will kick in its "laser component" routinely.

> ***Joy, the pleasure of finding things out, is central to the learning process.***

The approach suggested in this book will ensure that joy is always present in your studies. We can grant our spirits permission to flourish. We can change how we feel. Control comes not from will power or force, but from paying attention to the demands of the spirit and making sure that we do not interfere with its signals. *Control is letting nature prevail, not beating it into submission.*

3. *Store*

At some point you will have set up a structure for what you want to get into your computer, and you will have translated it into your own unique language. You know you are at that place when it makes sense to you. Notice that what "makes sense" means, literally: You have it on your senses, on your nerve endings. There is no longer a separation between you and the target material. It has become part of what you are. *You and the target material are one.*

This is the goal of any new learning. You know you are there when you can talk about it in your own language or can *do* it, as in riding a bike or typing. If the process described for getting there *makes sense* to you, you know that there is a natural way of going about it and that the way is actually pleasant, even exciting.

When you are that far along, you understand and you feel good. The learning session is complete . . . almost. I am typing this on a WordPerfect word-processing program. If I do not want to lose everything I have done so far, I have to punch certain keys before I exit the program: I have to *save.* This guarantees my work is stored or filed and I can get it back. It is the same with the mental computer. The program is there, but the traces are faint. The imprint has to be protected from fading.

> *If you walk away without reinforcing, you will lose 90 percent of your work.*

When you think you have finished and are ready for a break, do a quick check.

> *See if you can say, in your own words, what you have just learned.*

You can tell it to someone else or you can write it down, in which case it can be as brief as you want.

This accomplishes two things at once: You get a chance to see if you do indeed understand, and at the same time you start pressing those traces permanently into your neurons. This step does have to be in your own words, of course, because until the translation is accomplished, you really have not interfaced.

You have to be able to say it or do it. If you cannot rephrase some part of the material, go back and touch up that part—*before* you take your break. It is much easier to clear up a misunderstanding while still in a study session than to try to unlearn the error later on.

> *Never consider a session complete without first reinforcing.*

If you don't "save before exiting," you will have to redo a lot of your work and waste valuable time when you start up the program again. A few minutes at the end of a session will store your material and avoid needless effort trying to retrieve what you studied. Reinforcing is a simple but powerful final step.

Effortless Effort

> *Natural learning involves* getting ready, doing something *and then* checking it out. *We could also call it* formatting, interfacing, *and* storing.

The process of natural learning is described in three parts to give you a conscious idea of how it works, but of course, it is much messier in practice. Learning is actually one harmonious activity. It really does not feel like one, two, three. We move forward, sometimes backtrack, hang around one spot a while, review, check over the whole thing, go back over a part again, and so on.

Learning is more like a blueprint that gets filled in more and more completely until you end up with a solid, three-dimensional house. In a sense, the house is complete with the first pass-through, but the outline is faint and only vaguely perceived. Increasing absorption of the material, and the natural pleasure in finding things out (the joy of learning) will guide the interaction, the play, until the process is complete.

This chapter simply reminds you of how you always learn. You have used the method all your life but—if you are like most people—without being conscious of it. The one place where most people do *not* use their natural learning power is in school. Most educators act as if all learning is left-brained, conscious and logical. But trying to learn in a left-brain straitjacket is limiting and ineffectual.

Emphasizing the wrong hemisphere makes drudgery and hard work what human beings were born to do, love to do and can do brilliantly. You don't have to accept such limitations. You are in charge of your computer; you know it better than anyone else.

In school you are free to do whatever works.

If your natural way is 100 percent more efficient than methods used in schools, why not use it?

You will see as you go though *Get Your A Out of College* that test taking, memorizing, doing assignments—anything you have to do in school—can be reduced to the process described here:

Format

Interface

Store

This book is patterned after the *natural way of learning*. This first chapter is a way of *formatting* your computer, making it easy for you to *interface* with each new concept. Each chapter is a subprogram that contains all the elements of the process, including review and *reinforcement*. Each chapter has an advance organizer to help set up your mental program for easy *absorption.*

Main sections are headlined, and key ideas are highlighted with key icons, check icons, and with words emphasized in italic. So each chapter is also a chance to practice the process. By the time you interface with the whole book, you will be a skilled and efficient student if you aren't already, and an expert grade-getter as well.

To reinforce this chapter, try telling someone all about it or jot it down. Does the following version come close to yours?

The Tao of Learning

Get ready. Do something. Check it out.

Look the job over.

When relaxed and comfortable, take a brief, playful look through the material. Don't decide in advance what to look for. Let the material itself be your guide. If you start to feel anxious, set the task aside and come back to it at some predetermined time. Repeat this step as needed until you have a clear picture of what does and doesn't need to be done—a *format* for complete understanding.

Put the concept, task or skill into your own terms.

This is really an extension of the first step. Continue playing with the new concept, spending as much time with subsections as needed. At some point the target material will be in your own computer and in your own language. As you continue a playful examination of the task, you are already *absorbing* the concept or skill. You have *translated* it into your own language or, in computer terminology, *interfaced* between two programs, yours and the message sender's.

Don't forget joy.

The learning machine won't even start up without a *motive*—instructions from your midbrain, the feeling center that activates the whole system and keeps it fired up. If learning starts to feel like something you *have* to do and not something you *want* to do, stop and do something else or try another approach.

Compare your file with the original.

Yours will be in your own language, but the two should match up with no glitches. If any part is still unclear, play some more with that and then check out the whole thing again. To verify your version, tell it to someone or jot it down. If it works and you feel good about it, take a break. The session is complete.

If you don't *reinforce* or *review* at the end of the session, you will lose 90 percent of your understanding overnight.

> *The three parts of this natural way of learning are in reality one* **interactive seamless activity,** *a series of passes through the target material, producing at some point a permanent imprint on the nerve endings of the learner.*

The Hidden Rules of the Game

The remaining chapters of this book apply the natural learning process to school subjects. Most students think school subjects are mathematics, electronics, English, history. They are not.

> *School subjects are memorizing, reading textbooks, taking tests, doing assignments, handling stress.*

These activities are what really make up the structure of schooling. They are what is learned or not learned. If you master them, you can actually enjoy your school days.

All academic disciplines can indeed be fascinating. But to gain access to them, you need to know how to master the *hidden* school subjects.

Familiarity with *Get Your A Out of College* will show you how.

CHAPTER

2

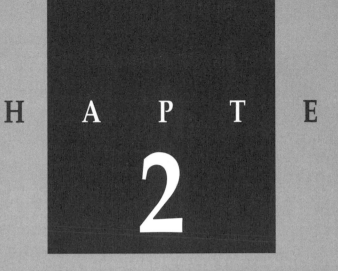

The Art of Remembering

Natural Memorizing and Remembering Processes

"There is nothing you have to do.
Let the flesh know.
Let the heart recognize.
Let the bones remember.
Your job is to be awake.
Travel light."
—*The Mullah*

Natural Memorizing

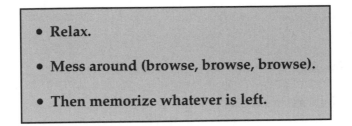

- **Relax.**
- **Mess around (browse, browse, browse).**
- **Then memorize whatever is left.**

We memorize constantly and effortlessly. We relax and mess around. That's it.

Relax

Play background music.

Try the largo (slow) movements from classical music pieces (Bach, Corelli, Handel, Telemann, Vivaldi).

Quiet the body and mind.

Take a half-speed walk, one pace per second.

Or shut your eyes and pay attention to your body, starting with your toes.

Or imagine yourself in a pool of red color, and let it change color, working through the spectrum: ROY G. BIV (Red, Orange, Yellow, Green, Blue, Indigo, Violet)

Mess Around

Browse. Browse. Browse.

Format your mind by playing with the material. Trust the nonconscious to do the programming.

Memorize

Relax. Mess around. Memorize.

Memory Inventory

Mark only the ideas you agree with. Then read the commentary that follows.

- ☐ **1.** Intelligent people have better memories.
- ☐ **2.** Memorizing requires effort and discipline.
- ☐ **3.** Memorizing is a logical, step-by-step process.
- ☐ **4.** Adults have better memory techniques than children.
- ☐ **5.** Memorizing must be conscious and purposeful.
- ☐ **6.** In most grading systems, memory skill is not graded.
- ☐ **7.** More time spent studying will result in more that is remembered.
- ☐ **8.** A good way to memorize something is to say it over and over.
- ☐ **9.** Memorizing should be vigorous and aggressive, not laid back and random.
- ☐ **10.** Some subjects are harder to memorize than others.

Commentary: What Is Memorizing, Really?

The ten statements in the Memory Inventory are commonly held beliefs. But, as you might guess, none of them is true, and acting as if they were will only interfere with your efforts to memorize. Your own experience will bear out this assertion. The following comments, as well, may not surprise you.

1. *Intelligent people have better memories?*

Think of the huge amounts of data any organism stores routinely. Then think of the amount even a brain-damaged human has available among all those neurons and synapses. A typical human brain stores billions of bits of information. The extra data a flashy "memory entertainer" can display are insignificant compared to the total that *any* human brain contains. *Everyone's memory bank is about the same size.* You yourself have done a brilliant job of storing masses of data—without breaking a sweat.

From birth, you began processing information and fitting it into interconnecting networks of meaning. By the time you were 2, you had broken the language code, a system so complex even the best linguists have not yet been able to describe it. If you smoothed out all the wrinkles in your brain, you would have a three-foot-square computer grid, infinitely better than the smartest microchip. Regardless of how intelligent or unintelligent you may think you are, you are far too smart to be floored by the trivial amount of information you may be asked to store while in school.

Not only have you already stored vast amounts of data, you retrieve and use what you need effortlessly. Imagine what is involved just to read this sentence. *Your body is designed to use its memory banks automatically.* Without interference from anyone, it knew from birth exactly what to do and how.

Unquestionably, you do have an excellent memory and substantial capacity to retrieve and use what you have stored. Strangely, schools have set up unnatural learning situations that make it seem to many students that remembering is impossible, or that some subjects are much more difficult than others. Once you recognize and remove those barriers, you can learn any new subject as easily as you have mastered just about everything else in life.

Even people who *are* "intelligent" don't have "better" memories.

Intelligence

If you are reading this page, you are perfectly capable of achieving any GPA you want. Under the right circumstances people can do anything they need to do: walk a tightrope, climb a mountain, run a VCR, sing at Carnegie Hall. If there is such a thing as higher intelligence—and the definition of intelligence is up for grabs—it doesn't seem to have much to do with getting things done.

> ***Will and need and circumstance are much more powerful than intelligence.***

Intelligence might well be pictured as a pie, each human being having his or her own unique slice. Although we have much in common, each of us processes information in our own way, from our own unique aspect of the continuum.

So-called mentally retarded individuals have a special window on the world, as each of us does. Our different mind-sets are our special strengths. *When people use their natural traits, they can do amazing things.*

2. *Memorizing requires effort and discipline?*

Take a look at all the things you know—150,000 words or more, automatic use of your native language, and complex skills like walking, tying your shoes, using eating utensils. Virtually everything you truly know was learned in a comfortable, effortless way. You didn't torture yourself, and you didn't get up at 5:00 a.m. to study or lose valuable sleep poring bleary-eyed over mountains of data. Clearly, the best memory techniques are nothing like the puritan methods almost universally recommended and practiced in schools. Memorizing is a natural biological process—if it's not interfered with it. No one knows how this imprinting on your memory circuits is accomplished, but a nonconscious part of the mental computer *does* know and does it routinely, unless you or well-meaning teachers gum up the works.

But there *are* things you can do to help set these processes in motion—the actual work will be done without conscious awareness. This chapter will remind you of the conditions under which you do learn well. You can actually have a good time doing schoolwork and even feel refreshed after a couple of hours at your desk.

3. *Memorizing is a logical, step-by-step process?*

The part of one's brain assigned to language patterns (the conscious part, which includes all logical and systematic processes) is a wetware chip about the size of a book of matches. It is the part we are somewhat aware of. It performs valuable services. It is our automatic talking machine. We can use it to check and verify the results of our thinking. We can use it to boot up or start the learning or memorizing programs in the nonconscious part of our brains. However, once we turn over the data to the nonconscious, the rest is automatic and we can go do something else.

We have no certainty of what goes on during learning or memorizing, but whatever it is, it seems to be anything but logical and systematic. It appears to start in the middle, jump around, go off in tangents, move back and forth between parts of the whole picture. In the end, we get a completed printout that we can *describe* logically and systematically.

4. *Adults have better memory techniques than children?*

Unless they are reminded of how they really learn, most adults try to do all their learning and remembering in their conscious minds. That is not how they did it when they were children. Kids have complete confidence in their computers and don't interfere with the excellent learning machinery they were born with. The one thing an adult can do that children cannot is to be aware of how this process works and *set it in motion deliberately.*

5. *Memorizing must be conscious and purposeful?*

Once the process of learning is started, it is best to take cues from the nonconscious. *If you do, your behavior will not seem very sensible.* You may experience periods of intense scrutiny with abrupt changes of direction, crazy word games, going on in illogical directions, circling, resting, doing something else entirely, sleeping on it. If you trust your wetware, the way a child does, you will always do the right thing—and it will be more efficient than any artificial study method you try. The more you trust your wetware, the better you get at it.

6. *In most grading systems, memory skill is not graded?*

On the contrary, it is almost the only thing that *is* graded. Grading for most courses is based on tests. Whether in short answers or essays, students are asked to remember or recall data. Even if teachers were interested in what a student understands or can do that he or she couldn't do before, few teachers know of any reliable ways to find that out. So they resort to checking *quantities* of stored data.

Learning is growth and change. Considerable quantities of data are accumulated along the way—but not necessarily the data that the teacher would find interesting or useful. If you speak and understand French, for example, your particular word horde is your own business. Nevertheless, the way the game goes in schools, first you are tested on the *vocabulary* of a subject—and then, of course, there is never any time left for how well you understand it.

The greatest concern most students have is whether they will be able to remember data for a test. Generally, students who get the highest grades are those who have developed a knack for storing and retrieving random bits of information. Such a knack has very little real use outside of schools. (Hence the phenomenal success of trivia games.)

But once a student catches on that remembering is indeed the essence of the school game, it is easy to develop the skill of memorizing. We all have a vocabulary of 50,000 to 300,000 words or more. A few thousand more is child's play—or should be. This chapter will show you that you already know exactly how to go about adding school tidbits to your cache.

7. *More time spent studying will result in more that is remembered?*

Time spent isn't the key. *How you use the time is much more relevant.* Most students could cut study time in half and get higher grades or get them more easily. The section on doing assignments in Chapter 5 offers ideas about making study time more pleasant and productive. Memory is a by-product of learning. A little time spent in understanding *how* we learn and remember will reduce considerably the slave labor of grinding away at books. Very little of your time will be spent in trying to remember, yet you will be able to recall anything you want.

8. *A good way to memorize something is to say it over and over?*

Rote memory (mindless repetition) is the poorest way to commit something to memory. It attempts to do the memorizing in the conscious mind. It doesn't take long for the repetition to turn into meaningless gibberish, and the mind simply turns off. Without some sort of structure to capture the data, they just float in irretrievable isolation. Ironically, most students, when they are desperate, resort to repetition. If you are asked to store trivia, there are pleasant, efficient ways of doing it—but not as a mantra.

9. *Memorizing should be vigorous and aggressive, not laid back and random?*

When the conscious and nonconscious parts of the mind are not in harmony, the memorizing process slows or stops. *We cannot bully our minds.* All parts of the brain must agree that the proposed behavior is desirable. Sitting up straight, beating our breasts and frowning will only interfere.

For example, a family-life teacher wondered why her quiet 8:00 a.m. section scored higher on tests than did her energetic 11:00 a.m. section of the same course. It is likely the students in the early class were closer to their natural learning state than were the more "intense" students. When the mind has time to play, it is in optimum learning mode.

Relaxation exercises will reduce stress and renew self-trust and self-confidence. The centered mind learns and retains. This chapter shows how to set the stage. Not surprisingly, the setting resembles a sandbox.

10. Some subjects are harder to memorize than others?

All knowledge involves placing information into meaning networks. Every language user is thoroughly experienced in creating blueprints of reality. *Difficulty* is a synonym for *unfamiliar.* Getting the hang of chemistry is no different from getting the hang of driving or serving cocktails or carrying mail. There are no difficult subjects, only areas of experience distant from our daily involvement. If one plays around with a new subject as a child does with new experiences, in due time the code will be revealed, and the new field will be just as easy as anything else. The key is to know how the brain works, to relax and allow it to do its job.

Remembering, the Key to Top Grades

What is the main requirement for good grades? Intelligence? Talent? Hard work? Honesty? Your own experience reveals that none of these is as important as being able to remember things.

> *Retrieval of information is the main task in getting a decent grade.*

No matter how much they profess to value thinking and learning, schools rarely test for those things. There are ways to discover how students are truly coming along in a subject, but those methods take time and involvement and care. It is much easier to test for quantities of data. So schools test for facts. And recall of raw facts calls for memory strategies.

If schools *did* emphasize understanding, the facts would be stored in meaning networks and easily recalled. *But course objectives and lesson plans almost never provide for memory training.* This needed skill is ignored.

Having that skill perhaps would make it *too* easy for students to win. It would spoil the ranking system.

Meanwhile, dutiful students spend most of their time trying to remember and usually doing a rotten job of it. That's because, although ordinary brains are expert at learning and remembering, storing *raw* data is unnatural. It can be done, and easily, but it requires conscious awareness of how memory works. Most students have had little or no education on this subject—even though it is more vital to school success than anything else. *Yet even a little attention to memory processes yields dramatic results.*

Some students do stumble on some useful memory tricks, but almost none give *mnemonics* (memory techniques) much attention. (We'll look at mnemonics shortly.) Ironically, however, the least effective method is the one most commonly used: passive repetition. Rote learning doesn't work. It is monotonous. The results are disappointing and depressing. Relaxing over late-night TV would prepare you better for a test than two hours of passive repetition.

Don't try to learn and remember in a passive state of mind.

Everyone already knows intuitively how to store and retrieve information effortlessly. We do it 24 hours a day without even thinking about it. So this chapter won't tell you anything you don't already know—but it can bring these natural abilities to your *awareness,* so that you can use them consciously and deliberately.

All You Really Need to Know About Memorizing

You have an excellent memory, and you use it effectively most of the time.

If you have trouble with a school subject, you are most likely trying to master it in a way that is unnatural to you.

Your memory programs will work well only in a warm and friendly environment. Fear or pride or force will abort the process.

Remind yourself of what really works for you, use it when working on your school subjects, and you will have the same success that enables you to function so well out of school. The more conscious you are of how you actually do learn and the more you trust yourself to do the right thing, the more fun you will have with your college subjects and the easier it will be to master them. Your method is uniquely your own, but it will be a variation of the Mess-Around Theory.

The Mess-Around Theory

Don't try to memorize anything up front. That is not natural. It *is* natural initially to play around. At some point, things will start to click and to fall into a *pattern* that makes sense. At another stage you will say, "I see." At another stage you will say, "I really do understand this." If you browse through your material at this point, you will find there is hardly anything left to memorize. The data have magically been caught in your memory net, and the whole process will have been a delight.

The Mess-Around Theory

- Play around until you understand.
- Check for any leftovers. Then digest them.

Too simple? It is what you have been doing all along—effortlessly. You do pay attention; you are never passive. *It is a matter of allowing your nature to guide you and trusting that it does work.*

There are certainly complicated things going on, but not in your conscious mind. The conscious mind pays attention. The nonconscious part processes the material and generates meaning patterns.

It may seem undignified for adults to "play around" with serious matters, but the play is purposeful. Just as a computer disk cannot store information until it is formatted, the brain cannot do much with random data, either.

Messing around is a formatting activity. The mind needs to create a framework. It knows perfectly well how to do this, but the conscious part of yourself has to cooperate.

> *Play around until you understand. Check for any leftovers; then digest them.*

The Natural Memorizing Process

RELAX.

Children don't learn language under stress, and college students can't use their abilities efficiently if they are tense and anxious. Think about how you feel when you learn to do things you love. You feel alive and well, and every bit of energy you use counts. You are at ease but not passive, like a cat. All parts of body and mind work in harmony. *Don't try to study until your senses are awake and relaxed.* One way to induce this harmony is to put on some appropriate music and go through a simple relaxation exercise.

Play Background Music

Sheila Ostrander and Lynn Schroeder in their book *Superlearning* recommend the slow movement of certain classical compositions of such composers as Bach, Corelli, Handel, Telemann and Vivaldi. The music should be instrumental and should be paced at about one beat per second. Of all the kinds of music tried, classical compositions have proven to be the most effective.

No one knows why music enhances the learning process, but it is known that the alpha rhythms of the brain have a similar pace, which is also about the same as that of a someone taking a leisurely stroll. Some have speculated that the gates between the right and left hemispheres of the brain (the network of neurons called the *corpus callosum*) are open wide to these rhythms, allowing information to pass back and forth freely. Whatever the reason, you will learn more easily when you are in this state of mind.

Quiet Your Body and Mind

There a number of simple and effective ways to achieve the relaxed aliveness of a cat—that is, of minimum energy and maximum results. Try one or all of these:

1. **Stroll around your house or backyard at half-speed, one pace per second.**

   "One and two and three and four," and so forth. Listen to the music, take a walk. The idea is to give your conscious mind something to do so that it can't play distracting, self-critical tapes, and so the mind and body get a chance to pull themselves together.

2. **Do a relaxation exercise.**

   Sit in a comfortable chair, play the music, shut your eyes, and give your attention to your toes. As soon as you are aware of all your toes and can actually feel them (without moving them), move your attention back along the feet, the heels, the ankles, and so on, up the legs, up the torso, the arms, the back of the head, until all parts of the body are activated and you feel a slight tingly sensation throughout.

3. **Mentally work your way through the visual spectrum: red, orange, yellow, green, blue, indigo, and violet.**

   Sit in your chair with your eyes closed, put on the music, and imagine yourself floating in a pool of rich, sensuous deep red. Then go on to the orange pool and then the yellow, and so on, allowing a minute or so for each of the seven colors. (A memory device for this color sequence is *ROY G. BIV.*)

4. **Make the music and the relaxation a habit.**

   Soon the right frame of mind for learning and memorizing will be automatic.

MESS AROUND.

For many, a study session is a frustrating, unpleasant, and unproductive experience: Start with the first paragraph and try to pound it into submission, then do the next paragraph and then the next. The words blur and the mind numbs. No wonder. That is not the way the human organism processes information.

Before anything will stick, the mind has to find a framework or create one. Beginning at the beginning is going blindly into the wilderness without a map. Without an overview, any effort to memorize is futile. The circuits have to be set up, formatted.

Messing around is *another name for* formatting.

So browse.

First set the stage with music and relaxation. You should feel good—comfortable and awake and not tense, no sense of pressure. Then look over the material you want to master. Do a pass through it. It doesn't matter where you start. You can move in any direction and pause anywhere, for as long as you like. Let your curiosity guide you. When you feel saturated, take a break.

When you are ready, come back and do another pass through the whole thing again. Keep on messing around in this fashion until you become aware of the pattern. Meaning will begin to emerge and take form.

Keep playing with the material. At some point you will become aware of an outline; gradually you will flesh out your understanding. Don't try to memorize anything until you can say, "Yes. I really do understand this."

If you have no experience with the subject at all, your first encounter might last only a minute or two. You may start feeling nervous and inadequate, so go away for a while. Your nonconscious will be working on it in the meantime. But

Keep coming back.

Seemingly on their own, things that appeared hopelessly vague will suddenly start making sense. Just let it happen. There can be a number of sessions, some long, some short, some superficial, some intense.

Sometimes you may want to interact. Go right ahead. *Try problems, draw pictures, fool around with possibilities.* The total time spent will be no longer than that of conventional, fruitless methods, but the results will be amazing. You will have shifted the learning to your brilliant nonconscious mind, which does this sort of thing effortlessly. Your conscious and nonconscious programs will be working in harmony, and you will actually feel refreshed.

The process, then, is

Browse, Browse, Browse.

When you feel thoroughly comfortable and familiar with the material and confident that you do understand, then see if there is anything left to memorize. You will find there is hardly anything left to worry about. Without even trying, you will have done most of the memorizing, and the material will be lodged far more permanently in your mind than it would have been with conventional study methods.

MEMORIZE.

To see if there is anything left to do, jot the material down in your own words, as briefly as possible, and examine your understanding of what you have been exploring. If you're studying a skill, try it out. If you discover some gaps, go to those parts and play some more.

You will have noticed by now that *memorizing* and *learning* are often used interchangeably in this book. After trying out the mess-around theory, you will see why. *Learning is growth and change,* and when you have learned a new thing, it has become part of you, as much as your own name or an ability to swim. These are not things you worry about forgetting. In other words,

> *If you learn something, you don't need to memorize it. It's the same thing.*

But we know that most tests are trivia tests, understanding and learning being too hard to assess in quizzes and essay tests. So for the school game, *your final pass through the material is for creating a listing of trivia likely to appear on a test.*

Make a Trivia List

Using your hand as a guide, skim through the material, making a list of items your teacher will probably test. You will discover you have already learned most of the list without even trying. Terminology is usually acquired incidentally, as a background of understanding.

If you do find some items that haven't been important to you but that may be to your teacher, or if you feel you might panic during a test and blank out, the next section provides some tricks that will get you through the test with confidence and a quiet mind.

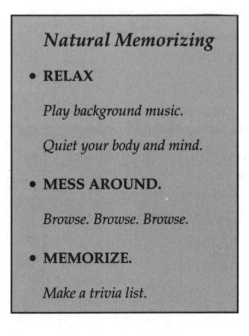

Natural Memorizing

- **RELAX**

  Play background music.

  Quiet your body and mind.

- **MESS AROUND.**

  Browse. Browse. Browse.

- **MEMORIZE.**

  Make a trivia list.

Memorizing Raw Data

Storing masses of *unrelated* data is impossible. The mind is a connecting organ. If it doesn't see relationships, bits of data float loosely and cannot be summoned by the conscious mind. It doesn't know where to look. The data may indeed be in there, but there is no way to gain access to all those isolated pieces.

In almost all of our learning experiences outside of school—when we study ballet, or auto mechanics or baseball or oceanography, for instance—we become absorbed in the experience itself. Sometime we later realize we have amassed hundreds of terms—without even trying. They are part of the *pattern* the nonconscious mind has created for us.

> *Vocabulary and terminology follow interest. They don't precede it.*

Unfortunately, in far too many courses students are typically asked to memorize the terminology first. If they were allowed to play with the new subject for a while, absorption of the language and ideas would be automatic.

An Example of Natural Memorizing

My colleague, Karl Staubach, was a forester for some time on Mt. Adams in Washington. When I was working on the first edition of this book, I decided to give Karl a little memory quiz.

"Karl, what's the height of Mt. Adams?"

"Oh, it's 12,326 feet."

"What about Rainier?" (which you can see from the west side of Mt. Adams)

"That's 14,444."

"And Mt. Hood?" (visible to the south)

"11,245."

"OK. How about Fujiyama?"

"12,365."

"All right. Everest, the highest mountain in the world?"

"It's 29,002. It's really 29,000, but that doesn't look scientific, so they added 2 feet."

"One more. Mt. Diablo." (That's a mountain near the college where we taught.)

"The biggest mud pile in the United States: 3,849."

The point is, Karl never *tried* to memorize those elevations. Knowing them is a by-product of his interest in nature. (If you look these up, you may find a few feet of difference, depending on which cartographer provided the data). No doubt he could tell me the elevation of just about every other major mountain in the world. He knows all sorts of things about trees, too, and spiders and rocks and snakes. But he did not "study" these things; he would consider such behavior undignified. This encyclopedic knowledge is the result of fascination, absorption and love.

> *Fall in love with something, and you won't need to memorize it.*

Before bar codes, the checkers at my supermarket learned hundreds of new prices every week. A student of mine who served cocktails in a bar could remember the drinks of a dozen people at a table and automatically bring a second round, getting each person's drink mixed exactly as ordered. When I was a division chairman, I knew the office numbers of all 37 division members, most of their phone extensions, their schedules, all course numbers and titles. I never tried to memorize any of that information. Some part of the cocktail server, the checker, and the division chairman knew how to store the data and make it accessible for retrieval.

But what if you're a student in a required course and a teacher demands that everyone memorize the elevations of six mountains (or 12 or

100)—without your ever setting foot on any of them, or smelling the air or swimming in an icy mountain lake or seeing paw prints of a cougar on the trail? This situation is fairly typical of schooling, and it happened to me.

Since I was not very interested in mountains at the time, I thought this would be a good chance to try out a memory strategy, to commit raw data to memory long enough to pass a test, even though I couldn't care less about the subject. Here's a description of how it went, at least that part of the process I was aware of.

An Example of Making Raw Data Meaningful

First, I jotted down the data I needed to learn. Since they meant nothing, there was no order:

Adams 12,326

Diablo 3,849

Hood 11,245

Everest 29,002

Fuji 12,365 Rainier 14,444

I started playing around to see what I noticed, light and easy and not really *trying*. Right away I noticed Rainier: 14,444—a 1 and all those 4's. And look at Everest: so much higher than any of the others—29,002, a little over *twice* as high as Rainier. (And that 2 at the end seemed so odd that I doubted I would forget it.)

Wait a minute! Look at Fuji: 12,365, a natural memory device built right into it—12 and 365, the number of months in a year and the number of days in a year. (I have never forgotten the height of Fuji since I first saw that. How could I?)

Then I put Fuji and Adams side by side: 12,365 and 12,326—a 39-foot difference, practically no significance at all. Look again at Adams: the digit sequence is almost the same as Fuji, and four of the five digits are indeed the same. Move the 6 to the right and stick in a 2; it boils down to the last two digits, and one is unchanged but moved to the right. *Only the 2 is new.* So if I could, retrieve Fuji (and who couldn't), Adams was duck soup.

Now look at Hood: 11,245, about 1,100 feet less than Adams or Fuji. Take a good look at the digits: 1, 1, and 2, then doubled to 4, plus one for a 5—11,245, a nice pattern of digits.

As you can see, Diablo doesn't come up to even half the elevation of the least of the others. It's about one-third the height of Fuji or Adams. And look at the digits. Three-eight, four-nine: 3–8, 4–9. Take the 38 and add one each: 49.

Continuing to play, I remembered that I had backpacked on Adams. Looking north, I could see Rainier. Hood could be seen to the south. You go "up north" and down south." Rainier is "up" and higher. Hood is "down" and lower. Rainier is about 2,100 feet *higher* than Adams. Hood is about 1,100 feet *lower.*

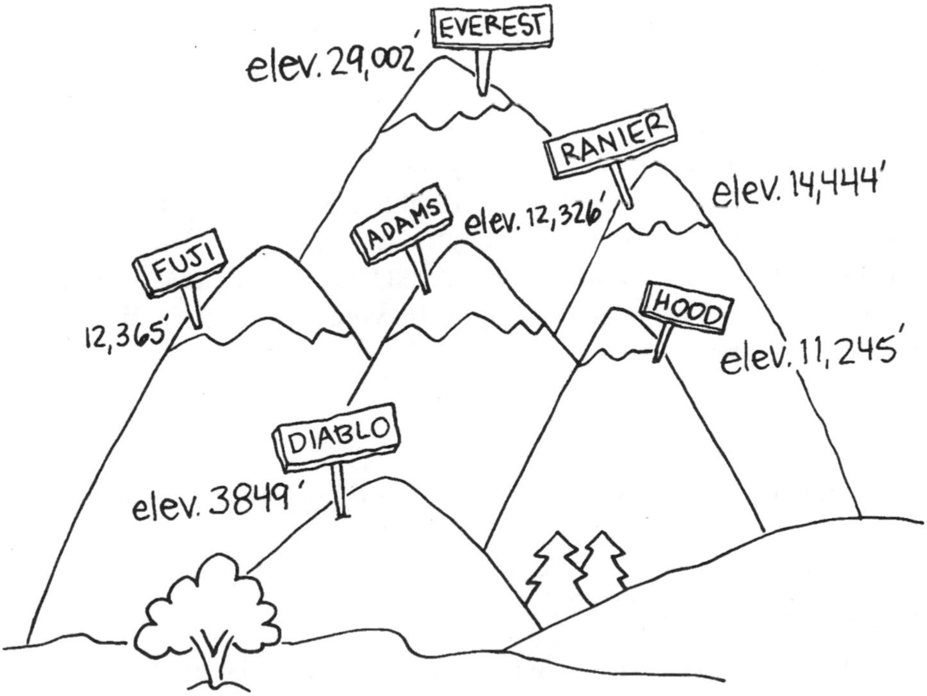

Look what happened. Merely by playing, *messing around,* I began building relationships. Starting with Mt. Fujiyama as the kingpin, I was able to retrieve the elevations of all the others or come close enough to get them all correct on a multiple-guess test.

We do not know what the process *really* is that stored this information in the memory banks. We do know some of the things that were done consciously. In no particular order, I used the following:

Coincidence

The elevation of Fuji just happened to be the same as the 12 months of the year and the 365 days of the year. Coincidence is always a wonderful bonus. Surprisingly, once we catch on to this powerful memory aid, we began to notice coincidence all over the place. The more of this sort of thing we see, the less we have to memorize.

Visualization

Another powerful imprinter for the memory circuits. I pictured myself on Adams looking north ("up") and then south ("down").

Association

I started noticing connections among the mountains, even making a more meaningful sketch. (Using a pencil to trace, to draw, to copy, to connect, gets the motor neurons into the process, too.) "Fuji and Adams are about the same. Rainier is about 2,000 feet higher. Hood is about 1,000 feet lower. Diablo is about a third. Everest is twice the highest of the American group."

Comparison and Contrast

I was noticing how aspects were similar and how they were different, at the same time.

Rhythm and Grouping

The elevation of Diablo can be read "Three thousand eight hundred and forty-nine feet." That is more connected and meaningful than "Three, eight, four, nine," But the mind seems to respond much more to a poetic mode: "Thirty-eight, forty-nine." Or, "Three-eight, four-nine," which also contains some coincidence.

Luck

It just happens that the digits in some of the elevations make interesting patterns. One, one, two, four, five (11,245). One, four, four, four, four (14,444). When we are on the alert for such lucky accidents, they "just happen" all over the place.

Thus, numerous memory devices seem to be natural and become available to any of us if we approach an assignment in a relaxed and comfortable way. You may have noticed others in the example. A few more will be called to your attention later in this chapter.

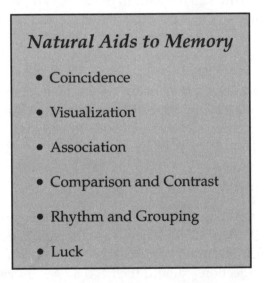

Natural Aids to Memory

- Coincidence
- Visualization
- Association
- Comparison and Contrast
- Rhythm and Grouping
- Luck

Since these aids and many more are part of everyone's natural equipment for getting along on the planet, they don't have to be memorized. (I hope no teacher will insist on students memorizing the memory list.) If initial study sessions are treated as play, these memory aids will crop up automatically.

More Natural Memory Strategies

Awareness of memory techniques (*mnemonics*) does yield higher grades, or at least an easier time getting them. In one experiment, for example, two groups were given the same amount of material to "learn" and the same amount of time. One group was simply told to learn the material and given no suggestions. The experimenter used most of the other group's time showing them memory techniques. Even though they had hardly any time left to learn the material, the recall of this group was eight times better.

> *The best general approach to memorization is relaxed playfulness. It all boils down to* messing around: formatting.

If data remain that are still difficult to retrieve, look over the list of natural aids to memory and try out any device that seems suitable. Or invent one of your own. Knowing that you do have effective resources will ease your mind and build your confidence.

Following are additional observations about these memory techniques (coincidence, visualization, association, comparison and contrast, rhythm and grouping, luck) and some others known to work.

1. Association: Making Connections

The mind is a connecting organ. Just about anything stored is caught up in a meaning network with links in all directions and even among diverse categories. The mind has access to all of them and can yield the most extreme connections, should the need arise. *Association* is known to be the most effective technique we can consciously use to imitate this natural process.

You've seen how linking the elevation of Mt. Fujiyama with something already permanently stored (the months and days of the year) effectively hooks the new fact into the memory bank. Once that is accomplished, Fuji's height can be a hook for some other fact, such as the elevation of Mt. Adams.

It is a *coincidence* that Fuji's height is the same as the months and days of the year, but we can create coincidences on purpose. And the more we do, the easier remembering is. Relaxed playfulness is the enabling mode.

The more hooks you see or create, the more ways you will have to access the information later on. Making connections is involved in all deliberate, conscious memory work. All other memory strategies are variations of the basic approach: association.

Association is the most powerful memory tool.

2. *Visualization*

See it.

The best spellers "see" the word and copy it from their mental screen. Use a pencil to write the problem word in big letters. Make the troublesome part even larger. For instance, it you can't remember whether *parallel* has two l's or one, print it big.

PARAllEL

Not only do you "see" the word more vividly, but the act of printing it and tracing over the letters helps imprint the word on the motor neurons. Did you see there are parallel letters in *para ll el*?

To spell *piece* correctly, notice the piece of *pie* in pieces. There, their, and they're all start with THE: THEre, THEir, THEy're.

Get the picture.

After you've spelled the words correctly a few times, you won't need the memory device.

Play Charades and PICTIONARY®

A technique of memory entertainers is to translate people's names into something tangible, something they can see. *Steve* becomes *stove,* and Steve is pictured with a stove atop his black, wavy *hair.* When the entertainer sees this individual in the audience and notices his distinctive characteristic (black wavy hair), there that stove is, right on top. Stove: *Steve!* An *association* is used. *Steve* is associated with *stove,* and *stove* is associated with *hair,* Steve's noticeable feature. But the emphasis is on *seeing* the connection.

The games of charades and PICTIONARY® use these devices, too. *Antimony* sounds like *ante money* (poker chips). Picture poker chips as your peg or hook (we'll discuss pegs and hooks later). See poker chips, think of ante money: *antimony.* See a red flag; think of *communism.* You can review for tests by making up PICTIONARY® games or playing charades: "Sounds like . . . ," "Looks like . . ."

Here's another visualization technique: No one knows why, but students who first take time to visualize the *place where they prepared for the test* score higher than those who take the test cold. A possible explanation is that the setting contains nonconscious connections with the material—all sorts of hooks and associations we are unaware of but are there nonetheless. Seeing the study setting may make these connections available to the conscious mind.

During a test, visualize the place where you studied.

3. Rhyme

Make a rhyme or a poem out of it. Or set it to music. Here are some examples.

Spelling:

I ***before e***
except after ***c***
or when sounded as a
as in ***neighbor*** *and* ***weigh.***

Sesame Street:

♪ C is for cookie.
That's good enough for me.
Oh! Cookie, cookie, cookie
Starts with C. ♫

The Old Mickey Mouse Club:

♪ M–I–C
K–E–Y
M–O–U–S–E ♫ ♫

Alliteration:

Peter Piper picked a peck of pickled peppers.

How can you lose? Child psychologists know how powerful rhythm and rhyme are in storing information and making it accessible. Music appears to be a fundamental aspect of information processing. In fact, an inharmonious, nonmelodic setting is actually counterproductive. Foreign language classes that incorporate musical lyrics are more productive than those that don't. "The man who has no music in his soul/is fit for treason, stratagems, and spoils." To teach himself English, a student from Peru watched *Sesame Street* and learned songs in the English language.

- ***Make a poem out of it.***

  Set it to music. Tap your fingers.

- ***Remember to play slow classical music and quiet your mind before each study session.***

  Many students keep the music on while they study.

- ***Learn math and chemistry musically.***

  The corpus callosum will let the information pass freely between your two hemispheres.

Fall in Love with the Assignment

Usually when one becomes absorbed in, falls in love with, a poem, a speech, a part in a play, remembering it happens without conscious effort. All of a sudden it has been "memorized." For example, scores of poems are stored in my memory, but I did not "try" to memorize or learn any of them. They were fascinating; the rest was done for me by my nonconscious mind.

If you are not interested to begin with, browse. More often than not, you will find yourself becoming curious. As patterns emerge, you will get more absorbed.

Browsing leads to absorption.

To learn something, fall in love with it. You will love anything you have seen clearly. Veterans of foreign wars say the best place to learn a foreign language is in bed. Naturally. The mind is most responsive in a warm and loving environment. Once we have allowed ourselves to browse long enough to become absorbed, we see clearly.

4. *Rhythm and Grouping*

We never have more than one thing to learn at a time. A Social Security number, 169 23 1566, is not nine separate things: 1, 6, 9, 2, 3, 1, 5, 4, 4. At the most it is three: 169, 23, 1566. Add rhythm and emphasis to the grouping and you get "One sixty-nine, twenty-THREE, fifTEEN sixty-six." They become one rhythmic phrase, much easier to store and retrieve. Give them a cadence.

A sixth-grader says: "MIS—Miss, SIS—sis, SIP—sip, P I—pi."

Whenever the material seems to call for it, see if a poem or song would help. It works for kids; it will work equally well for adults.

Allow your mind to create patterns.

Any batch of random information can be grouped one way or another. One result of playing around with a pile of facts is that they will fall into a pattern on their own, like yarrow sticks—if we don't interfere. No doubt what really happens is that the nonconscious mind sees connections and passes the suggestion over to the conscious part. John Philip Sousa, the March King, said he took dictation from the inner chambers of his mind. His compositions "came to him" complete. A sincere composer has a compelling reason for believing in God, he said. It is the same for anyone.

All we have to do is be quiet and listen. The mind insists on making connections. It is very old and very wise. Trust it.

Meaning Leads to Memory

To memorize "Ode on a Grecian Urn" or "The Gettysburg Address," first Browse it enough times to get the feel of it. Keep making passes through until you feel the whole thing makes sense. Don't try to memorize until you understand and feel comfortable with the piece. By the time you are ready for a deliberate memorizing session, you will already have done most of the work. The rest will be fine-tuning.

Having listened to relaxation music and having quieted your mind and body,

Break the material into meaningful parts.

Master each part in sequence, adding to what you already know and reviewing the remainder in each practice.

The trick is to work in meaning units. Artificial breaks make no sense and don't stick. But if you remember *meaning,* the right words will flow along with the memory.

Let your nonconscious mind create meaning. Memory follows.

5. *Coined Words*

We never have to remember more than one thing at once. Once you have played with and gotten the feel of the colors of the visual spectrum (red, orange, yellow, green, blue, indigo, violet), they can be retrieved *in order.* All you need to have is just one thing in mind—the made-up name

ROY G. BIV

We introduced you to Roy in the relaxation exercise suggested earlier for quieting the mind. Now imagine ROY G. BIV in a vertical column, and let yourself float in each pool of color as you descend toward deep violet:

R

O

Y

G

B

I

V

Here are some other examples of using coined words as memory aids. One student examined the key vocabulary of his geology course, and after some relaxed messing around, reduced them to the coined word

SAM GALOPAGUS

After grade-school kids first get familiar with the Great Lakes (Erie, Huron, Ontario, Superior, Michigan), they can remember them if they memorize only the acronym

HOMES

Or, better, they can set them up for location on the map, with

SHO

ME

> An *acronym* reduces several words to a familiar word or a coined word, such as MADD, NASA, NRA, and DOS.

6. Sentences

For the lines of the musical staff (E G B D F), young music students can make up a sentence: *Every Good Boy Does Fine.* The sentence strategy is effective in reducing test anxiety for adults, too.

Another example: For the planets and their order out from the sun (Mercury, Venus, Earth, Mars, Jupiter, Saturn, Uranus, Neptune, Pluto), storing them in the following sentence makes them accessible for a test: *Mother Very Energetically Made a Jelly Sandwich Under No Protest.*

7. Stories

Students in every field, from surgery to mathematics, have created memory devices such as acronyms, coined words and sentences for storing essential facts. With use, the device drops away and the desired material remains.

For longer lists, a story can be created. The 12 cranial nerves (olfactory, optic, oculomotor, trochlear, trigeminal, abducens, facial, auditory, glossopharyngeal, vagus, accessory, and hypoglossal) could be stored in order in a sentence like the following. Notice it has been put into a rhyming verse, as well:

On Old Olympus's Towering Top
A Fat-Assed German Vaults And Hops.

But a story has more built-in hooks to remember these terms. In this one, the key words *sound like* the terms to be remembered, making them even more accessible:

> At the **oil factory** (olfactory) the **optician** (optic) looked for the **occupant** (oculomotor) of the **truck** (trochlear). And so on.[1]

The increased involvement of your brain in creating a story and the resulting network of meaning make the data more permanent and more accessible. A story is a variation of the link method—commonly used by memory entertainers and widely applied by students who have long lists to recall—described later in this section.

8. Humor, Exaggeration, Irreverence

> *Make it funny, make it big, make it little, make it disreputable.*

The mind delights in far-out, irrational connections. If you have fun and think up socially unacceptable or humorous connections, you will be more likely to remember. Don't be too serious.

Years ago, my fellow students in a Navy electronics program had an off-color sentence to represent the color code for resistors. Even though that was in 1952, I still remember it.

9. Linking Method for Long Lists

People who like ballet, stock cars, computers, cooking, or poetry, discover they accumulate hundreds of terms from those subjects without even trying. But schooling too often gets things backwards. Students are expected to memorize the terminology up front, before they have a chance to format their disks for the new field. All at once, they are confronted with scores of unrelated items and expected to recall them for a test.

---

[1] Gordon H. Bower, *Psychology Today*, October 1973.

With the *link method*, you can create connections as you go along, never having more than one new item to consider at a time. Each new item is linked to the preceding one until a chain of the entire list has been forged.

For example, let's see how to use linking to memorize these words in order:

1. rice

2. road

3. rain

4. ram

5. roar

6. rail

7. rich

8. rock

9. roof

10. rope

Since the first item, **rice**, has no connections initially with anything else, we have to make it vivid. We can use any memory trick that works. Try visualization and exaggeration: Bags and bags of rice blocking traffic. *See* them. BIG PILE. When it is time to retrieve the first item, bring it up on your mental scanner. There it is, a big pile of **rice**.

From here on, the process is easier. Make a connection between **rice**—already in the memory bank—and the second item, **road**. You don't have all ten items to think about, only **road**. How about a **road** through **rice** fields, or those **rice** bags all over the **road**—anything that will link **road** to **rice**.

Once **road** is firmly in place and connected to **rice**, we can move on to **rain**. **Rice** is already in the memory bank, so we set it aside and work only with the next link, connecting **rain** to **road**. There is just one item, **rain**, to work on. Even the list had 100 or 200 items, you would never play with more than one item at a time.

The **road** is almost flooded out by a blinding **rain**. Pouring down **rain**, buckets of **rain** blotting out the **road**. Make the connection stick, using any device you like. This particular list seems to want to become a story about **rice** blocking the **road** in a **rain**storm.

Take a moment to notice what has happened. If we wanted to retrieve the second item on the list but couldn't think of it, we could look at the third item and see the **rain** on the **road**. If that didn't work, we could try the first item and discover **rice** all over the **road**. We have artificial links in two directions, along with other hooks such as visualization and a story. Playing around, we might notice that all the words in the list start with **r.**

> *Because of the many hooks it can sink into each item, the link method is one of the most used mnemonic tools.*

Item four, is the next (*and only*) item we have to think about. We connect it to **rain**. We could keep the story going, with a huge **ram** suddenly appearing through the windshield in the driving **rain**. Or we could simply see a **ram** in the barnyard getting totally drenched by a heavy **rain**. ((Notice the third item, **rain**, now has connections in two directions; we can retrieve it in at least two ways.)

Just before pouncing on the **ram**, a cougar lets out a mighty **roar**, thus linking **roar** into the chain. Now, in one direction, **ram** is linked to the **roar**ing cougar, and in the other, to the driving **rain**.

For the sixth item, **rail**, we could keep the story going, or we could make up a totally new connection between **roar** and **rail**: The train is **roar**ing down the **rail**s, for instance.

Take as much time as you need to fix each item into the chain, working with *only* one new one at a time. Of course, there is everything to gain by making these connections in a playful, relaxed manner. It is fine to run through the list whenever you feel like it.

Item seven, the **rich** man, elegantly dressed, stands at a bar **rail** made of solid gold. A **rich** man at the bar **rail**.

Look at that **rock**, item eight, on the **rich** man's little finger! Wow!

A **rock** has rolled down the mountain and crashed through the **roof**, item nine, of the shack. The **rock** really big. There it is, protruding through the **roof** of the little shack.

Finally, you are using a **rope**, item ten, to climb up the **roof** of your house.

Vivid Connections

Once you've made a vivid connection between each new item and the preceding one, you can start anywhere in the chain and work backward or forward and retrieve every item, even if the list is quite long. If you draw a blank in one direction, try the other. During review, if an item is connected too tenuously, go back and create a more memorable link.

Once the chain has been completed, review the list. See if you can write all the items in order. Try starting at different places and work backward or forward. Treat the whole review as play.

It is better to create your own links than to use someone else's. The more of your mental processes actively involved the better the retrieval.

10. Grid Method

The *grid* method is a streamlined *method of places*, which has been around since the time of Ancient Greece. Visualizing each new item in a special place makes it easy to recall later, to bring up the *place* on one's mental screen and "see" the wanted item just where it was placed.

Using the method of places, you could put your first item "in the first place," say, your front porch. The second item could go "in the second place," your entrance hall. The next would go "in the third place," perhaps your living room, and so on throughout your house. That is how the Greek orators did it. Without the luxury of notes, they could retrieve the first item they wanted to talk about from the "first place."

When it came time to go on to the next topic. They could say, "in the second place . . . ," and pick off the second item from the second spot in their home, where they had stored it.

Today's method of places—the *grid method*—along with the *link method,* together are the most popular devices used by stage performers. They work. The simplified method of places substitutes a tidy grid for the front porch, the entrance hall, the living room, and so forth, as shown here:

1	**2**	**3**
6	**5**	**4**
7	**8**	**9**

Picture the floor of a room laid out in nine large squares as in the drawing. Place the first item in the first square in the far-left corner. The second item goes to the right in square 2. Link the two items together. Then put the next item in square 3, then move down for the 4th, left for 5 and 6, down for 7 and to the right for 8 and 9. In this way you can build a continuous *chain,* adding items one by one, and "seeing" each in its own special place.

An Example Using the Grid Method

Use the grid to place these words in permanent memory:

1. hat
2. hen
3. ham
4. hair
5. hill
6. hash
7. hook
8. hoof
9. hoop

(These items are the basis for another powerful method of memorizing. If you put these nine words in your memory bank now, the next technique will be easy to understand and use.)

Begin with **hat** and put it in the first place, square 1. Since there is nothing else to hook it into our memory network, artificially emphasize it by exaggeration, humor, whatever makes it visually vivid. You want to "see" that **hat** when you bring the grid up on your mental screen. It could be a funny hat, or a BIG one, maybe a sombrero big enough to dance on. You could even sketch a **hat** on the grid:

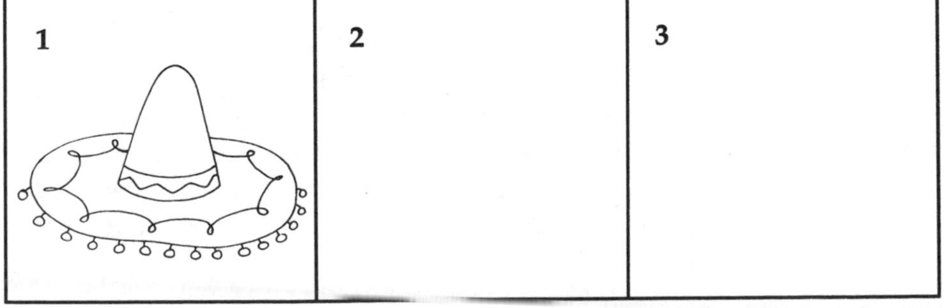

Once the **hat** has been put in its place with as much visual emphasis as possible, place the **hen** in square 2. "See" the **hen** in its place to the right of the **hat**. Now we can begin linking to connect items, finding a good strong bond for **hat** and **hen**. Picture the **hen** sitting on a **hat** full of eggs, perhaps, or wearing a top **hat**:

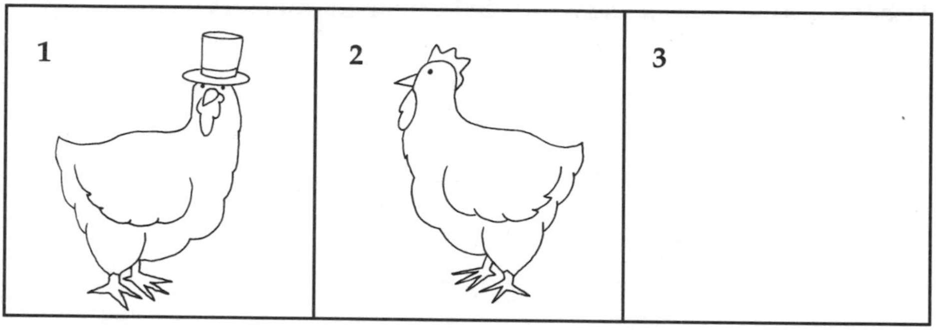

Once the **hen** has a strong image in its place in square 2, and vividly linked to **hat**, we can give our attention to the third item, **ham**, in square 3. **Hat** can be set aside for now, and *only* the new item, **ham**, needs to be worked on. Connect **ham** to **hen**—perhaps a plate of **ham** and eggs, the eggs being our cue for **hen**:

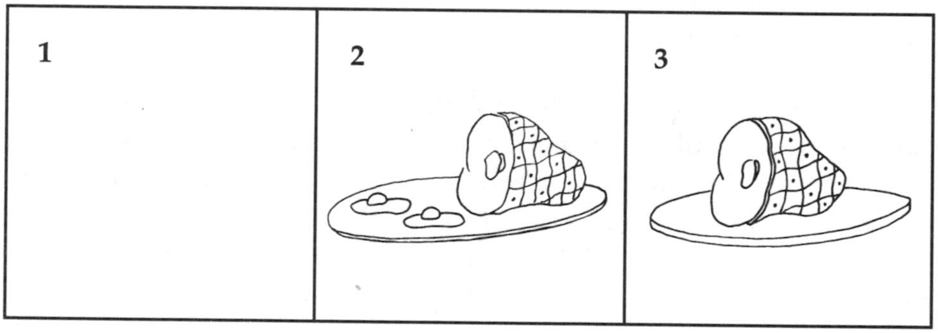

Continue placing items, one by one, in the squares. The fourth item, **hair**, is placed in square 4. (Notice that **hair** has four letters instead of three, in contrast to the words in the top row.) We link **hair** visually with **ham** in the square above. Set **hen** aside for now. Perhaps we could picture a strand of **hair** on a plate with the **ham**. That ought to do it.

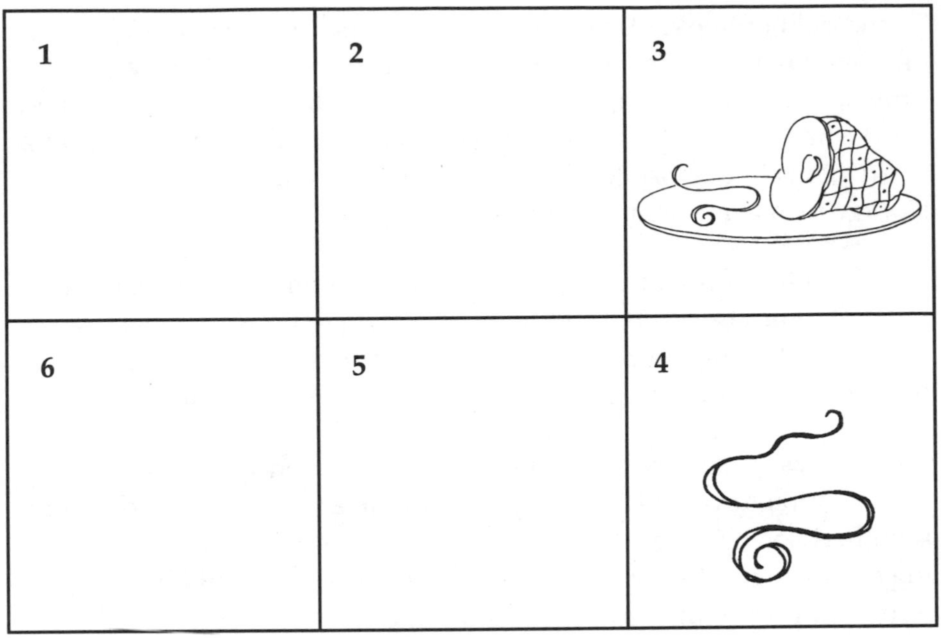

Go on placing each item in its square and making a visual link with the item that precedes it. Use any other devices that occur to you, too. The more you notice about each word and its relationship to the others, the easier it will be to retrieve.

The next item, **hill**, must be placed in square 5 and connected to **hair** in square 4. You could see a field of golden wheat, waving in the breeze, like **hair**. Work only with **hill** and **hair**; ignore **ham** for now.

Hash goes in square 6 and must be connected with **hill**, to its right. It could be quite a pile of **hash**, in fact a whole **hill** of **hash**—or any other connection that works for you and brings a vivid, memorable picture to your mind in square 6 whenever you want to retrieve the item, **hash**, that you placed there.

Three more items to go. **Hook** is placed in square 7 below **hash**. How about a big crane **hook** lifting a pallet loaded with cases of **hash**, each case labeled in big letters, HASH: HASH, HASH, HASH, HASH, HASH. "See" the cases suspended in the air by the big crane **hook**. Make the **hook** silver or gold, extra big and shiny.

To the right of **hook**, place **hoof** in square 8. Set **hash** aside, and work only with **hoof**, connecting it with **hook**. Use the crane **hook** again, this time having it lifting a horse into the air, by its **hoof**. Horse is our cue for the **hoof**, attached to the **hook**. (Any other connection that makes a vivid visual image would do. Making your own links is better for storage than using someone else's.)

Finally, at the bottom right of the grid, place **hoop** in square 9. For the link with **hoof** to its left, "see" a circus setting with a horse leaping through a flaming **hoop**, his **hoof**s showing first. Or you could "see" the horse on its hind legs, twirling a **hoop** on each front **hoof**.

For retrieval purposes, take advantage of coincidence: All three words in the bottom row begin with the letters **hoo**, and *all* nine words begin with **h**. Also, the top row consists of three-letter words. The remaining six are four-letter words. To retrieve the list, you could begin by numbering a column from 1 to 9 and put **h**_ _ for 1, 2 and 3. Put down an **h**_ _ _ for 4, 5 and 6. And write **hoo** _ for 7, 8 and 9.

If you are one of the many who panic or get nervous during a test, having just this much on paper is soothing. You can begin filling in the blanks anywhere on the grid, working backward and forward and jumping around, until you complete the list. If you can convince yourself to treat the retrieval as a game and can approach it playfully, taking a test can turn out to be fun.

That completes the nine-square grid. If you had nine more words, they could be stored on a wall. Twenty-seven more could go on the other three walls and nine more on the ceiling.

Why the Grid Method Is Powerful

The grid method is so effective because it can incorporate several memory devices all at once: Each item gets its own place, and it is imprinted *visually* on our memory. When we summon the grid, we can "see" the item right where it was placed. But we can make a chain of the items, using *linking*, and we can use *exaggeration*, a *story* if we wish, and *coincidence*. Notice, for example, that all of the first three words begin with *h* and all three are spelled with three letters. And we used a *cue* (eggs) to remind us of *hen.*

We treat the whole process *playfully.* When we want to retrieve a word, if one hook fails, we have lots of others to try. Each word is safely stored in its place. If necessary, we can go back and play with any word that doesn't come to mind easily and create more hooks.

> ***The* grid method *is a method of* places, *but it can use any other memory device, too, including visualization, linking, exaggeration and humor, a story, coincidence, cueing, and play.***

11. *Peg Method*

> *The peg method is a variation on the grid method, but instead of putting each item in a square, you hang it on its own special peg.*

Let's say you already have some pegs in your memory bank. All you have to do is hang a term you want to remember on the first peg, hang the next term on the second peg, and so on, peg by peg. When it comes time to retrieve a term, go to the peg and see what you hung there. The peg system is a method of places using pegs instead of squares.

An Example Using the Peg System: You already have nine pegs stored in your memory banks: the items placed in the grid above. You can use these words as your first nine pegs, so you won't have to make up new ones (If you haven't tried the *grid method* yet, go back and learn these nine words before going on.)

1. hat
2. hen
3. ham
4. hair
5. hill
6. hash
7. hook
8. hoof
9. hoop

Suppose you want to remember a list and the items must be in order—let's try the planets (Mercury, Venus, Earth, Mars, Jupiter, Uranus, Neptune, Pluto). Simply make some visual connection between Mercury and the first peg, Venus and the second peg, Earth and the third, and so on. To see what you attached to the forth peg, you go to **hair** and you will find Mars attached.

1. Put a thermometer in the band of the peg word **hat**. **Mercury** is the stuff in thermometers, isn't it?

2. Next, hang a big red heart around the **hen**'s neck. **Venus**, the goddess of love, is thus hooked to the second peg, **hen**.

3. Put a clod of dirt on the plate with the **ham**. The third planet Earth, is now nicely hung on the peg **ham**.

4. Picture a cannon growing **hair** (the fourth peg word). **Mars** is the god of war, so that connection ought to work.

Notice that visual cues *stand in for less visual items.*

5. **Jupiter** was the supreme god of Roman mythology. So, to cue yourself to the fifth planet, **Jupiter**, just put a cross on a **hill**, since a cross is likely to remind people in Western societies of God. The peg **hill** has a cross on top, and the cross leads to God and **Jupiter**. (If this one doesn't work for you, think of some other visual cue.)

6. **Saturn** has to be hooked to the sixth peg, **hash**. **Satur**day is associated with **Saturn**. Picture a leaf from a calendar sticking up in a bowl of **hash**. The word SATURDAY is printed there in large letters. So the sixth peg, **hash**, leads to **Satur**day, and that leads to the word you want to recall: **Saturn**.

7. **Uranus** is the seventh planet to recall, so attach it to **hook**, the seventh peg. Make your own visual cue for this one.

8. Of course, **Neptune** is the god of the seas, so a boat, perhaps, should be linked to **hoof**, the eighth peg. Ah—someone using a horse's **hoof** instead of an oar to row the boat. **Hoof—boat—Neptune**.

9. The last planet is **Pluto**, Mickey's dog. **Pluto** is jumping through a **hoop**, of course.

Hat with thermometer in hat band

Mercury

Hen with big heart pendant

Venus

Ham with clump of dirt

Earth

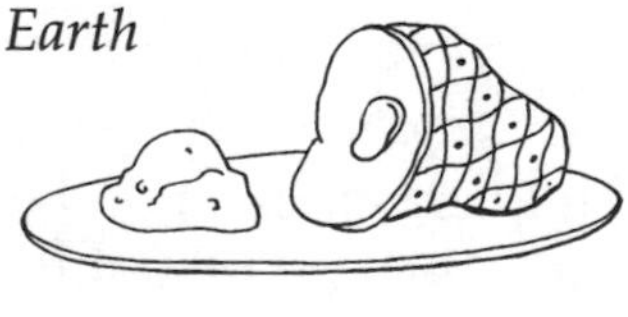

Hash with page from calendar sticking out; date: Saturday

Saturn

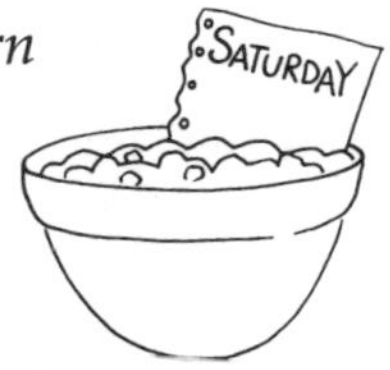

Hook in bedpan

Uranus

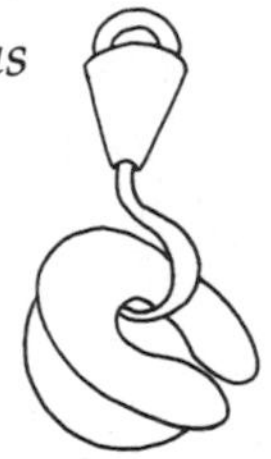

Hoof being used as an oar

Neptune

Hairy cannon

Mars

Cross on hill

Jupiter

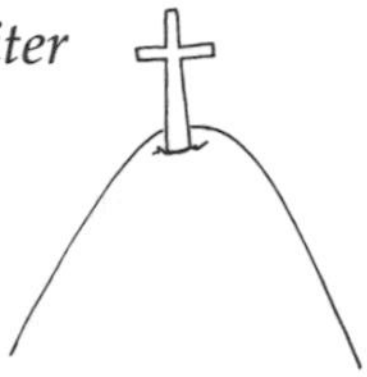

Pluto jumping through a hoop

Pluto

Retrieving Words from Pegs: On a test, if asked to list the nine planets, in order outward from the Sun, you would unhook them from their pegs, one by one. The **hat** holds a thermometer, so you write down **Mercury**. The **hen** is wearing a heart: **Venus**. Dirt on the **ham**? **Earth**. **Hair**y cannon: **Mars**. Cross on the **hill**: **Jupiter**. The seventh peg is **hook**: **Uranus**. The eighth peg is **hoof**; it is being used to row a boat: Sea-**Neptune**. Going through the ninth peg, **hoop**, we see Mickey's dog, **Pluto**.

Since the pegs in this example are already part of the permanent memory network, you can use them over and over. The task is simply to attach the new word firmly to the known peg. Then, for the test, if you need to retrieve your fourth item, think of the fourth peg, **hair**, and there the new word is, hanging on its peg, right where you left it.

100 Pegs: Lasting Value in No Time at All

If you had 100 pegs permanently in your memory instead of just nine, you would have convenient hooks for storing any new list you needed to save and retrieve for a test. The same pegs could be used over and over throughout college. What a pleasant thought!

But wouldn't adding 100 extra items to our memory be a lot of work? Not really. Memorizing 100 pegs is a one-time task with long-term value.

Stage entertainers find even 500 pegs can be learned, to provide a major support to their impressive performances. They are introduced to each member of the audience, for example, and later identify everyone by name, mentally picking off each name from the peg word on which it was hung earlier.

Learn the pegs—even 100 of them—once only, and they are available whenever you need them.

The Digit-Consonant method is a way to master 100 pegs in no time at all and have fun doing it. (If you learned the lists in the grid and link method examples, you already know 19 of the pegs, including the 9 that are the basis for the whole list.)

12. Digit-Consonant Method

You already know that the 100-peg list is built from a basic list: **hat**, **hen**, **ham**, **hair**, **hill**, **hash**, **hook**, **hoof**, **hoop**. The emphasized sounds from these words can be recombined, as you will see, to produce a memorable sequence of peg words.

In the Digit-Consonant method, **hat** has already been established as the first peg of our list. **Hen** is always the second peg, **ham** is third, and so on. But let's streamline the list and pay attention just to the consonant sound of each word. In **hat** it is the **t** sound. In **hen** it is the **n** sound. In **hash** it is the **sh** sound. For this method, we pay attention to the *sounds*, not the spelling.

The digits 1 through 9, then, can easily be associated with the consonant sound of the peg that goes with it:

1. ha**t**
2. he**n**
3. ha**m**
4. hai**r**
5. hi**ll**
6. ha**sh**
7. hoo**k**
8. hoo**f**
9. hoo**p**

To associate a sound with each of these digits, you use the sound emphasized in bold above. And if you should happen to forget, you can always retrieve it from the peg. From here on, the **p** sound is always going to be associated with 9. The **k** sound will always call up **7**, and so on through the list.

Here is the list again, showing just the sounds:

1. **t**
2. **n**
3. **m**
4. **r**
5. **l**
6. **sh**
7. **k**
8. **f**
9. **p**

You will never have to worry about forgetting that **r** stands for **4** because that sound is imbedded in the peg word **hair**, which is permanently in the memory bank. It is the same with the other eight sounds. You can always retrieve them from the peg words. These nine sounds, plus a few others, will be the building blocks for the Digit-Consonant system and for the 100-peg list.

Why Bother with the Digit-Consonant System?

Some people have trouble remembering telephone numbers, Social Security numbers, license numbers, constants in math, and so on. It can be annoying having to look them up, and on tests students are often expected to remember them. What if the number could be converted into a word or two? *Mom,* for example, is much easier to remember than 33. *Rail* is a lot easier to remember than 45.

And *potash river frogs* is a lot easier to store and retrieve than the raw phone number for American River College in Sacramento. Using digit-consonants, I stored *potash river frogs* in my memory network over ten years ago. Picking digits off that phrase, I can still call American River College without going to a phone book. I have never had trouble remembering the phrase. Read on, and you will be able to figure out the phone number for yourself and build your own phrases for numbers you need to store.

To create the associated word or phrase, you use the basic nine sounds in various combinations: **t** is always **1**, **m** is always **3**, and **sh** is always **6**. So, suppose you want to turn **44** into a word. Look at the list. What sound is associated with **4**? Right—you need two **r** sounds. You already have **roar** from the list in the link method example.

Ignore all vowel sounds. What number would be represented by **rock**? Ignore the vowel and the silent **c**, and you have an **r** sound and **k** sound. **R** represents **4** from the above list, and **k** is the sound for **7**. So the number is **47**. How about **43**? You need an **r** sound and an **m** sound: **Ram**.

That is all there is to it. You already have the basic nine sounds memorized. See what sounds you need, and find a word that fits. For a three-digit number, simply add another appropriate sound: **474** would need **r k r**. "**R**o**ck**e**r**" would do.

But nine sounds are rather confining. A few more would make the system more flexible. Fortunately, we can add some without unduly burdening our memory banks. Here are some sounds to add that are easy to remember:

T and **d** sound a lot alike, so let either one stand for **1**.

Sh and **ch** are close sounds, too. So, let either one stand for **6**. Let's throw in the **j** sound, too, as in **j**udge. You now can use **sh**, **ch**, and **j** interchangeably. Any of the three sounds means **6**.

Let either **k** or **g** (as in **g**un) stand for **7**. And throw in **ng** for flexibility. So **7** can be represented by **k** or **g** or **ng**.

The **f** and **v** in hoof and hooves sound quite similar, so let either represent **8**.

Either **b** or **p** will work for **9**.

You have ignored zero until now. So to complete your list, assign **s** or **z** sounds to **0**.

The complete sound list:

0 s, z

1 t, d

2 n

3 m

4 r

5 l

6 sh, ch, j

7 k, g, ng

8 f, v

9 p, b

Now, using your list, try to figure out what the phone number is for American River College. Remember, the phrase I made up is

potash river frogs

As you can see, there are three digits stored in **potash**: **p t sh**. To find the digit for **p**, look at the list. It stands for **9**. Figure out the rest of the phone number and check (below) to verify your results—or call up!

Notice this coincidence: The **sh** in *potash* is a different sound from that of the **s** in *frogs*. By luck, *river* is also in the name of the college; it is also luck that frogs hang out around rivers. Such coincidences are always a pleasant bonus.

(9 1 6) 4 8 4 – 8 4 7 0
P~~O~~T~~A~~S H R~~I~~V~~E~~R F R~~O~~G S

Another coincidence: I used to call Marg in our college bookstore from time to time and would have to dig out her extension number. For fun, I checked the digits against the consonant sounds to see if I could devise a memory word and not have to look up the number all the time. The word turned out to be **marg**. Figure out what Marg's extension is:

M~~A~~R G

M is **3**; **r** is **4**; and **g** is **7**. Marg's number is **347**. I never had to look it up again.

Now we can go ahead and use this technique of associating a sound with a digit, the Digit-Consonant method, to create 100 pegs for storing raw data.

Creating 100 Peg Words from a Few Basic Sounds

When you're at the front end of four or more years of college, it's wise to develop a reliable system for storing data (facts, terms, names, events). Knowing you have an effective system always on hand takes considerable stress out of schooling. As you will see, committing 100 pegs to memory can be done quickly, using the method of associating sounds with digits (the Digit-Consonant method).

Because the basic sounds are used over and over in a systematic way to create these pegs, there is far less to remember than you might assume. Look at the list that follows and notice, for example, how pegs 40 through 49 have built-in memory aids. If you worked through the link method described earlier, you will recognize these ten words. They were stored in memory using the link method, and you may have them in your memory network already. But now let's look at these words on page 71 from another angle.

Notice that the beginning letter of all ten words is **r**. You will recall that the sound we always associate with digit **4** is **r**. You would *expect* the left-hand digit of all ten numbers in this group to be represented by an **r**.

Now notice the helpful pattern of sounds associated with the right-hand digit as we go from 40 to 49: the very same sounds we learned in the basic list, the sounds in ha**t**, he**n**, ha**m**, hai**r**, hil**l**, ha**sh**, hoo**k**, hoo**f**, hoo**p**. (The first number in the series, 40, is made up of an **r** sound and an **s** sound: "rice" *sounds like* **r** ~~ĭ~~ **s**.)

Look at the pegs for 30 through 39: The first sound is always an **m** sound, and the right-hand consonant sound goes through the basic list—from the **s** sound for **0**, to the **p** sound for **9**.

So you don't really have 100 new things to memorize. If you play with each set of ten, they naturally fit into a memory network. In a relaxed and playful way, you could become familiar with the entire list in one or two short sessions and have the whole list available to hang terms on within a week. From then on, it will be easy to store any list for retrieval on a test.

Learning the List

First look over the entire 100 pegs. Notice the patterns and anything else that interests you—that is, *mess around* some and get your computer *formatted* to take in this information.

One Hundred Pegs[1]

0	ooze, **s**, **z**	20	nose	50	lace	80	face
1	ha**t**, **d**	21	knot	51	lad	81	foot
2	he**n**	22	nun	52	lawn	82	fan
3	ha**m**	23	name	53	loom	83	foam
4	hai**r**	24	near	54	lair	84	fire
5	hi**ll**	25	nail	55	lily	85	file
6	ha**sh**, **ch**, **j**	26	notch	56	lash	86	fish
7	hoo**k**, **g**, **ng**	27	neck	57	lock	87	fig
8	hoo**f**, **v**	28	knife	58	leaf	88	fife
9	hoo**p**, **b**	29	knob	59	lip	89	fob
10	dice	30	mouse	60	juice	90	pass
11	deed	31	mat	61	jet	91	pot
12	down	32	moon	62	john	92	pen
13	dam	33	mom	63	jam	93	poem
14	deer	34	mare	64	jar	94	pear
15	doll	35	mail	65	jail	95	pool
16	dish	36	match	66	judge	96	pooch
17	deck	37	mug	67	jack	97	pike
18	dove	38	muff	68	jive	98	puff
19	dope	39	map	69	job	99	pipe
		40	rice	70	goose	100	passes
		41	road	71	goat		
		42	rain	72	gun		
		43	ram	73	gum		
		44	roar	74	gear		
		45	rail	75	gale		
		46	rich	76	gash		
		47	rock	77	gag		
		48	roof	78	gaffe		
		49	rope	79	gap		

[1] Modified from M. N. Young and W. B. Gibson. *How to Develop an Exceptional Memory.* Hollywood: Wilshire Book Company, 1962.

Then work with a set of ten pegs at a time. Play with these words and notice any coincidences or other peculiarities about the group. Once you are familiar with the words and the pattern they form, use any memory technique you like and put the finishing touches to storing the pegs in your memory network. The link, grid, or story methods would work well, but always use the simplest and easiest way for you. With so many memory hooks already stored in the pegs, they will fall into a natural sequence. You will soon see that the whole list has found its way into your memory bank with very little conscious effort from you.

Zen and the Art of Memorizing: Doing it Blindfolded

This chapter could be called "The Zen of Memorizing." It is based on the idea of effortless effort. The 100 pegs in the preceding section can be installed into memory with scarcely any effort. If you have followed the suggestions in this chapter so far, 90% of the process is complete. We now add one final, powerful step, and in this technique you literally

Memorize with your eyes shut.

When mind and body are in harmony, we can learn the way children do. The entire process is one of playful, absorbed messing around. We trust our natural processes to do their job. The work of our conscious minds is simply to remove obstacles so that the whole being functions harmoniously.

Trying without trying means calming the mind and giving it interesting material to absorb. The nonconscious part, as we have shown, does the rest.

The Calming Process

Sitting quietly, playing appropriate classical music and quieting the body and mind are described earlier in this chapter.

- *Sit quietly.*
- *Play music,* such as the largo (slow) movements of classical compositions.
- *Relax the body and mind* through a technique that works best for you—a slow walk or a progression through pools of color attending to each part of the toes to the head.

The Final Memorizing Process

With eyes closed, listen to a tape of the material to be learned. Once your body and mind are ready, sit in a comfortable chair with your eyes closed. With music of largo tempo in the background, listen to a tape that contains the material you wish to store in your mind. The pacing of the tape—which does require a precise distribution of bits of information and intervals of silence—is explained in memory strategy no. 13.

13. *How to Make a Learning Tape*

> *Never try to "memorize" anything until you are* familiar with the material *and have allowed your mind to set up a* structure *in which to store it. Always play with the information first in a relaxed but attentive way.*

All of the techniques described in this chapter set up the mind so that it can convert raw data into meaning. Only after you have allowed patterns and relationships to emerge and feel comfortable with the new subject is there any point in making a learning tape. But once you are at this stage, a learning tape will be magically effective.

After years of experimentation and research, Sheila Ostrander and Lynn Schroeder, who explain this method in detail in their book *Superlearning,* have found this format to be the best for information processing. For optimal retention, record no more than four seconds of information at a time and fill the remainder of every eight-second segment with silence. Here is how it works:

1. Break up your material into parts that you can say out loud in no more than four seconds each.
2. Tape the first item. If it fills up four seconds, add four seconds of silence. If it fills less than four seconds, add enough silence to make eight seconds altogether.
3. Tape the second item in the same manner, and so on throughout your list.

Note: The total pattern of information and silence must always come to eight seconds altogether.

Example

Example

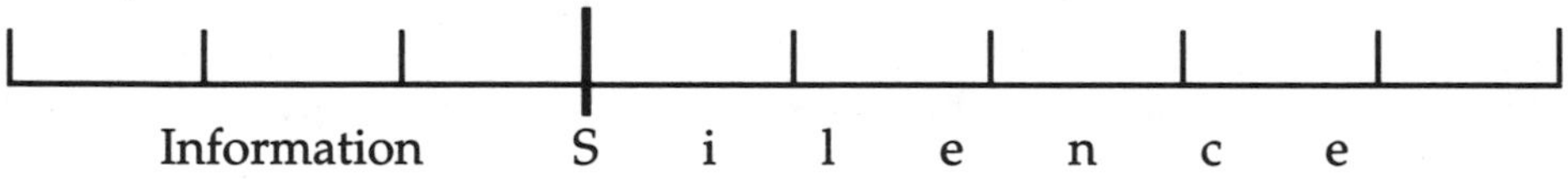

Example

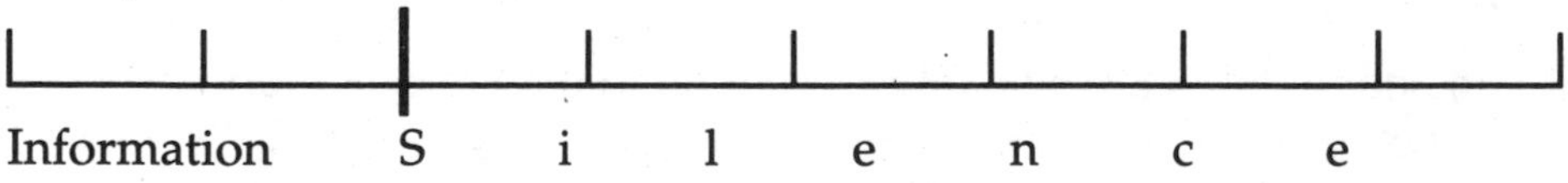

You can record 100 segments of information in about 13 minutes. Each part that you record should "make sense" by itself. For example, you can say, "no more than four seconds each," in about four seconds, and it becomes a *meaning unit*. But it would be pointless to set "and it is a . . ." all by itself.

To avoid monotony, say the first item in a normal tone, the next item softly, and the third loudly. Do the same with the next three items, and so on. (If an item is short, you can fill the four seconds allowed by repeating it.) Here is an example:

"One, hat; one, hat." (normal)

(silence)

"*Two, hen; two hen.*" (soft)

(silence)

"**Three, ham; three, ham.**" (loud)

(silence)

"Four, hair, four, hair." (normal)

(silence)

"*Five, hill; five, hill.*" (soft)

(silence)

"**Six, hash; six, hash.**" (loud)

(silence)

Making and Using a Learning Tape

1. Break the material into parts of no more than four seconds each.

2. Tape each bit, and add enough silence to round out an eight-second interval for each bit.

   Say the first bit in a normal tone, the second, *softly,* and the third in a **loud** tone, and so on throughout the tape.

3. Listen to your tape, sitting quietly with your eyes closed, relaxed and attentive, with appropriate music in the background.

The Magical Results of Learning Tapes

As yet unexplained are the amazing and superior results people get when they listen to a tape made under these conditions. For learning foreign language vocabulary, even whole phrases; for facts, events, formulas, names, and dates; for speeches and poems—this method of effortless effort yields much better retention than any other method attempted. Highly motivated adults, even "problem" eighth-graders find the process rewarding. With increased success, many students become enthusiastic about their studies for the first time.

Success does breed success. *Remembering is more a matter of confidence than anything else.* Once you realize you really can commit information to memory on purpose and retrieve it later, school becomes *possible.*

Try it out for yourself: Make a tape of the 100 pegs. Listen to the tape, relaxed and attentive, with the music in the background. *Don't try to remember; let it happen.* If your mind wanders, let it. You will be surprised at how quickly and easily these words are absorbed into your memory network.

After you have used the tape method a couple of times, notice what your conscious mind is doing as you listen. The four seconds or more of silence seem to be a comfortable length of time to wander around the most recent words on the tape. But the tape moves on before you have time to become passive. Possibly what happens in the nonconscious is that it has time to pay attention to the phrase and fit it into a meaning network—just what is needed for retention.

Whatever the reason, the process feels good, it is productive and active, and you finish a 13-minute session refreshed.

Preventing Memory Loss

If you turn off your computer without executing the Save command, you lose all your work for that session. *Then* you turn off the machine.

The memory strategies presented in this chapter are already fading from your mind. If you start thinking about something else right now, the memory traces of what you've read here will fade even more quickly. No matter how well you grasp these ideas, within a day you could easily forget 90 percent.

How can you stop this memory loss? Experiments show that a few minutes of *reinforcing* at the end of a learning session will save you from having to redo the whole thing later. A good reinforcing session right away, with occasional touch-ups, is the swiftest way through school work.

Immediate reinforcement yields maximum retention.

No matter how short your learning session, always save some time at the end to reinforce your understanding and give your nonconscious mind a chance to make a meaning network of the material. You can have 90 percent retention or better in far less time than most students spend studying inefficiently and getting poor results. In fact, 15 minutes of efficient study and review are more productive than 2 hours of the typical approaches to study.

A good review of the memory techniques in this chapter could take just a couple of minutes. This review should be attentive, relaxed and playful—as for all learning.

REINFORCE for Long-Term Retention

Be sure to review at the end of any learning session. Even a minute or two will reinforce memory traces that otherwise fade and disappear. Work that is done in the conscious mind is like RAM in computers. If you turn off your mind before storing your work on your mental hard disk, you will not be able to retrieve the data.

To reinforce your short-term memory at the end of each work session, try this self-test:

1. After a study session, jot down all the key ideas you can. Then browse and add any you missed. Try again. Try it again a day later. Compress and simplify.

2. Browse and make a trivia list. Use a mnemonic (memory) device to commit these items to memory.

3. Make up your own test, with questions of the sort your teacher is likely to ask. Many of these questions are likely to appear on your teacher's test.

Try these steps to reinforce the ideas about memorizing in this chapter.

1. Browse back through the material, looking at headings, boxed text, examples, and so forth, to bring them up on your mental screen.

2. Jot down in your own words as many techniques as you can recall. Use your hand to help you scan and check through the text for any you missed and add them to your list.

3. Look over the list. When you approach review playfully, you will notice *natural groupings* or other *coincidences* that will help you recall these concepts. Grouping, of course, makes storage more manageable. (It is easier to recall 1544 than 1, 5, 4, 4.) Here

are some of the memory techniques you might recall from this chapter. How would you group them?

Association, making connections	Humor, exaggeration, irreverence
Visualization	Link method
Rhyme	Grid method
Rhythm and grouping	Peg method
Coined words (acronyms)	Digit-Consonant method
Sentences	Learning tape
Stories	

4. We have taken 12 separate ideas and arranged them into 5 meaningful and more manageable groups. Examine your groups of techniques. Do they compare to the following?

- **Rhyme, rhythm** and **grouping** are *poetic* devices.
- **Coined words, acronyms, sentences** and **stories** are *grammatical* devices, going from simple to more complex.
- **Linking** is involved in all memory work, as are **association** and **making connections**. These concepts are virtually interchangeable.
- The **grid, peg,** and **Digit-Consonant** methods are all variations on the ancient *method of places.*
- In any memory work, we use **visualization** wherever we can—as well as **humor, exaggeration,** and **irreverence**.
- The **learning tape** enlists the nonconscious part of the mind in the job.

5. Make a memory *hologram;* in other words, *visualize.*

How Visualization Helps

When you use visualization to help you remember the lists of memory aids, you make remembering even simpler. Instead of the names of the concepts, you could store most of the list in two *images:* a hen wearing a hat and a person blindfolded.

Simply, simplify, simplify

Look at how many memory devices are stored in the image of the hen wearing a hat: It comes from the *grid* method, which is a *method of places. Humor* and/or *exaggeration* are involved. We used *visualization* to "see" the ha*t* in square 1 and the he*n* in square 2. We used the *grid method* to create nine *pegs.* We used *linking* to add one new item at a time and even began creating a little *story* as we went along. We took advantage of *coincidence.* We noticed all the pegs began with *h,* the top row were all three-letter words, and the rest were four-letter words. The nine words memorized in the grid example were the basis for the *Digit-Consonant* method.

The person in the blindfold shown here contains all the information about trusting the nonconscious:

The blindfolded person calls to mind *sitting quietly* with eyes closed, body and mind *relaxed* and *attentive,* with *appropriate music* in the background, and playing a *learning tape.*

Just as computer disks can compress data into "zipped" bundles that can be unzipped later, each part of a compressed image or example can be unzipped to release associated data. Each part contains its own bundle of details that can be plucked from the image or example, as if you are looking at a photograph and ticking off the features of the person pictured there. If you have the photo, you don't have to memorize the features.

If you have an image, you don't have to memorize the details.

Analogy: A Fundamental Memory Device

Making an *analogy* means comparing one thing to another. In memorizing that means looking at the new thing and asking *What is this like that I already know?* Use this process on anything new, strange or difficult, to fit it into your picture of the world.

For example, students get familiar with how electricity works with this by analogy: The flow of electricity through a wire is like the flow of water through a pipe. Voltage, current and resistance compare with water pressure, amount of flow, and size of pipe.

Even the most advanced investigations are carried forward through theoretical "models," which are the same as analogies. Toy with difficult concepts until they remind you of a structure you are familiar with. These analogies or models often come from ordinary experience. Once you "see" a connection, it will be hard to forget.

Analogy is the most powerful tool of thought.

Harmony: The Ideal Condition for Learning and Remembering

Most of the things you can do deliberately with the conscious mind (the left hemisphere of the brain in most people) are embedded in the image of the hen in a top hat. Thus the key to remembering is to store as much as possible in the smallest package—a visual image.

Most of the information about how to make the nonconscious (the right hemisphere of the brain) an equal partner in the learning process is available in the image of the blindfolded person.

Thus the human organism in a state of harmony is the ideal condition for learning and remembering.

For most people, it is easier to retrieve a general concept from an example or an image than to try to remember an abstract idea or title directly. During the review at the end of a learning session, look for patterns and see if they can be stored in an image or example.

An image or example is the ideal mnemonic (memory) device.

For example, SAM GALOPAGUS might be a a marvelous reduction of baggage to carry around in the mind, but an image of SAM would be an elegant simplification.

A Potpourri: Tips, Tricks, and Techniques

Make remembering as easy on yourself as possible. When you are messing around with your material, be on the alert for some simple way to remember. Your nonconscious mind will drop hints. Take advantage of them. Here are a few examples. Make your own collection using the blank page that follows. You and your fellow students—and teachers, too—can easily fill it to overflowing.

For Typing and Music and Other Motor Skills: Practice!

Go as slowly as necessary to strike every note or key correctly with *no* mistakes. These are motor skills—you want your fingers to "remember" with no thinking at all. Every wrong move interrupts the process.

Rewrite Your Notes for Better Retention

1. Rewrite your notes in a shorter form. Later, make the shorter version shorter yet. Then do it again. The process allows the mind to notice patterns and to distinguish concepts from trivia. You will find the material ending up in your memory banks instead of being scattered randomly all over your folder.

2. Make a separate list for your trivia. Then use your favorite memory technique to store the items that won't stick.

3. A variation is simply to type up your notes. You will be surprised at how much gets transferred into your long-term memory.

For Dance Steps, Golf, etc.: Observe the Experts

Track the teacher or model. Watch his or her movements. Mentally rehearse your swing, your steps, your speech. Imagine yourself going through the motions.

For Biology: Store Classifications in a Sentence

King Philip Came Over From Germany Saturday.

(kingdom, phylum, class, order, family, genus, species)

For Formulas, Equations

Ohm's Law in a nutshell:

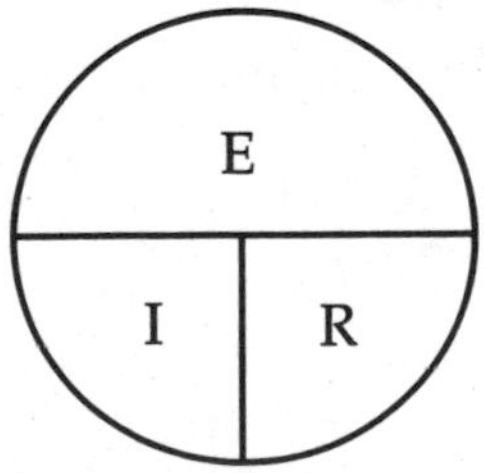

Hold your finger over the one you want to find. Then do the math that is indicated. Thus, if you want I, it is E over R. (Divide voltage by resistance.) If you want E, it is I × R. (Multiply current by resistance.) If you want R, it is E over I. (Divide voltage by current.)

Rehearse Out Loud

You will be amazed at how much you will retain, simply by saying out loud what you want to remember. But make it a dress rehearsal.

For Drama: Advice for Learning Your Lines

1. Don't try to learn your lines until you understand the play. Read through it a few times first. You will have absorbed a lot of your role without even trying.

2. Highlight the cue in one color, your part in another.

3. Tape the cues in the scenes where you have lines. Leave the tape blank where your part would be said. Listen to the tape in the car or while ironing or shaving. Say your part when appropriate.

4. In early stages of practice, tape the cue *and* your part. Leave enough blank space for you to repeat your part.

How to Find Things

Put things where you will bump into them when you need them. *Hmm. How come this sunblock is in my way on the sink? Ah, yes!* Leave your car keys on the floor by the door when you come *into* the house. They will be in the way when you leave.

The Notepad: A Sure-Fire Memory Device

Why load up your short-term memory? Put things to be done or remembered on a small notepad. Cross them off as you finish with them.

Review Within 24 Hours

A short review within a day of a learning session is a powerful aid to retention. Try saying the key ideas out loud. Even with just a few minutes of review, you will see great results.

How to Tip in Restaurants Without Doing the Math

1. For 15 percent, look at the bill and move the decimal point one place to the left. That will be 10 percent. Add half of that and you have your tip. Example: The bill is $28.57. Ten percent is $2.85 or so. Half of that is about $1.40. So $2.80 plus $1.40 is $4.20. (No one is going to worry about the pennies. But if it would make you feel better, you could round it out to $4.50.)

2. If you have low self-esteem, or if you got really good service, you can make it 20 percent by doubling the result of moving the decimal point. In our example, twice $2.80 is $5.60. Make it $5.50.

3. Whip out a calculator.

Use Flash Cards for Odd Moments

Flash cards work for vocabulary, dates and events, formulas and their meanings, artists and their works. After becoming familiar with the material, make up a pack of cards to carry with you. Use them while waiting at the check-out counter, at the movies, at the hair dresser's.

Rehearse only a few minutes at a time, and shuffle the deck each time. Short, intense practice is best. Rehearsal works only when the mind is fresh and attentive. A new setting and time can provide additional memory links you are not even aware of.

Overlearn. A few extra rounds make all the difference in the amount you will retain.

Once a card is learned, take it out of the pack.

Use this page to collect other memory devices.

Remembering as Problem Solving

Actually, remembering *is* problem solving. Both remembering and problem solving use the same approach:

- What am I being asked?
- Is it possible for me to get an answer? (Is it stored there in the first place?)
- Where will I find it?
- How will I find it?

To retrieve stuff, you must have a structure. Even so, once things have been properly stored, how do you get them back? The answer is

> *You have to put together information you can find, see what the combination yields, and go on from there—and go about it in an orderly way.*

We actually apply systematic rules whenever we try to find something in our memory banks, though probably we are not conscious of this. Some part of the mind knows immediately whether or not even to try. We seem to know before we even start whether the search is futile. When asked, "Where were you a week ago?" we know somehow that we were *somewhere.* But can we actually recover the information? Often our minimal expectations of ourselves are such that we don't even try. And often we give up too soon.

But experience can alter our attitude. *The greater the persistence, the greater the chance of success.* What did you have yesterday for dinner? Most people would tackle that. What were you doing Tuesday afternoon two weeks ago? Many would give up on that, but with encouragement and prompting almost everyone would recover the information. What were you doing on Valentine's Day three years ago? Impossible? With persistence and conscious search procedures there is a good chance you can recall this information, too.

If you feel you can make reasonable decisions, if you can guide your own life, if you can function well as a cook or carpenter, then you should have no trouble remembering. It is exactly the same mechanism, though you may not realize it.

Retrieval Processes

How do we go about this business of retrieval? We know we don't just punch in the question and out comes the answer. It is much more involved.

Who are you? Even a question as basic as that requires interpretation: Should I even answer? Should I give a false answer? What is actually being asked? My name, my occupation, my authority, my social class? (If asked by a Zen priest or someone like Socrates, you may decide you don't know.) Nevertheless, almost instantly you can select from all the possible answers and respond appropriately. (Sometimes you misunderstand and give the wrong answer.)

Other kinds of questions may require elaborate search procedures. For example: *Figure out what you were doing on Valentine's Day three years ago. Do this now. Work your way through the problem out loud—into a cassette if possible. Or write it down. What steps do you observe? What strategies?*

STOP

If you are typical (though no one can say you have to be), you didn't try to get the answer all at once. You probably started with a smaller piece, a subgroup:

> What was I doing on Valentine's Day three years ago? Let's see. This year the 14th will be on a Sunday. In '92 it was a leap year, so it was a Friday. In '91, a Thursday, and in '90 a Wednesday. Okay, so it was a school day. I would certainly have been teaching. School schedules are easier than weekends to retrieve. I'll bet we did something in class for the occasion. I'd started to have afternoon classes by then. I can "see" a 2:00 class sitting in a circle—no, it's that dumb room in the TE building with the noisy heating system and the

> pipes showing. They weren't in a circle. The middle part was rows, but there was a U shape around the three walls. Yeah. That class had a big ethnic diversity. Okay. I gave everyone a pink heart about three inches or so cut out of construction paper, and each person was assigned to give the person next to him or her a valentine message on that heart. I can sort of see some of the students, some brash, some shy. The more I look into this scene, the more vivid it becomes. The morning class would have been in that crummy ET Annex. I don't think we did the valentines in that class. Let's see. Was that a lit class? The afternoon class was freshman English, so this was critical thinking. I can "see" Jeff Briggs and Edward over on the side. . . .
>
> Well, and the evening: We always celebrate the day, and we like to go to La Cigale. I could easily say what I had for dinner: rack of lamb. An early dinner, before the crowds. Was that the year I had a ruby pendant for Ruth? Claudette was our waitress. . . .

And so on. Was your process similar? Notice there is some subgrouping, some looping back to prior questions, and moving ahead again. Perhaps this series of steps is similar to what you did:

- I try to *reconstruct* the setting. *A visual image is full of information.*
- I look for *contexts* or *associations* that may yield the answer.
- I get lots more information than I actually need, more than was included in the shorter version. This helps me *visualize* the scene in which the information is stored.
- Later on I thought about other Valentine's Days before and after, for *contrast* and *triggering.*
- Also, I explored how I was *feeling* at the time, my *emotions.*

- Gradually more and more of the pictures is filled in. When I can't find the answer, I work on smaller parts or take a side trip and try again. *There are lots of tries and blind alleys.*

- But I begin to feel it is possible I really can find the answer. That sparks my *enthusiasm.* I sharpen up my questions and strengthen my *persistence.* Now I am really going for that answer.

- I use both logic and hunches.

- I play with possibilities. I reason with myself.

No doubt these steps seem perfectly reasonable to you. When we are not anxious, we use them. It is often fun. (In fact, it has to be fun to work. We have to be relaxed and alert and playful.) The trouble is, we forget these natural retrieval approaches if we are in a chemistry exam and behave instead as if we are not the brilliant creatures we quite clearly are. As you can see, you have all sorts of options.

Could you remember the names of all the people in your high-school class? For such a task, persistence does indeed pay off. The longer people stick to it, for days and days and sometimes even months, the more they can remember.

The longer we persist the more we can recall.

Thus, we do have strategies within us for retrieval. We don't have to throw up our hands and hope for lightning to strike. "Even if I don't know Napoleon's birth date, I can use this process to narrow down the possible dates considerably." On a multiple-choice test that could be close enough. And we can activate these recall strategies at any time.

We can activate recall strategies deliberately.

Let's take a look at some of these recall strategies.

RECALL STRATEGIES: How to Find It Again

Memory is system. Memory is not a junk pile. Put a bit of information in a good place to begin with, using a good cross-referencing system, and you *will* be able to find it. Something is "memorized" when it is well placed.

Think of memory as a filing system, not the hall closet.

Recall Strategies

Note: Don't try to remember these strategies word for word. Just browse and play with them a while. See if you do use them. During tests, allow yourself the freedom to make use of whatever approach feels right.

To trigger recall, we must *loop* and *detour* as needed. During tests, allow yourself the freedom to play.

- ***Persist.***

  If you have the time, have the self-esteem to use it. One or two points could raise your grade. In retrieval, persistence pays off.

- ***Play. Treat it as a game.***

  Anxiety paralyzes the retrieval process. Play a more positive self-image tape in your mind and get back in the game. You have to feel free; then you will see alternatives.

- ***Divide up the question.***

  Browsing diverts our sensors so that solutions get a chance to pop into our heads. "If I figure out B, that may lead to C. Oh! There's the answer over there. Where did *that* come from? I wasn't even looking there."

- ***Rephrase the original question.***

  Go back from time to time and see how you are doing; try another path.

- ***Reconstruct a setting or several settings.***

  Call up on your mental screen the place *where* you were when you processed the material and entered it into your memory banks. Search the setting for clues. They may lead to other groupings that may contain the answer.

- ***Use leftovers.***

  Recalled contexts usually contain more details than are actually needed. Scan them for accidental aids.

- ***Visualize.***

  Remember—an image is full of data. You can hold the picture in your mind's eye and examine it for information. Be willing to suspend your search while you stroll around looking.

- ***Use your own analogy.***

  If you made up your own example or if you thought up a great comparison (such as the water-through-a-pipe analogy for electricity; see "Analogy: A Fundamental Memory Device" earlier in this chapter) bring the example or analogy to mind. Then derive the target formula, equation or whatever from the example.

  Work backward, from the example or image to the formula or concept.

- ***Try alternatives.***

  At blind alleys, back up and try a new path. Realize there are dozens of ways to accomplish your goal.

- ***Feel free to back up, defer, move ahead, relax or get intense, as needed.***

  If a path is temporarily blocked, set the question aside. Do some other parts of the problem. When your mind is quieter, come back to the question.

- ***Use both logic and hunches.***

  Memory is coy. Retrieval requires both rhyme and reason.

You have used all of these retrieval strategies at one time or another. *They are part of everyone's natural thinking processes.* The key is to be conscious of them, as you now are.

> *Become conscious of your retrieval tactics and recognize that you do have all these resources available.*

If you approach retrieval in a relaxed and playful way, you can use it deliberately and effortlessly.

Troubleshooting: Handling Failure and Anxiety

If you blank out on a test, go ahead and feel sorry for yourself—for a minute or two. Then fight back. Look at your failure as an opportunity to perfect your game. In the background of virtually every amazing human being is a history of failure after failure. For the wise, failure is a chance to learn. *The only fatal mistake is giving up.*

The way to deal with failure is to analyze what went wrong. To become great at the school game,

Always analyze your mistakes.

Only three things are likely to interfere with remembering:

- Panic
- Wrong filing strategies
- Wrong recall tactics

There are remedies for each of these mistakes.

Panic

Panic arises from fear of the unknown, insecurity, lack of confidence, poor self-esteem. You can reduce the likelihood of panic by doing dry runs beforehand. First, of course, you need to get the stuff into your memory banks using your natural memorizing abilities—those described in this book. But then:

Do Some Confidence Building

Don't exaggerate the importance of the school game. *No test score measures your character or worth or knowledge.* Test taking is just a game, like basketball or tennis. So don't allow a school test to have undue power of you. Instead, do something productive.

Practice Remembering

Practice in the same circumstances in which the test will be given. Make up the test questions like those your teacher uses. Check out the room, the setting, the timing. Take your own test as if it were the real thing—just as you would practice for the low hurdles.

Find out all you can about your teacher and the kind of test he or she gives. Talk to former students. Analyze any test you can get your hands on. It is money in the bank.

Practice the stressful situation until you are used to it. It is just like learning to drive.

Wrong Filing Strategies

When you get your test back, always do an item analysis. What went wrong? How and where did you file that bit of data? Could you have anticipated the problem that caused you to miss this item?

See if you left out any part of the general storing process:

1. Relax. Quiet your body and mind.

2. Browse, Browse, Browse.

3. Use a memorizing device for trivia.

Whatever happened, once you can see what went wrong, your performance *will be better next time.*

Handling Trivia

Failing a test may not your fault—at least not the first time.

Memory is not literal.

The mind digests *ideas,* not exact wording. If your teacher tests word-for-word recall, your first quiz will show that. In that case, your only recourse is to apply a memory device to the raw data. It's a trivia game, so you may as well arm yourself. Following the general rules will store the data for you, and using the memory devices will bring back the trivia verbatim.

Wrong Recall Tactics

If your item analysis reveals that you *did* file the material well, you may need to brush up on your recall tactics.

Next time, when you hit a brick wall, stop. Do some easy questions for a while until you calm down. Then go back and put your recall strategies to work.

Treat the search for the answer as a game. Have some fun doing this detective work.

And always keep in the back of your mind the knowledge that school is not the only game in town. What is the worst possible scenario? So you flunk—not only the test but COLLEGE! Will you die?

You cannot possibly know *in advance* the importance of any single event. Who knows—flunking could be the best thing that ever happened to you. So relax. Worrying about some imagined or uncontrollable event in the future is fruitless. Get in the habit of treating a test as a game and approach it playfully.

The best thing you can do is free your mind to play with alternatives.

- Try associations, tangents, clues in other questions on the test, rephrasing, and so forth.
- Persist until they throw you out of the room.
- Play to win.

Fantastic Built-In Computers

If schools were modeled on how animals *really* learn, there would be no need for a chapter on memorizing. Under normal conditions, creatures learn effortlessly whatever is appropriate to their circumstances. Even ants have miraculous little computers that enable them to do remarkable things. So, too, are we humans splendidly equipped to learn well and easily whatever is appropriate for our needs. We know perfectly well how to use fantastic built-in computers—unless the process is interfered with.

Unfortunately, teachers who understand learning theory and use it efficiently are rare. Most of the time the whole process is upside-down. Clearly, fear is a lousy motivator, and extrinsic reward encourages dependency. Insisting on terminology *before* providing experience sandbags the learning process.

The least schools could do for you, the students, is provide education on how memory does work. That would give you a fighting chance. Even a little awareness of how your mental computer works can dramatically ease the artificial process of "memorizing." Once you know what the game really is, you can activate your memory circuits deliberately—with the assurance that no job of processing information need be difficult.

Memorizing, as described here, is not the amassing of bits of raw data. It is an *integration,* the fleshing out and expanding of a picture of reality that every creature creates. As Piaget and others have suggested, our understanding is limited to the completeness of our field of vision.

Understanding is limited to the field of vision.

If we step back, we see a larger picture, clearer and more complete. Our view grows from a simple whole to a more detailed and completed, but always integrated, entity.

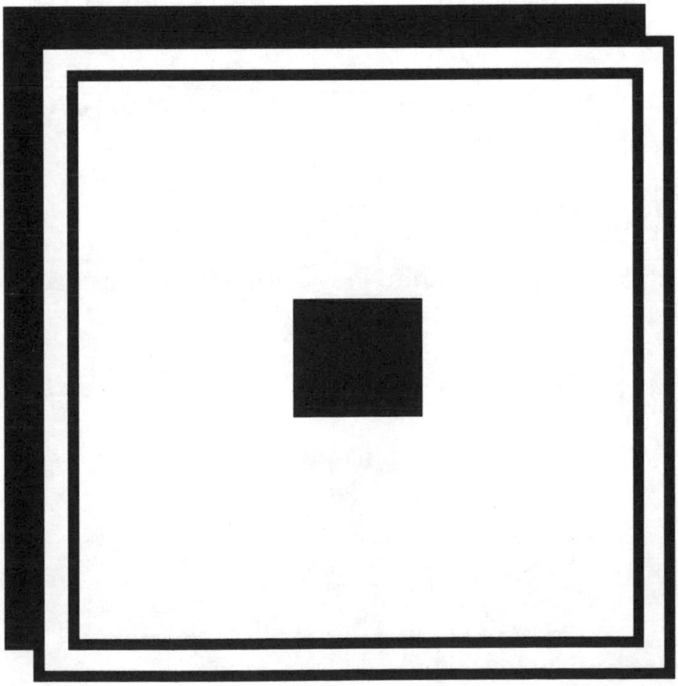

Since learning and "memorizing" are really the same thing, any time spent on this chapter pays off in every other aspect of your education. Awareness of how you really do learn—quite a different process from what goes on in most classrooms—is the foundation of purposeful, lifelong growth and change. When a human being takes charge of the furnishing of his or her own mind, the process of education really begins. So an intelligent approach to the school game is both an assured *and* confident educational adventure.

> *Students need to know that school is essentially a memory game, and every student—that's you—is already an expert player.*

The memory strategies outlined in this chapter are in harmony with this kind of growth.

Power Play

All the ideas in this chapter can be compressed into the powerful idea of "child's play":

> ***Play around until you understand. Check for leftovers. Then digest them.***

- Get into a playful mode of behavior.
- Quiet your body and mind. Play appropriate music and relax with some exercise that works for you.
- Format your conscious mind.
- Mess around with the new material—like a kid in a sandbox—until it makes sense.
- Do a trivia check.
- Apply a memory device to any raw data left over that the teacher is likely to test for.

C H A P T E R

3

Raising Test Scores

Turning Tests into Crosswords Puzzles

"I have resented to this day
When any but myself presumed to say
That there was anything I could not be."
—Robert Frost

For Frost Poem on page 99

MYTHS ABOUT TESTS

Mark only the ideas you agree with. Then read the commentary that follows.

☐ **1.** Tests measure how much a student has learned.

☐ **2.** Tests are objective.

☐ **3.** Tests are fair.

☐ **4.** Tests show teachers how well they are teaching.

☐ **5.** Tests help students learn.

☐ **6.** Essay tests measure understanding better than short-answer tests do.

☐ **7.** If it is taught, it must be tested.

☐ **8.** The best insurance for a high test score is thorough understanding of the subject.

☐ **9.** Tests can predict performance on the job.

☐ **10.** SATs identify the best students for college.

Commentary: What Testing Really Tests

Most people think the statements in the "Myths About Tests" box are true; research, however, shows they are not. Most students believe them and suffer the consequences. But a little reflection will show that testing actually interferes with learning.

Most tests impede education.

To break down this barrier, a student must understand what is really going on, what testing really is, and then learn the rules of *that* game.

Tests are deeply embedded in the system, but you need not let them have significant power over your life. In fact, if not taken seriously, tests can be somewhat entertaining diversions. But you must *play to win.*

Otherwise, why play?

Take another look at these myths. From what point of view are they *not* true? What is your own experience? Have tests really helped you? Are tests really for your benefit?

1. Tests measure how much a student has learned?

We all know better: *Tests really measure skill in taking tests.* Change, growth, and understanding are not sought, nor can they be revealed, by conventional tests. Do 150 random bits and pieces of data reflect the complex changes in you? Does the test consist of items everyone is likely to know? Or "tough" questions that only a few will know?

As plenty of studies show, a good test score does not mean you will remember.[1] Neither is it a good predictor of performance or of success in a field of study.[2] Course grades indicate neither what a student knows nor what he or she can do.[3]

[1] Jennings and Nathan.
[2] *Ibid.*
[3] Glaser.

Tests are games in which large numbers of students guess what the test maker wants and then give responses in uniform signals that can be machined-scored, if possible. Every student knows that two people with the same score can have vastly different understanding or capability. Like any other game, tests have rules: time and space limits, playing fields, equipment, scoring procedures, codes of conduct, number of players, winners, losers, referees.

Playing the test game is an end in itself. Furthermore, time spent on these games is time stolen from involvement in the subject you wish to master. Preparing for a test is a very different process from getting good at French or engineering. Still, the game can be mastered, and it can even yield educational by-products. It makes sense to gain control over whatever curves life may throw you.

Thus, you can think of tests as just one more problem-solving challenge. What you accomplish in literature, mathematics or welding is one thing; tests are something else again. That's all.

2. *Tests are objective?*

Whole books have been written showing that even national "standardized" tests are riddled with bias.[4] The socioeconomic slant of IQ tests is notorious.[5] Indeed, entire groups of human beings have been declared substandard because of tests results. The tests—even today—serve to discriminate between social groups and ethnic groups. When the tests were given in the cultural and linguistic setting familiar to the test takers, the scores suddenly soared. There is no such thing as an objective test.

How conscious the test makers are of inevitable flaws in an "objective" test varies. No one could ever convince the Educational Testing Service (ETS) of the defects in its products. Only recently have some of its

---

[4] See Owen, David. *None of the Above,* Houghton Mifflin Company, Boston, 1985. See also, *The Myth of Measurability,* edited by Houts, Paul L., Hart Publishing Company, Inc., New York, 1977.

[5] See also Whimbey, Arthur, "You Can Learn to Raise Your IQ Score," *Psychology Today,* January 1976.

practices been challenged successfully in the courts. This private organization, with a "nonprofit" classification, has no external oversight. *ETS polices itself.*[6] Of course, it always turns out to have a marvelous product. Fox looking after the hens.

But even a casual examination reveals that test items vary widely (and wildly) in the level of thinking or kind of thinking required to answer them. Yet the test items are usually weighted the same. A student could answer all the thought questions well and miss all the fact questions. Someone else could do the opposite and come out with the same score.

The Limitations of Written Tests

The more we examine what can go wrong in making, giving, interpreting, and taking a written test, the more we see its limitations. Even expensively researched and carefully controlled "standardized" tests are subject to all these dangers—as test makers themselves readily admit. Their attempts to persuade school people to recognize test limitations have met with little success.

As William G. Perry notes, "Intelligence tests require thought, but generally in little spurts and restricted operations that are incapable of revealing its larger outlines. Questionnaires prohibit thought by setting *precast alternatives* and forbidding the respondent to say how he would form the question and qualify the answer."[7]

To get any real sense out of a score, you'd have to do an item-by-item analysis for each student. A simple raw score means nothing.[8] As research shows, without a conversation with the student about his or her reasoning on each item, a teacher cannot know what influenced the answer.[9] A "right" answer could be so shaky or so illogical as to be useless. *Right/wrong testing ignores complex reasoning processes.*[10]

---

[6] Owen.

[7] *Forms of Intellectual and Ethical Development in the College Years,* New York: Holt, Rinehart, and Winston, 1968.

[8] Ruth.

[9] Jennings and Nathan

[10] Ruth.

Trivial Pursuits

Ever wondered why Trivial Pursuit® and TV game shows are so popular? It may be there is no other use for such thinking in the real world.

Since schools have not figured out any other way of sorting huge numbers of students, it is not likely that standardized tests will go away soon. Society wants it this way. The Soviet Union in 1936, did away with IQ tests. It had no political interest in classifying its citizens, it was able to save the state huge bundles of money. *IQ tests serve no educational purpose.*

Do We Need College Entrance Tests?

There is evidence that colleges could use a lottery to choose among high-school graduates, with no ill effects. In California, students for many years were allowed to enroll in community colleges with no screening whatever. By and large, they fared as well as those chosen for other schools through SAT scores and high-school grades.

What about tests designed by teachers? How could they possibly be objective? Most teachers have little or no training in test making. Even if teachers had time to weed out obviously flawed items, how can it be maintained that one pattern of samplings does indeed assess a whole complex of interrelated changes in 30 or 40 unique human beings? The idea is contrary to everything we know of the mind and how it changes.

Unfortunately, tests remain the dominant means of assigning grades today. Innocence of the true nature of tests puts a test taker at a disadvantage. The only recourse is awareness and skill at test taking. *An hour spent on learning how to take a test will net you a higher score than an hour spent studying the subject.*

3. *Tests are fair?*

People who get high scores think so. But consider this: *High scores merely show that the student has had prior experience with that kind of test.* High-scorers may be neither smarter nor more apt than someone to whom the course is brand-new. These high-scorers may actually have learned and changed the least. They may have learned the answers before they signed up for the course. Their wetware disks are already formatted for the teacher's point of view. Naturally, the questions compute for them. So a good score may actually reflect the least learning.

A good score may simply reflect speed. (Is the ability to do things fast listed as a goal in any courses *you* have ever taken?) Timed "objective" tests ignore differences in the way people learn and in their biological clocks. The most learning usually occurs with beginners, with those to whom the subject is extremely strange or unusual. But these students never get a chance to reveal their growth. Teachers wish they would go away.

In fact, some teachers lighten their load by testing students right out of classes, giving monster tests at the beginning to scare students into dropping the course. Teachers subjectively select and phrase test items and are the final judges of their own creations. Thus a test can be made difficult or easy, depending entirely on the mood of the teacher.

Tests can be so worded that everyone passes or everyone fails. Your Department of Motor Vehicles may give a written test that is "easy." It wants most people to pass the test. It avoids test games. Consequently, just about everyone passes, and one may repeat the test with no stigma. If a person can't read, there are special provisions to get around the problem. In a Texas school district, too many students were failing a standardized reading test, and the superintendent was getting criticism on the poor teaching. A bond election was coming up. The superintendent solved the problem by lowering the passing grade. Suddenly the students were doing much better. Fair?

The only thing you can be sure a test measures is experience in taking that kind of test. If students are treated inequitably, if difficulty depends on the whim of the test maker, if the instrument doesn't measure what it purports to, something is wrong.

4. *Tests show teachers how well they are teaching?*

Tests give teachers a way of ranking students. What educational purpose is served by this? It is a rare teacher whose test actually measures the progress of a class toward meeting long-term goals. Seldom do they analyze student responses to individual test items and use the findings to improve teaching procedures. "Objective" tests would not help much, anyway. How you answer test questions tells nothing about how much you understand a subject. They are two different experiences.

A high score shows only one thing: test-taking skill.

5. *Tests help students learn?*

Tests have all sorts of purposes, but hardly any of them are educational. They are really for sorting students, ranking them, putting them in competition, coercing them into doing assignments. The results even become permanent records for registrars and employers.

Tests actually interfere with learning. Suppose your understanding of a subject is shaky. You find out a day or a week after a test that you missed 10 or 15 items. All that time, your wrong responses are settling in your mind as the *right* ones! Even worse, a multiple-guess test contains 75 percent inaccurate or misleading information. Think how hard it is to get all that confusion sorted out. A pro doesn't teach someone to play golf by showing three wrong ways and only one right one.

A tester who tries to honor learning theory will give students immediate knowledge of results, item by item. The correct response would be discussed and made clear then and there. No external records would be kept. (At the very least, when tests are returned to the students, the teacher could append the preferred, annotated answers for the students to compare with their own. That would suggest *some* educational intent.)

Obviously, the purpose of in-class tests is not educational. We learn what we do. Look at your behavior during a test; *that* is what you are learning.

6. *Essay tests measure understanding better than short-answer tests do?*

Essay tests contain the same flaws as objective tests, plus a few of their own. They usually solicit a batch of facts sewn together into sentences and paragraphs. In other words, they are objective tests in disguise. Evaluators score tests based on a list of items sought. Sometimes points are added or subtracted for composition and editing skill, even though the test is supposed to be measuring something else. Of course, someone has to think up the questions and their wording. But who decides the questions are clear, that each student understands what response is being sought? How is it determined that these questions do reveal competence in the subject—or skill in writing answers to them? Only one person makes these decisions.

What essay tests really measure is skill in taking essay tests.

7. *If it's taught, it must be tested?*

When something is really learned, both the learner and the teacher know testing is pointless. Answering 100 questions about bicycles is not the same as riding one; that goes for school subjects, too. You either have the feel of riding the bicycle, or you don't. You either know the discipline of history or you don't. You can't be a 90-percent or a 95-percent or a 99-percent bicycle rider or speaker of French. *The time spent making, taking and worrying about tests of any sort would, in a healthier learning atmosphere, go toward mastery.*

There are many ways other than testing to see how a student is coming along in a subject. The teacher might ask, "How are you doing?" It is natural to want to understand or get good at something. If students don't feel threatened, they are glad to tell teachers exactly how they are doing. When people are self-educating, they *use* their teachers and other available resources. Hiding their weaknesses makes no sense.

Most of the five billion people on this globe never encounter such a thing as a short-answer or essay test. "Objective" tests and "essay" tests are a recent peculiarity of Western society. *Riding a bike, driving a car, doing surgery, setting type, communicating with someone in another language—these are the tests that matter and that cannot be faked.* To discover real progress, then, a student might keep a folder of work from beginning to end of a course of study. Portfolios contain abundant evidence. In fact, there are lots of unobtrusive ways of measuring, such as observation.

But the question remains, do students *have* to be measured? The answer almost always is no. Even if it were desirable, it may not ever be possible, as *The Myth of Measurability,* edited by Paul Houts,[11] demonstrates.

8. *The best insurance for getting a high test score is to have thorough understanding of the subject?*

When you are taking a test, the subject is test taking, not literature or economics. If two students understand a subject equally well but one has mastered test taking, guess who will get the higher score.

In fact, it is possible to do well on lots of tests without having studied the subject at all. To get firsthand experience of this idea, my colleague Karl Staubach, who is the best test-taker I know, took a standardized reading test without reading the article it was based on. He scored 20 out of 20! I tried it, too, and scored 18 out of 20. Clearly the test could not have been a reading test for us. In fact, there is no doubt whatever that *the best insurance for getting a high score is thorough understanding of the test-taking process.*

This chapter contains some of the strategies we have used that can turn horrendous college tests into academic crossword puzzles.

9. *Tests can predict performance on the job?*

There is no connection between your success at work and your test scores or school grades. Apart from the research, experience shows that good scores mean nothing "in the field." Some people are good at taking tests. But the irony is that getting through an employer's door often does depend on school records. So it makes good sense to master

[11] Hart Publishing Company, Inc., New York, 1977.

test-taking skills. It is not very hard to do. Like any other skill, you get better with enlightened practice. When you realize early what the game is and get good at it, you'll breeze through school with scarcely any stress.

Getting good at a job, too, is a matter of experience. To be good in your chosen field, get hands-on practice now—every chance you can. Take part-time jobs that provide work experience while you're still in school.

*Use your test-taking skills to get the job. Use **experience** to keep it.*

10. SATs identify the best students for college?

There *is* a strong relationship between SAT scores and your high-school and college grades. What it boils down to is that *schools and the tests mirror each other more and more as the years roll on.*

But human beings have multiple knowledge systems, and various ways of representing the world. They put varying emphasis on ways of processing information, use different parts of the brain for understanding, and have different kinds of memory structures. Nevertheless, schools today focus more and more on only a narrow range of skills and behavior, perhaps with an eye on SAT emphasis. Schools teach the sort of things found on the tests, and even plan and present material in short bursts of data, like sound bites.

Consequently, many fine minds with unique ways of interacting with the world never get a chance in school to develop their strengths. Music, art and dancing, for example, are considered cocurricular or extracurricular. Yet most societies of the world nurture the arts as essential to every citizen's humanity.

In an enlightened college, every student is an excellent student. Do you feel out of place in college? The reason might be the way your college restricts diversity. Schools that recognize the varieties of learning styles and diverse patterns of talent and provide flexible curricula find all sorts of people can do splendidly in college. The community college experience in California, for example, is that higher education for everyone is a workable idea—SAT mindsets notwithstanding.

The Truth about Testing

- The only thing a test measures is experience in test taking.
- There is no such thing as an "objective" test.
- IQ tests serve no educational purpose.
- To master a subject, fall in love with it. To do well on tests, study the art of test taking.
- A higher score may actually reflect less learning.
- Tests show neither what a student knows nor what he or she can do.
- Essay tests are "objective" tests with words strung between the facts.
- Tests do not help students learn, and they do not help teachers teach.
- Ranking students serves no educational purpose.
- In an enlightened college, every student is an excellent student.

The Effect of Test-Taking Skills on Grades

Next to skill in remembering, knowing how to take tests will have the most direct effect on your grades. As little as 15 to 20 percent of your grade will be for what you know about the subject being learned; the rest reflects your test-taking know-how.

> *Grade-point average is affected more by test-taking dexterity than by just about anything else.*

Unfortunately, as you no doubt already know, test-taking (and memory techniques) are among the least taught skills. Learning how tests work and discovering how to take them can make the difference between a C and an A. (Perhaps that is why schools give so little help in this vital area—aware students could wreck the curve!) You can change your "IQ" and your SAT dramatically simply by using the right test-taking techniques.

Test taking is a skill like any other and can be learned. As you will see, much of what you need to know is common sense. If you are not already aware of your own test-taking skills, you will discover them in this chapter, and this awareness will alter your scores significantly. Even better, you will reduce your school anxiety to a healthy level.

In fact, you will know more about tests than most teachers do. Hardly any of them have studied even conventional test-making procedures. Far fewer have ever examined the evils of scoring human behavior. By studying this chapter you will know what most don't: what a test actually measures, how it is put together, its weaknesses, and most important, how to get a high score with no more knowledge than you usually have.

How Tests Work: The Rules of the Game

The following analysis of the test game is based on a paper by my colleague, Karl Staubach, expert test-taker and test-analyst. He points out that any situation with artificial, contrived elements is a game and should be played as such. When you have lots of money riding on the outcome, as all students do,

Play the game to win.

Motives

Find out your opponent's motives, and while you are at it, know your own. In the school game, your opponent is the test maker.

Competition

Test makers want to rank test takers. They deliberately leave out questions everyone gets right—that throws players into competition. There is no escape. A high score for you means a low score for someone else.

Artificial Grading

When tests compare students, the grades are artificial. A teacher or test maker can set the cut-off points anywhere. He or she may think, "I'm seeing too many A grades. I'm going to set the cut-off at 95 instead of 90." And there goes your head. "I made the test too tough. I'll lower the cut-off to 65 instead of 70." Happy days are here again. "Too many kids are getting high scores on these entrance tests. We'd better raise the cut-off score." And your allowance gets cut off.

For every test, someone invents the grade categories.

Failure and Guilt

The test game requires that you agree with the test maker. False, incorrect, unsatisfactory, or wrong answers are *bad* answers. You should be ashamed of yourself.

The Looking Glass

Students who think and perform like their teachers get the best grades.[13] Of course, since they already see the world the way their teachers do, they have less to learn. In contrast, you know what happens to those who are *least* like their teachers: They find themselves in a foreign country. They learn more, but their grades are rotten. You may have to think a while about this startling finding.

Biases

When the same person who teaches you also prepares and/or evaluates your test, watch out. His or her biases cannot help but influence the grading. With the best intentions, teachers are bound to think behavior like their own is good or right—or even charming.

---

[13] Unpublished research report by Dr. James Doerter, Southern Oregon College, Ashland, Oregon.

Performance Criteria

All the existing testing paraphernalia could be junked with no harm done. In real life, a simple *"How are you coming along?"* does the trick. On the job, performance is self-evident. You drive the car or speak the language, or you don't.

Play to Win

- **It's Business**

  In a money game, don't get emotionally involved. This is business.

- **Forget Sentiment**

  Don't get sentimental about your opponent during a game.

- **Maintain Humor**

  If you take a test seriously, you will not play well. Develop a sense of humor—you will notice all sorts of clues that you miss when your palms are sweaty. Imagine you are the test maker planning your next move.

- **Develop Expertise**

  Become an expert on testing. Make up ridiculous tests as part of your study routine. You will be surprised how many of your crazy questions actually appear on the next test.

Developing Test Awareness

Some people have no trouble at all reasoning their way through life, but they get low test scores. It is not that they are stupid. It is simply that they have a *mind-set for failure.* They feel sure the game is hopeless, so they take tests passively. But once these same people catch on, scores and grades go up.

Make the test-taking process visible. Be sure to

- Get a good look at how tests are made, their *structure.*
- When you make mistakes, use item analysis to find out how and where your thinking went wrong.
- Practice answering questions by working your way through, *out loud,* or by writing down your thoughts as you go. Hearing or seeing what you are thinking makes you conscious of your thought processes.

The object is to learn to reason your way through a problem *on purpose.*

Out loud, reason through the items you missed.

Use this approach and you will see a marked changed in your test results.[14]

Academic Crossword Puzzles: Analysis of a Sample Test 1

There is only one way to get good at taking tests. You have to look cold-bloodedly under the academic window dressing. When the content is stripped away, you get a skeleton like the one that follows. Some years ago, Karl Staubach published this "test" in the Diablo Valley College faculty *Forum.* Try it yourself. Then read the Item Analysis.

[14]Whimbey

Your Pickpocket Education

How to Take a Test Without Knowing Anything
(Time Limit 15 Minutes)

I. Quantitative Reasoning

A. What is the diameter of the circle in Figure (a)?

(a)

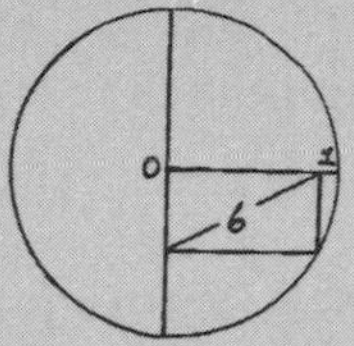

B. Develop an equation for apparent loss of elevation due to curvature of the Earth; express unknowns in terms of feet and miles; show your work.

C. How long does it take an inchworm to go a foot?

II. Critical Analysis

A. This statement is false. True/False

B. Unscramble the following words:

1. TUTIWHO
2. TEERMAID
3. PANETRAP
4. MORNWICH
5. RILACTIC

III. Reading Comprehension

A. Blah ba blah blah because . . . ?

1. blah ba blah blah.
2. blah blah ba blah.
3. blah ba blah ba blah, blah, blah blah.
4. bah ba blah ba blah.

B. Blah ba blah no blah . . . ?

1. blah not blah ba blah.
2. no blah ba blah blah.
3. blah ba blah ba blah.
4. ba blah isn't blah blah

C. Blah ba never blah ba blah. . . . . True/False

D. Blah ba blah ba blah . . . ?

1. blah ba blah.
2. blah blah ba.
3. blah: ½ blah
4. ba blah blah.

E. Unknowns in equations for the Earth's curvature are usually expressed in

1. millimeters
2. feet and inches.
3. miles and feet.
4. hundredths of inches

Item Analysis of Sample Test 1: Your Key to Top Grades

One reason YOUR PICKPOCKET EDUCATION is a good skeleton test for practice is that there is hardly any content. A player has to look at the structure for clues. The game itself is clearly the subject, not English or calculus.

Ruthless analysis of the game is the only way to get good at tests. So learn to think like your opponent. Better still, use your opponent's mistakes to your advantage. In test analysis, missed items are invaluable for developing awareness and skill.

All of the following guidelines will be familiar to you.

Play Around Until You Understand the Game

But let's back up. Even before we start messing around, we need to

Relax

You'll want to review Chapter 2 for details, but here are the essentials:

Before the Test

- Play background music. The largo (slow) movement of a classical piece is the best.

- Quiet your body and mind. Take a half-speed walk, one pace per second. Or shut your eyes and pay attention to each part of the surface of your body, starting with your toes. Or imagine yourself in a pool of red color and work your way through the spectrum: ROY G. BIV (Red, Orange, Yellow, Green, Blue, Indigo, and Violet).

During the Test

When you start in on the test, try to be in a relaxed and playful mood. "In a money game, don't get emotionally involved." From here on in, it is simply

Mess around. Mess around. Mess around.

First, browse. Like most games, this one has a time limit: 15 minutes. It's a point game, so *do whatever is easiest first.*

Unless you see an easy solution, skip the second question and maybe even the first. There might be some calculating to do. Build points *and confidence* by doing the easy ones first.

The Mess-Around Theory of Test Taking

Play around until you understand the game (format).

Rack up all the points you can. Then do the leftovers.

Item Analysis of Sample Test 1

The Reading Comprehension section of Your Pickpocket Education looks like sheer nonsense so let's start there. Any sort of subject knowledge would be useless here.

A. *Blah ba blah blah because . . . .?*

Answers 1, 2, 3 and 4 look pretty much alike, except that the third one is longer. There being nothing else to go on, choose the most different one. If you chose it for that reason, you were "right." Rack up a point.

B. *Blah ba blah no blah?*

Again, only one answer stands out as different. Three of the four contain a negative: *not, isn't, no.* Answer 3 is the exception—that is a good reason to choose it. Also, if you chose any of the others, that *ain't* such a swell idea. (Double negatives are discouraged in school English.) So there are two reasons to go with the third answer.

C. *Blah ba never blah ba blah. . . . . .* True/False

False. Academics rarely go out on a limb. Statements that contain the words *always, never* or any other sort of definite, absolute statement is a sign to be careful. Other things being equal, don't choose them. If the definite answer indeed *is* the wanted answer, it will have been pounded in so much that you will know that and will choose it anyway.

D. *Blah ba blah ba blah . . . ?*

The gibberish in three of the four answers, again, looks pretty much the same. But answer 3, *blah:* $^1/_2$ *blah,* is different. Choose it.

E. *Unknowns in equations for the Earth's curvature are usually expressed in . . .*

How refreshing: This question and the answers are in regular English! But if you follow the reasoning for the four questions above, you can answer this one "correctly" even without knowing anything. Three of the answers offered are teeny-tiny measurements: *millimeters, feet and inches, hundredths of inches.* But answer 3 is in *miles and feet.* Again, it is the answer that's most different. That is one reason to choose it.

Another reason is common sense: Millimeters, inches, or hundredths of inches won't cut it.

Ah, but there is another wonderful reason: the principle of *Academic Crossword Puzzles.* If you were playfully messing around, *browsing,*

browsing, browsing, you could not help but notice question B in the Quantitative Reasoning section. It contains your answer! Until you have analyzed a few tests, you will not believe how often that happens. If you are relaxed enough to notice it, tests are full of information you can use to piece together a pattern of "correct" responses.

Use the test to answer the test.

Every test is a mass of random data stored in the questions and in the answers, even in all the "wrong" answers. This random information—amazingly often—contains the exact answer you are looking for, or it will remind you of the answers. *The best place to find help on a question is in the test itself.*

When All Else Fails, Choose the Third Answer

Watch for a *pattern of answers.* Answer 3 on this "test" has been the "right" answer three times. If that pattern continues throughout, it might be a tip-off, should you find yourself completely at a loss. Indeed, in most teacher-made tests, the third answer is "right" more often than any other. That holds true even is some "standardized" tests. Use your common sense, of course, but if you have absolutely nothing else to go on, choose the third answer.

Examine the answer pattern of your tests and see which answer is favored.

So far, as promised, we have found five answers anyone could get without knowing anything. Let's see if that works for the Critical Analysis section of the test, too. Start with question B.

B. *Unscramble the following words:*

If you think playing around with these words might take too long, look again. The answer to RILACTIC is CRITICAL. It appears on the test itself, just five lines up. Remember, use the test to answer the test. You will find the other four answers on the test, too.

Tests are indeed loaded with information a good player can use to figure out the wanted answers. Approached playfully, the game can be stimulating, delightful fun.

Now how about Critical Analysis, question A?

A. *This statement is false. . . .* True/False

> Karl included this question to emphasize the poor wording of so many test questions. If the statement *is* indeed false, then it's telling the truth, so it's "true." But then how can it be false? So we have to say it's "false" that it's false. Whew! Without knowing what the test maker really wanted to know, no one can answer with a simple True or False. Unfortunately, *test questions are often ambiguous.*

Analysis shows that almost any question can be interpreted in many ways. Until there is a meeting of minds about what indeed is being asked, the response cannot be judged. And no short answer is adequate. The questioner must discover the context of the answer and what is meant by it. In other words, the tester and respondent must *communicate* with each other, and that is virtually impossible with short-answer tests.

Answering Ambiguous Questions

If the test is teacher-made or if it will be scored by a human being and not a machine, answer the question, *but explain your reasoning in the margin.*

> *If the test is "standardized,"* think like your opponent. *This is where* messing around *earlier pays off. You will have noticed the level of sophistication of the questions and will have* psyched out the test maker. *This is a point game; answer accordingly. If you must insist on justice, take that up later.*

How about Quantitative Reasoning?

C. *How long does it take an inchworm to go a foot?*

This question isn't ambiguous, but there is something missing. If you take the test seriously or if you think teachers or test makers are infallible, you will waste a lot of time trying to figure this out. Call the tester over and point out that the information on how fast the MORNWICH is going (the rate), is missing. Otherwise, point that out in the margin.

If messing around reveals that the tester has a silly streak, you might consider giving an equally silly answer and cover your bet with an explanation in the margin.

Flawed questions are the rule, not the exception. It takes time to weed out obvious defects—time teachers do not have. Even the "experts" screw up routinely. Rather than assume the tester is perfect, ask for clarification. If refused, continue with the crossword-puzzle approach. Remember—it's a game. Rack up points.

A. *What is the diameter of the circle in Figure (a)?*

Even if you assume you do not have enough math to solve the problem, always

> *Give yourself the benefit of the doubt. Never leave a question unanswered.*

Some students who analyzed this test with me didn't know and had to ask what a diameter is. Unless you're working on a vocabulary test, you ought to be allowed to ask what a word means—and then proceed to answer the question. The vertical (up-and-down) line in the drawing is the diameter. There. How long is it?

Never leave a question unanswered. In real life, an approximation is all that is necessary in most cases. If you are playfully relaxed, you could figure out how long that line is without any math at all. Give up?

See that 6 in the drawing? Tear off a piece of paper and mark off the length of the 6. Now see how many of those lengths it takes to get across the vertical line Gee, two! So the diameter is twice 6, or 12. There are more respectable ways to find 12,[15] but any home carpenter could easily find a piece of plywood to cover the circle, or a homemaker could buy a large enough table cloth. In other words,

Answer test questions with common sense.

That is 14 out of 15 questions answered without knowing anything! Now for the last question under Quantitative Reasoning.

B. *Develop an equation for apparent loss of elevation due to curvature of the Earth.*

The question clearly *does* call for some background and experience and might actually require calculation. That is why we saved it for last. If you are comfortable with your answers to all the other questions, you could play with this one in the time left.

But more likely, most students would miss this question. In a point game, decide where you want to take your losses. After all, 14 out of 15 on most tests is quite respectable. You can simply decide to let that one go. (Otherwise, if you really want to try it, you can call Karl Staubach at Diablo Valley College, Pleasant Hill, California 94523, and compare your solution with his.)

The message here is simple:

Build your score with the questions you can do easily. Don't get anxious about a few points you can afford to miss.

[15] You might have noticed that 6 is a *diagonal* of the *rectangle*. And in the other direction, 6 happens to run from the center to the edge of the circle (the radius) and happens to be half the full distance across the circle, or 12. But you do not have to know that to answer the question.

Mastering the Game I

Item Analysis is the key to top grades.

- Take tests in a relaxed and playful mood.
- Get formatted first: Browse, Browse, Browse.
- Rack up points and build confidence: Do easiest questions first.
- Use structural clues: Longest, shortest, most different. Grammatical tip-offs.
- Beware of absolute, definite answers.
- Answer all questions. When all else fails, choose the third answer.
- Don't make the test tough. Use common sense and your own natural intelligence. Use approximations.
- Tests are academic crossword puzzles. Use the amassed information for clues or even exact answers.
- Ask for clarification of ambiguous or flawed questions. If necessary, explain your answer in the margin.
- Psych out the test maker. Think like your opponent.
- Don't sweat questions you can afford to miss. Mess around. Mess around. Mess around.

Academic Crossword Puzzles: Analysis of a Sample Test 2

Tests are games; taking tests is a playing skill.

If studying the test itself is a new idea to you, you may need a few tries before you catch on. Here is a second chance. Every test maker has a unique mind-set. *Messing around* or *browsing* is a way of *formatting* yourself to the way the test works and what to notice. Try it on this test. Be sure to be *relaxed* and *playful* before you start, and be sure to *browse the whole test first.*

Test Your . . . What?

(Time Limit 8 Minutes)

1. Allow yourself five minutes to rearrange the letters O-W-D-E-N-A-R-W to spell a new word—but not a proper name, nor anything foreign or "unnatural." Write it out.
2. Quickly now: How many animals of each species did Adam take aboard the Ark with him? (Note that the question is not how many *pairs,* but how many *animals.*)
3. What unusual characteristic do these six words have in common? DEFT SIGHING CALMNESS CANOPY FIRST STUN (Please complete your answer within five minutes.)
4. Figure out this problem in diplomatic relations: If an international airliner crashed *exactly* on the U.S.-Canadian border, where would they be required by international law to bury the survivors? (If you can't decide within *one minute* what your answer will be, please go on to the next item.)
5. What is the minimum number of active baseball players on the playing field during any part of an inning?
6. Figure out this problem within one minute: If one face of a cube measures 2" by 4", what is the area of *each* of the faces, and what is the *total* area of all eight faces? (Jot down your answer in the margin.)
7. A farmer had 17 sheep. All but 9 died. How many did he have left?

8. An archeologist reported finding two gold coins dated 46 B.C. At a dinner in his honor, he was thoroughly and openly discredited by a disgruntled fellow archeologist. Why?

9. A man living in Winston-Salem, North Carolina, cannot be buried in a state west of the Mississippi River—nor in Hawaii or Alaska—even in the event of presidential intervention. Why is this?

10. If you went to bed at 8 o'clock last night and set your alarm clock to get up at 9 o'clock this morning, why on earth—after 13 hours rest, especially—are you sleepy today?

11. If you had only one match and you entered a room to start up a kerosene lamp, an oil heater, and a wood-burning stove, which would you light first and why?

12. Quickly: Divide 30 by $\frac{1}{2}$, and add 10. What is the answer?

13. If your doctor gave you three pills and told you to take one every half-hour, how long would it require for you to take all of them?

14. Two men played checkers. They played five games, and each man won three. How do you explain this?

15. Look at these phrases for a moment to get them firmly in mind:

PARIS
IN THE
THE SPRING

ONCE
IN A
A LIFETIME

BIRD
IN THE
THE HAND

SLOW
MEN AT
AT WORK

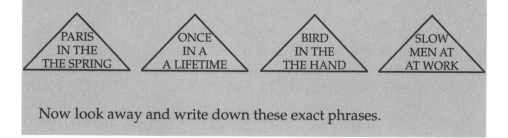

Now look away and write down these exact phrases.

Item Analysis of Sample Test 2: Building Awareness

What does this test test? Like all other tests, it is a test of test-taking skill. As always, approach the test in a relaxed, playful mode. Begin by *messing around.*

Browse. Browse. Browse.

No matter how short the time allowed, get *formatted.* You have to know what kind of game you are playing. It would be foolish to think you're playing hearts when the game is really poker. Yet students who are not test-wise make that mistake routinely.

Messing around reveals that TEST YOUR . . . WHAT? is a trick test, and logical reasoning is actually a hindrance. If you are playful and relaxed, you may see the answer to a couple of questions right off. (They are all old chestnuts, so you may recognize some of them) That happens on conventional tests, too, all the time. Everyone has a vast store of common knowledge that can answer many test questions, with no recourse to schooling whatever.

When appropriate, use common knowledge.

Once you catch on to the game, you know how to respond to the questions. In TEST YOUR . . . WHAT? you should score at least 12 points. You do not really have to know anything to do this.

1. *. . . spell a new word.*

You certainly should not give five of the allowed eight minutes to one question. So either save this one until last or ignore the five minutes suggested. After all, you have less than half a minute for each question.

Pace yourself.

Do the easy questions first. You will soon see that the answers are right there on the page, but in this game the test maker tries to hide them from you.

The "correct" answer is *a new word.* The writer tries to distract you first by making it seem hard: "Allow yourself five minutes . . ." Then, to take your eyes away from the phrase *a new word,* a raft of useless instructions immediately follows. Well-worded instructions would help guide you, but here your reading strength is turned against you. Once you catch on to the ploy, however, it is no longer a barrier. In fact, the question becomes easy.

Examine the motives of the test maker.

2. *How many did Adam take on board?*

It was *Noah,* not Adam. We are onto the game now. The "Quickly now" and the parentheses ( ) and underlining are all to keep you from noticing the word *Adam.* In this question and in the first question, *italic* is not used where it would help. It is used only where it will distract. Underhanded! But that is the game, and we are onto it, so why grumble? Use these tricks to your advantage.

Use the test to answer the test.

3. *DEFT SIGHING CALMNESS CANOPY FIRST STUN*

Browsing shows that most of the questions on this test call for the same *level* of thinking and the same *kind* of thinking. But this one is different—it requires different behavior and may take too long, unless you stumble on the answer accidentally. It is really not a trick. But you have to change gears to discover the *DEF, GHI, LMN, NOP, RST,* and *STU* sequences.

Every test has few clinkers, and it is all right to miss them. Fiddle with them only if you have time left over. Before you begin, always mess around to determine *the test's level of sophistication* so that you will know the kind of thinking the test maker accepts as "correct." Is the game bridge or canasta?

Find the right mind-set.

4. *. . . bury survivors?*

They are still alive. We know the underlining and helpful hints are just dust in the eyes. So we strip the junk away and the real question stands revealed: Where are survivors buried? Ah.

Remember, all tests are reading tests. You always have to browse until you are sure what is really being asked. That is usually the hard part. Once the question is clear, answering is much easier.

Find out what the question is really asking.

Nervous students often skim questions and misread them. Don't make this mistake.

Never get emotional in a money game.

5. *How many active baseball players?*

This question is written poorly. There are too many "right" answers. What does the writer mean by *active*? If you are calm enough during a test, ask the test giver to define confusing words or instructions—*before* the test starts, if possible. Make sure you are answering the question that's in the test maker's head, not the question in yours.

Answer the test maker's question, not your version of it.

If the test giver will not help, choose *your* best guess and write your reasoning in the margin.

6. *Area of each face of the cube and total area of the eight faces.*

A cube's sides are *squares,* and it has only *six* faces. In addition to the pattern of diversions we have discovered, the writer uses another of your bad habits against you. If you mechanically applied a math formula, you forgot this is a trick test. You don't have to know math for this test.

So, for any question, get the feel of it before answering. *Picture* the situation; even draw a picture to rough scale if you can. If the question is flawed, you cannot really answer it.

Visualize the problem; make a sketch.

On a regular test, ask about errors you see, or write a diplomatic note showing why the question cannot be answered. Test makers do make mistakes—including giving the test in the first place.

7. *All but 9 died.*

Too easy. You already caught on to this trick in number 4. *Use the test to answer the test.* A test is like a chapter in a textbook, but the information is scattered all over instead of in paragraphs. So if you browse around, you will find lots of help for almost any question on the test. What you need is right there on the page.

Helpful clues are scattered all over the test.

8. *Coins dated 46 B.C.*

Picture the situation. Get the feel of the question. Come back later. You know for sure that the clue is right on the surface and that you need no special information. B.C.!

9. *A man living in Winston-Salem.*

Same issue as in 2 and 4. Same tricks, too. Skilled test-takers notice such patterns and take advantage of them.

10. *. . . after 13 hours rest.*

Visualize.

You have to *see* the clock and imagine actually setting it. Then you will soon discover the problem. Of course, if you are used to 24-hour clocks, that won't help. But that is too sophisticated for this test.

Find the level of difficulty of the test and choose answers within that range.

11. *Which would you light first?*

Naturally, a good reader thinks the word *which* refers only to *lamp, heater,* and *stove.* To trick you, the test maker counts on your reading the way most people would. But you know this is a trick test—and not a very sophisticated one, either.

12. *Divide 30 by* $\frac{1}{2}$.

"Quickly" is what tries to throw you off. People get hurried and start multiplying instead of dividing. Again, make sure you *answer the question asked,* not your own version of it. This is where relaxed playfulness pays off: You *notice* more.

Put the question into your own words. Rephrase.

"If I divide something *by* half, I'm asking how many halves there are in it. In one pie there are two halves. In 30 pies, there are 60 halves. Plus 10 is 70." The wording of the question may be harder to figure out than the solution!

13. *One pill every half-hour.*

Visualize. Mentally take the pills. Picture the hands at, say, 7:00. Take one. Take the next at 7:30. Take the next at 8:00. See? *See.*

This is the third question on the test that could be solved by mentally going through the steps. Visualizing even a little bit of the process often reveals the answer.

14. *Each man won three games.*

Rotten question. The test maker leaves out information you need to answer correctly. In this trick test, it is deliberate, but teachers often omit needed data inadvertently, too. By this time, however, you—the skilled test taker—are onto the opponent's way of thinking.

Imagine you are the test maker planning your next move.

On school tests, if needed information is missing, ask for it.

15. *Write down these exact phrases.*

Of course, if you answered question 1 correctly, which required you to copy "A NEW WORD," you might think "these exact phrases" is what you should put down as your answer. Unfortunately, this test is not that consistent—a common circumstance with school tests, too.

This question is more on a par with questions 11 and 14 and uses your good reading habits against you. Good readers read *ideas,* not words. Here, the triangle camouflage the duplicated *the, a,* and *at.* But knowing the kind of test this is may alert you enough to

Slow down. Tick off the words out loud.

This is an editing or proofreading skill and requires changing gears.

Mastering the Game II

Always preview the test: Mess around.

- For clues, use the style of the test, level of sophistication, wording of questions or answers, and overall feel. What *level* of thinking; what *kind*?
- Pace yourself. Set the number of seconds per question and stick to your schedule. Use leftover time for the harder questions, *last.*
- Re-read a confusing question until you are sure of what is really wanted. Force yourself to read slowly, *saying* the question under your breath.
- Rephrase a tricky question in your own words. *Say* what it is really asking.
- Visualize. Make sketches. Run through a bit of the process to see if it works. Jot things down.

- A test is like a textbook chapter, but scrambled. The whole mass of information can be used to help answer any question.
- Use common knowledge and common sense.
- Imagine you are the test maker, planning your next move.
- Use natural recall and problem-solving strategies.

Always review your answers for clerical errors.

Item Analysis of Sample Test 3: Fine-Tuning

Following are questions taken from "real" tests. Try your test-taking skills on each one before reading the accompanying commentary. You will see that standardized tests call for the same approach used in the two sample tests you've already examined.

1. *Tales of giants in folklore and legend*

A. Usually refer to animal giants and only rarely to human giants.

B. Are workings of our imagination and are therefore totally untrue.

C. Are accurate reports of scientific facts.

D. Are sometimes true.

Cross off obviously wrong choices.

While messing around, *cross off any answer you notice won't work.* Sometimes you can eliminate three out of four without even trying. If you can eliminate just two, you go from one chance in four to fifty-fifty.

Let's see how it works here. *Common knowledge* eliminates A. Any kid can name lots of "human" giants (a really thoughtful person might wonder how the test maker defines *human.*) Cross out A.

Doesn't "totally untrue" in B send up a red flag? Just because we imagine it, does that mean it doesn't have a basis in fact? Cross out B. *Common sense* rules it out, but the *absolute, definite statement* is also a sign that it's "wrong."

Cross out C, also, since it is common knowledge that folklore and legend are anything but scientific facts. Now we can put D on the answer sheet without even looking at it! It's all that's left. Also, if you just choose the *most different* answer, D is the only answer that isn't definite and absolute. (It is also *the shortest*).

Next, see if you can guess which answer is "right" among the six below—even though I have not bothered to provide the question:

2.

A. He may run out of gas.

B. He will run out of gas.

C. He should not have taken this route.

D. He is lost.

E. He should turn right at the stop sign.

F. He should turn left at the stop sign.

The *most different answer* is A, and it happens to be the "right" one. Also, all the others are *definite,* but A is not so rigid. This item is from a test that purports to measure genius; if it does, test-taking skill must be a synonym for genius.

On this test of "genius" we found all 20 questions to be flawed. For example, two other questions had this wording:

3. *Which word does not belong in the following group?*

Here are the choices for one of the questions. Which would you choose and why?

A. knife	**B.** smile	**C.** lovely
D. swan	**E.** feather	**F.** thought

There are all sorts of reasons to include or exclude an item. So there is no way of knowing the test maker's viewpoint. Ask yourself in what *way* doesn't it belong? State the question properly, and it's more likely to be answered correctly.

In this example, students discussing possible "right" answers came up with cogent and imaginative justification for all six possibilities. The most common response was A, knife: "It is a metallic and sharp and feels out of place with the softer items." English teachers almost always choose C, lovely, because it's an adjective and the other's are nouns. But a linguist might question that, since lovely can be used as a noun.

What to do? *Think like the test maker.* He or she will label you a genius if you do. *The way to do that is to practice taking that kind of test.* Analyze the items you missed and see if there might have been a way to figure it out without knowing anything—that is, *get formatted* for that kind of test: GED, SAT, teacher-made, whatever kind you need to get good at.

So how do you get to Carnegie Hall?

Practice. Practice. Practice.
Always analyze items you missed.
See if there are clues or tip-offs you could have used.

Even a test of information is less foolproof than test makers think. This item from a standardized dental hygienist test is not atypical:

4. *The dental hygienist consults with administrators, conducts an education program with the residents and provides in-service training for the nursing staff. Which of the following would be appropriate for assessing the outcome of the completed project?*

A. Interviews with the nursing staff

B. Interviews with administrators

C. Comparison of pre- and post-indices

D. Survey of existing methods of dental care

E. Inventory of available oral physiotherapy aids and mobile dental equipment

1. A and B only
2. A, B and C
3. B and D
4. C only
5. C, D and E
6. All of the above

Common sense would rightly pinpoint (6), *All of the above*, as the wanted answer. If the item isn't ridiculous, of course it would be OK to do what it recommends. But common sense isn't even necessary here. On the original test, just above this question *on the same page*, we found a paragraph setting up a situation that calls for every one of the items in this question.

The test answers the test.

A good test taker can actually learn about dental hygiene while taking this test! Even technical terms are not indecipherable. In this test we were able to work out answers involving the terms OHI-S, DMFT, Russell's PI, caries, and peridontal, even without knowing for certain what they meant.

Here's another point—if you're worried sick about getting your dentistry license, you will not be relaxed and playful enough to lap up all this gravy. For most people, the difficulty with tests is emotions, not intellect. So remember this:

Emotion is a major barrier to getting high scores.

Incidentally, questions structured like those in the dental hygiene test are considered needlessly cumbersome by test-making specialists. Valuable time is consumed sorting out all those A's, B's, C's, D's and E's and then trying to keep them straight for the answer sheet.

Keep Track of Acceptable/Unacceptable Choices

For *all-of-the-above, none-of-the-above* options, put a T next to any answer that seem reasonable. Put an X next to any that are clearly not acceptable.

5. *A general rule for memorizing is:*

   A. Memorize by rote in half-hour to one-hour sessions.

   B. Put the material in your own words.

   C. Repeat the material over and over.

   D. No pain, no gain.

Similar answers may cancel each other out. Watch for them. Since A and C mean roughly the same thing, they are probably both wrong. That leaves B and D. If they both seem right, pick the one that seems better. Test makers cover themselves by the instruction "Choose the best answer," not "Choose the correct answer." Here, B is the wanted answer.

Cross out wrong answers as you go. It is less confusing.

6. *School may be defined as a game because*

   A. time limits are set.

   B. many people participate.

   C. there is a leader.

   D. it has artificial and arbitrary rules.

Chose the *most inclusive answer,* D. The other answers may be aspects of the game, but D is a more general description and is broad enough to include the others. In this case,

**Pick an answer that includes the others,
not just a single aspect or detail.**

7. *The best time to review for a test is*

   A. immediately before you go to bed.

   B. while concentrating on a different subject.

   C. during another class.

   D. immediately after you get up.

When opposites appear as choices, one is likely to be right.

Common sense would make B and C unlikely, anyway. Here A is the wanted answer.

8. *The saying "No rose but which has its thorns" means most nearly:*

   A. The sweetest smelling rose has its perfume.

   B. Touch not the thorn which grows on a rose.

   C. No rare gem without its flaw.

   D. Malice seldom wants a mark to aim at.

   E. Where there is smoke there is fire.

First try to put the saying into your own words and in more general terms.

"Any valued thing has its drawback." What relationship is emphasized (Valued thing plus negative aspect.) In A, perfume is a positive aspect. Cross it out. Answer B is a warning; the original statement is not. Cross out B. Answer D involves elements external to the original statement. Cross it out, too. Finally, E contains elements that go together. So that leaves C as the most likely answer.

Group Think

This type of question expects you to think like everybody else. A more interesting game my classes sometimes play is to think up points of view from which *each* answer is "right." Rather than merely retrieving stored data, everyone gets to use imagination, ingenuity and active mental processes.

Usually if there is one question like number 8 on a test, there will be several. The best defense is to practice in advance.

Get sample tests from the library and analyze your missed items until you get formatted for such tests.

If you come upon any new kind of test structure without warning, *play with a few questions until you know you are onto the game.* Then go back and work over the first ones again.

9. T/F: *It is not a matter of concern not to review your test answers.*

Untangle the tricky wording first.

"Let's see. The statement is saying it is OK not to review your answers. Wrong. It is so." Something like that. This item isn't too bad, but others of this sort can be a real mess. Just be sure to straighten it out before trying to answer. If the statement is too confusing altogether, save it till the end to play with. If you skim over the question, you may misunderstand what is actually being asked. And don't forget—*absolute, definite statements are likely to be false.* Watch for words like *always, never, all, none, impossible* or any flat-out statement.

In contrast, *tentative, wishy-washy statements are likely to be true.* Tip-offs are words like *seldom, usually, perhaps, may,* or *generally.* The wanted answer is usually True.

10. *Select the pair of words that has a relationship most like that of the original pair.*

TRIGGER : BULLET

A. handle : drawer

B. holster : gun

C. bulb : light

D. switch : current

E. pulley : rope

Translate the relationship into regular English.

"*Trigger* has the same relationship to *bullet* as *what* to *what*? Take some time first to see how *trigger* is related to *bullet*. The trigger *activates* the bullet. What relationship is just like that? If you think like the test maker, the only possible answer is D.

The item above is from an analogy test. It is supposed to test thinking ability. Such questions appear on aptitude and general-ability tests. But all they really measure is previous experience in working with such relationships and prior information. (What a field day independent, imaginative thinkers would have if asked to "Find at least one point of view from which each pair below has the same relationship as the original pair.")

Since such items are common fare on many standardized tests, a wise player would get good at them in advance.

Practice.

Libraries have sample tests and puzzle books. Like all tests, there is a knack to mastering them. Wouldn't it be nice if such "tests" were given and taken as recreational diversions rather than administered as valid indicators of intellectual ability and social worth?

Fall in Love with Tests

Whole books have been written about what is wrong with tests and what is wrong with testing. There are dozens more on how to take tests. *But the best way to get good at taking them is to do your own ongoing investigation.* Fall in love with tests, how they are made, what to look for. Make up your own tests. Take tests every chance you get. You will soon shift from being *content oriented* to *playing the game yourself*. You will also have a thoroughly good time.

- Get sample tests from the library.

- Review old tests to get used to the instructions and format. Often the directions are the hardest part.

- Play with puzzle-question books.
- Do item analysis—out loud.
- Analyze items you miss with an eye toward improving your game.

Mastering the Game III

Practice

- Learn to laugh. Test taking is a peculiar, amusing activity.

Practice

- Analyze missed items—out loud.

Practice

- Develop assurance through experience.

Practice

- Fall in love with tests.

Practice

Essay Tests: Stringing Beads

To get high scores on essay tests, practice writing answers to questions you yourself make up.

Writing answers to essay tests is not as complicated as you might believe. Supposedly, essay tests measure ability to organize, draw conclusions, relate ideas, and so on. In practice, however, they usually end up being simply recall tests but *with the facts embedded in sentences instead of listed in phrases.* So essay tests are really just another form of trivia test.

Commonly, tests makers have a list of facts they would like to see in your paper. When you get your scored exam back, you will see the points or checks noted in the margins.

Essay Tests are Recall Tests

- Make your own list of the facts your teacher is likely to look for in your essay.
- Use a reliable memory device.
- Jot down the data—your trivia list—somewhere *before* even looking at the test questions.
- Read over the test directions enough to be sure of what is really being asked. Why lose points because you misunderstood?
- See that your trivia list gets stuffed into your paper somehow.

Smooth connections from one fact to the next may help some, but your Social Science teacher, for instance, does not have time to consider the quality of your composition or of your thinking and originality. He or she is usually reduced to skimming for key ideas (facts). So make it easy on teachers and raise your score in the process.

Mastering Essay Tests I: Game Plan

- *When you get the test, jot down your memorized list first.* This will reduce anxiety about forgetting.
- *Preview the test.* Be sure of what is really being asked and what will be credited. Notice how much time is allowed, how many questions must be answered, which ones are easier, and if there is credit for answering extra questions.
- *Allot time for each answer and stick to this schedule.* If all questions are worth the same credit, give them equal time.

- *Do every question that will be credited.* Write *something*. You don't get any credit for a blank page.

- *Do easy questions first.* Answer exactly what is asked and then *stop*. Save leftover time for playing with questions you at first thought you couldn't answer. You *can*.

- *Don't change the subject*. You will not get much credit for a beautifully written wrong answer. There are more productive ways to address the problem of not really knowing anything.

- *Get used to what is meant by typical test directions.*

Some Common Directions Found in Essay Tests

"Compare and Contrast"

"Compare *Howard's End* with *Enchanted April.*" How are they alike? How are they different? Stuff in enough facts to make it stick. Your opinion is not usually wanted.

Think like the test maker.

"Define"

"Define *hollyfud.*" Just tell what it is. Give just enough information so that it will not get mixed up with something else. Tell what is unique about it.

"Discuss"

"Discuss the four main causes of the Civil War." Put down what both the *teacher and the text* say are important about them. (If you do not know, make up your own four causes. What would common sense say?) Describe each cause and tell how and why each helped to start the conflict. Put it in simple, straightforward English. Pretend you are telling it to a fifth-grader. Your teacher will be impressed.

Don't show off. Write as if you are having a conversation with a fifth-grader. What questions would a fifth-grader ask? Answer them.

"Criticize"

"Criticize the Monroe Doctrine." *Criticize* doesn't mean to give only the faults. Write about both good and bad points. Stick to conventional views, unless you are sure the teacher wants your opinion. Judge it good or bad, true or false, right or wrong according to whatever slant was *supported in class by your teacher or was expressed in your text.*

Be sure to read the directions carefully—a couple of times if necessary. "Criticize Shakespeare's *Hamlet*" is a distinctly different instruction from "Criticize the production of *Hamlet* performed here last Friday." The first is the play itself; the second is the production. If you're nervous or in a hurry, you could misread the instruction. So,

Deliberately slow down.

"Trace"

"Trace the development of economic stability in California from the beginning until 1990." Put the events in a time sequence. First, on scratch paper, jot down dates and events in a column. Then in your paper, put these facts into sentences and tie one into the next. Usually there will be three to five key items, with possibly a few minor facts tossed in.

"Illustrate"

"Two wrongs don't make a right. Illustrate." Tell a story of which the point reminds you. To put it another way, *illustrate* means to *draw a picture.* So draw a picture in words, or make a sketch, or both.

Other Words That Crop Up in Essay Tests

describe	enumerate	explain
list	outline	prove
justify	review	summarize

You probably know what they mean. But do not get spooked and change the directions inside your head. If asked to *enumerate,* do not write an evaluation as well.

Mastering Essay Tests II: Writing Strategies

- *Leave time to review and proofread for clerical and factual errors. Replace repeated words or phrases* with something else that means the same thing. Or *stuff in a fact.* The paper will seem more knowledgeable. Wherever possible, *replace pronouns* (words such as I, we, you, he, she, it, they, or who, me, us, your, his) *with nouns.*

- *Use lots of paragraphs to make the writing look organized.* Insert roughly one new fact for each paragraph. The test reader will find it easier to check the essay for the facts on his or her list.

- *Write neatly.* Research shows sloppy papers are often graded down one whole letter.

- *Leave lots of space between answers for things you remember later.*

- *In blue-book tests, leave the left-hand page blank.* If you think of something to add, put it there, and draw a neat arrow to where it belongs.

- Even at the cost of neatness, *do cross out or correct errors.*

- *Don't find fault with a test question in your essay answer*—unless you don't mind getting a lower grade.

- *Avoid being folksy, cute or apologetic. Say it and stop.* Some teachers do not care for "I think". . . , "It seems to me". . . , "In my opinion". . . , and the like. Avoid them.

- *If you run out of time for your last answer, put in an outline or list your facts.* You may get full credit. Give it a try. And next time, pace yourself.

Hanging-In Tactics

You Have a Mental Block

If the problem really is a mental block, activating some deliberate retrieval strategies should get things flowing again.

Get something on that blank sheet of paper.

This is a "where-were-you-on-Valentine's-Day-three-years-ago" situation. You know *something* about all sorts of things, and when you start tracing them back, you will find everything is connected. So mess around and see what happens. You are almost sure of getting *some* points.

A good way to get unstuck is just to start writing—anything remotely connected to the subject. Write anything at all. *As you write, you will begin to remember things.*

The brain is a connecting organ. One thing leads to another, and everything is interconnected. Use the natural retrieval strategies we all have, but be sure to put down the thoughts *as they come,* so that you will have some words on paper. *What you need is in there; it just needs to be teased out.*

"What were the four causes of the Civil War?" Believe that you *do* know some things about the Civil War: Lincoln, his assassination, slavery, cotton, the Grey and the Blue, England and France, Sumpter, Peachtree Street. The Mason-Dixon Line, John Brown, Carl Sandburg, Rhett Butler, Northern factories, transportation, Gettysburg, Lee, *Huckleberry Finn.*

Step back and see what you have on paper. By this time you may notice an overall pattern. If you do, you can go back and insert or cross out. Insert topic sentences (a sentence that puts it all in a nutshell) and connecting sentences to make it all seem organized. Write a summary. Anyone skimming for the facts you've written on your test will not normally have time to pay attention to your style. You have more information than you guessed and your paper will probably read much better than you thought possible.

To take this approach, you have to like yourself enough to want to give it a try.

Believe that you are as good as anyone else in the room. You have a right to top grades. *You would not give up in basketball; don't give up in this game, either.*

You're Unprepared

If you really did not study, the day of the test is not time to panic. You are there, it *is* a game; see what you can salvage.

Never give up in a school game.

Keep in mind that some of the papers that get top grades are written by BS artists. You can try that too. Never leave the page blank—even a wild guess might get you some credit.

Suppose you are asked to identify Franklin Roosevelt, for example. The grader will be looking for facts. Maybe you get five points for the question. Okay, let's dig up and stuff in some facts:

> Franklin Roosevelt was a *Twentieth Century U.S. president* who had a strong *influence on American life,* despite the *paralysis* (you saw two minutes of *Sunrise at Campobello* on late-night TV once) that confined him to a wheelchair. His wife *Eleanor* became famous herself. Franklin was the *second Roosevelt in the White House.*

It's not much, but you may pick up some credit, and that may be just enough to save your skin.

Always try.

Use this page to add your own tips, tricks and tactics for taking essay tests.

Common Questions About Taking Tests

What's the Best Attitude?

It is good to be a little but not too anxious. Get too smug and you will be careless with easy questions; too tense, and you will keep trying the wrong strategy (tunnel vision). Psychologist W. Lambert Gardiner puts it this way: "Sweat if it's easy; relax if it's hard."

Don't assume you will fail; but don't be nonchalant, either. Get every point you can.

What About Cramming?

If you did not pace your work earlier, sure, take every break you can get. But *plan your attack.* Don't just wade in and try to read everything you put off for all those weeks.

Get an overview of the stuff. Find the general outline and main points. Follow the steps of routine review given for "What's the best way to review?" below, and in the later section "Game Plan for Taking Tests."

Should I Stay Up All Night?

You can get along without sleep well beyond 24 hours. If you have your wits about you and remain cool, conceivably you could sit up all night preparing. Psychologically, however, people get more anxious the longer they spend going over material. In general, then, *the best strategy is to get a good night's sleep.*

Should I Take the Night Off Before a Test?

No. Living it up before a test is not really beneficial—at least there is no research to support it. There is *plenty,* however, to suggest you should put in a *reasonable* amount of study and go to bed. A couple of hours of review are plenty. Sleep reinforces and fixes what has been studied (like Jell-O)—provided nothing disruptive has happened in between.

What's the Best Way to Review?

If you made useful notes right in the text (more on this in Chapter 3 and 4), review these. Your own markings will provide the gist of the chapter.

What are the author's main points? There will be three to five or so per chapter. How does the writer support them? Once you have retrieved this overview from your earlier study, *make up questions like ones your teacher might ask.* Brush up on any weak areas.

Use exactly the same approach for cramming as for review. Outline the chapters, but don't try to read the material. Count on your test-taking skills to piece together specific answers.

Does Extra Study Work?

A little overlearning is good, but excessive study can wreck your nervous system. So *deliberately plan a length of time for review, proceed systematically, and STOP.*

Game Plan for Taking Tests

Before the Test

- *Review one or two hours just before bedtime.* If you used the study methods recommended in this book, you won't need this much time.

- *Get up at a normal time for you.* Treat the day as routinely as possible. Eat your normal breakfast.

> **Chop Wood. Carry Water**
>
> A high-protein breakfast helps keep blood sugar up all day and provides continuous necessary energy. A shower and light exercise will tone up the body—and the spirit. But *daily rituals* are the best insurance against panic.

- *Do a relaxation exercise, if at all possible.* Largo music; slow walk. Get into a playful but relaxed and alert state of mind.

- *Reinforce memory of key ideas and build confidence by leafing through your review materials for a few minutes.*

- *Get to class early enough to get seated and lay out necessary materials.* Getting there too early or too late increases tension. Talking with friends usually has that effect, too.

- *Sit in your usual seat.* Avoid distractions, including friends.

Virtual Reality

Before looking at the test, visualize the place where you studied. People who *see* the setting score more points than those who do not.

During the Test

In general, use the test-taking tips throughout this chapter. In addition:

- *If there is more than one way to interpret the general instructions for the test, ask the teacher which meaning is intended.* If any test items are unclear or ambiguous, ask for clarification. If necessary, write notes in the margin.

- *Remember to do easy questions first. Play with the hard ones.*

- *If you start to get tense, come back later.* Do some muscle tensing and relaxing exercises. Try breathing slowly and deeply and count your breaths for half a minute or so.

- *Answer every question, even if there are penalties for guessing.* People who guess get better scores than those who don't.

- *First answers are not always best.* Studies show that people who change their answers generally score higher than those who don't. When you review your answers, if something else looks better, select it.

- *Unless there is reason to do otherwise, treat questions as though they are being asked honestly.* The key is to think like the test maker.

- In math, *estimate the answer or solve the problem before looking at the multiple-guess answers.* Otherwise, you may tend to work the problem to fit one of the answers.

- Persist. People who make the highest scores stick with the test until forced to leave. Let the others leave. *Being passive is one of the main barriers to high scores.* Low-scorers think the answer must be there *now;* high-scorers play all the angles and figure it out. Squeeze out every point you can.

PLAY TO WIN.

Talk Yourself Through the Test

Skilled test-takers talk themselves through tough questions. Replace the *I'm-a-rotten-student-and-I-always-fail* tape in your mind and slap in the one that reminds you of your success.

Change the tape:

"I've done lots tougher things than this. I know plenty of recall strategies. Let's look for clues on the test. Hang in there. This is a game. I am a capable, intelligent human being. I have been successful in almost everything I ever tried."

After the Test: Perfecting Your Game

Study Your Mistakes

Become a skilled test-taker by knowing what went wrong. How was your game off? What strategies will prevent your getting caught again? Mistakes and failures are *information.* In a money game, don't get emotional. *No grade is ever final.*

- *Do an item analysis.*

- *Examine the first quiz in any class for clues to the test maker's style and format.* Figure out the level and kind of thinking called for by examining what answers were considered "right." Which of your strategies worked well or poorly? What kind of questions should you make up for practice next time?

- *Ask for an appointment to go over your wrong answers with your teacher.* Be diplomatic. Don't say the test was lousy. Most teachers consider their tests works of art. The real purpose of the visit is to touch bases. Make the teacher conscious of you, your name and your "interest" in the course. The idea is for the teacher to think that if you fail the course, he or she has failed, too. If your grade hovers between a C and B, the human factor can tip the scale.

- *Failure is never final.* Failure is information. *No test has ever been designed that can measure what you really know or how smart you are.*

  No test grade and no course grade is ever the last word. When you have self-esteem, there is always something more you can do. School is a game and there are lots of ways to score. Item analysis will reveal the right approach. Then go for it.

Here are some productive responses to failure:

- A make-up test
- An extra project
- A better game plan for future tests
- A conference with the teacher (let the teacher suggest something)
- A tutor
- A different approach to study
- Transfer to different teacher or college
- An extenuating-circumstance grade change
- Withdrawal from the course
- Re-assessment of what you really want out of life

You get the idea. But keep your solution in line with the problem. A popgun may be all that is needed.

- *Take your score with good humor.* Emotional reaction disrupts thinking processes. If you are playfully relaxed and alert, you will be more effective in planning your next move. Despair is self-destructive.

> *Self-esteem is the greatest gift you can give yourself. The only person who can give you a failing mark is you.*

Conquering Test Anxiety

Most people are too anxious during tests. Their concern clouds their reasoning and makes them less efficient. Off balance, they score far lower than they should. No one who is going to spend 12–16 years or more taking tests should endure this unnecessary handicap. The solution, of course, is to learn the rules and techniques of successful test taking.

Success builds assurance.

Self-assurance in turn frees us to perform better and better. Once we realize that 80 percent of our score depends on *how* we take the test, it becomes obvious that learning rules of the test-taking game is crucial. You don't have to be clever, brilliant, or dishonest to do it, either. It is a simple matter of observation and practice.

Oddly, hardly anyone thinks much about what it means to make, give and take tests. Once we see tests are school games that have little meaning in the real world, once we realize the game has a format that can be recognized and rules that can be mastered, playing strategies that can be learned, test taking becomes as entertaining as Trivial Pursuit® or crossword puzzles.

Mastering the skill of test taking, like learning to absorb and retrieve information, is part of the process of educating oneself. So the effort will not be wasted or pointless. Figuring out tests is a problem-solving experience. And *developing confidence to recognize and solve problems is not just a school game but a true education activity.*

In Real Life, There Are No Final Exams

Once you hit the streets, you will never, ever suffer a final exam. Bob Green ("One of Life's Closely Guarded Secrets," *Chicago Tribune,* 1981) is exactly right:

> "There are no cases in which you have to sit down in a crowded room, scrunch your eyes up in concentration and regurgitate obscure and ridiculous facts from memory. . . . The only place you'll ever encounter something as bizarre and frightening as a final exam is at college. . . . If someone did come up to you at work and asked you to do something like that, he'd soon be locked up in an institution somewhere. . . . If the real world were as bizarre and rotten as final exams, you'd see everyone on the street walking around in the same demented, pathetic state as college students during exam week."

Gamesmanship

High scores depend on test-taking skill. So:

- Learn to play the game.
- Develop skill through ITEM ANALYSIS.
- Develop assurance through PRACTICE.
- Have the self-esteem to PERSIST.
- Use the Mess-Around Theory of Test Taking.
- Play around until you understand the game.
- Format.
- Rack up all the points you can. Then do the leftovers.

FALL IN LOVE WITH TEST TAKING.

Use this page to collect additional test-taking tips.

The Wizard of Oz Revealed

It really is all smoke and mirrors. Go backstage and discover the tricks of test makers and you begin to laugh. It is impossible to take these curious rituals seriously. Once you see testing as an inconsequential game, you can put your full mind to getting good at it. You will perform at peak efficiency. Better still, you will be freed to enjoy your college years. It is good for your health.

Tests have only as much power over us as we give them. If we grant authority to test makers, then they *do* have it. We can retrieve that power by becoming test-wise. All it takes is paying attention to the structure itself. So examine it, fiddle with it, play around, and soon the whole scheme is unmasked.

Fair enough. Players ought to know as much about the game as the management, but a test-wise student usually knows *more.* Most teachers never think about the implications of making, giving and taking tests. It is just the way things were done when they got there, and they keep on doing it. It would be harder to get them to stop than to abolish cigarette smoking. We all know what entrenched habits are like.

The Mess-Around Theory will make you an expert. Playfully examine tests, make up questions, and you will soon develop a system of your own for playing the game. It's like going to Las Vegas: If you want to leave all your money there, then play blackjack the way college students typically take tests. Or learn how to count cards. Better still, STAY HOME. That is, don't get caught up emotionally in someone else's game. Create your *own* game.

Students who have their own agenda, who take guidance from their deepest selves, are the ones who prevail. Sticks and carrots are irrelevant. These are the joyous students—the ones who educate not only themselves but their teachers, as well. Imagine a critical mass of such autonomous creatures. The whole testing apparatus would topple, followed closely by the demise of registrars. It is not impossible.

31 Tips for Test Taking

1. Browse. Browse. Browse.
2. When appropriate, use common knowledge.
3. Pace yourself.
4. Examine the motives of the test maker.
5. Use the test to answer the test.
6. Find the right mind-set.
7. Find out what the question is really asking.
8. Never get emotional in a money game.
9. Answer the test maker's question, not your version of it.
10. Visualize the problem; make a sketch.
11. Helpful clues are scattered all over the test.
12. Visualize.
13. Put the question in your own words. Rephrase.
14. Imagine you are the test maker planning your next move.
15. On school tests, if needed information is missing, ask for it.
16. Slow down. Tick off the words out loud.
17. Cross off obviously wrong choices.
18. Practice. Practice. Practice.
19. Always analyze items you missed.
20. See if there are clues or tip-offs you could have used.
21. The test answers the test.
22. Emotion is a major barrier to getting high scores.
23. Cross out wrong answers as you go. It is less confusing.
24. Pick an answer that includes the others, not just a single aspect or detail.
25. When opposites appear as choices, one is likely to be right.
26. First try to put the saying into your own words and in more general terms.
27. Get sample tests from the library and analyze your missed items until you get formatted for such tests.
28. Untangle the tricky wording first.
29. Translate the relationship into regular English.
30. Practice.
31. Think like the test maker.

C H A P T E R

4

Reading Textbooks

Turning Textbooks into Love Letters

"Only art teaches.
Everything else is torture."
—G. B. Shaw

Browse

Focus

Absorb

Reinforce

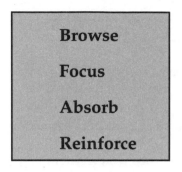

Taking Pleasure in Reading Textbooks

A nerd *has* to read. But a good reader knows that in all that manure there *must* be a pony. Active browsing will find it.

- **Browse**

  As you've learned to do, play suitable music and quiet the body and mind. Then, browse, browse, browse until some aspect becomes interesting.

- **Focus**

  Playful messing around will lead in a natural way to a focused awareness.

- **Absorb**

  Browsing with focused awareness brings pleasurable, effortless absorption.

- **Reinforce**

  Saying what is understood or writing it down fixes the absorbed information in memory.

Browse ⇨ ***Focus*** ⇨ ***Absorb*** ⇨ ***Reinforce***

What Makes A Good Reader?

Mark only the ideas you agree with. Then read the commentary that follows.

☐ **1.** Experts in a subject are the best textbooks writers.

☐ **2.** Most textbooks are well written.

☐ **3.** For most students, reading is a waste of time.

☐ **4.** Textbooks are difficult because subjects are.

☐ **5.** A good reader reads well no matter what the subject.

☐ **6.** Poor readers plunge in anywhere.

☐ **7.** Good readers read and understand every word of a chapter or book.

☐ **8.** The best readers begin at the beginning and work through each sentence to the end.

☐ **9.** Textbooks are designed to encourage good reading habits.

☐ **10.** Good reading is a talent of gifted human beings.

Commentary: What a Good Reader Really Is

1. Experts in a subject are the best textbook writers?

Most experts are not particularly good at writing and some are lousy at it. A writer is one kind of artist; a social scientist or a musician or a physicist is another. Rarely is one person good at both. Nevertheless, experts usually write the textbooks, and students are obliged to suffer the resultant mess.

2. *Most textbooks are well written?*

You will find few textbooks among the *belles-lettres.* They are usually pedestrian efforts to get the facts into print. Unfortunately, when a book is not well written, it is hard to read. "Only art teaches," said G. B. Shaw. "Everything else is torture." No wonder students fall asleep over an economics text or get headaches trying to decipher an anthropology chapter. It is hard to write beautifully. It is even harder to read what is not beautifully written.

Lay side by side two explanations of the binomial theorem and you will see immediately that one does a better job than the other. If a student is stuck with a particularly poor text, it is good practice to have a couple of versions of the subject at hand and make the best of a bad lot. Browse texts by other writers for better explanations of confusing topics. Learn to cross-reference.

Of course, if textbooks were indeed finely crafted, the prose would illuminate the subject, not obscure it. Some books take hundreds of words to make an obvious point while ignoring real difficulties, and are hypnotically monotonous. Textbooks are a major barrier to what the college experience should be: a joyous adventure of the mind. A student with self-esteem will take necessary steps to correct this.

It is possible to get the essence from a textbook and even have fun at it. To change the game, you must first of all stop taking textbooks seriously. Certainly you must not stand in awe of the writer. Reverence will only shackle you. In particular, the Mess-Around Theory must be applied boldly and freely and playfully. Self-confidence is all there is to it. This chapter amplifies the concept.

3. *For most students, reading is a waste of time?*

It certainly is. Time spent unproductively is time wasted, and the typical approach to reading schoolbooks is anything but efficient. Most students, for example, read all their texts as if they were written by the same author, or are all on the same subject, or have the same purpose, or are all packed with absolutely valuable information, however redundant or confused. Do you spend long evenings, with little profit for your efforts, poring over material that doesn't seem worth reading in the first place? It need not be that way.

I have often said to students, "Don't waste time on your schoolwork" or "Don't waste time reading." Wasting time on schoolbooks numbs the mind and senses and retards education. You don't get merit badges for drudgery; there has to be some pleasure in the undertaking. But surprising as it may be, extracting data from even the worst textbook *can* be stimulating. With a good strategy, the gold can be panned ten times faster than with the approach most people use.

4. Textbooks are difficult because subjects are?

A good teacher can explain calculus to a first grader. A good writer can make any subject fascinating. There is no such thing as a dull subject, but anything can be written about dully. Compare different versions of the Bible, for example, or look at the myriad ways to write about love.

One tactic is to find the best text on the subject. *Find a beautifully written text and your reading problems are virtually eliminated. Or begin with some other medium. Get formatted first with a good audio tape or a video or good fiction or a good conversation.*

To research this book, I talked with directors of several major schools of education. I began by asking for their metaphors for the concepts we discussed. Later, I read the materials they recommended. By then, I had an *overview,* a *map.* My mind was *formatted,* so it was easy to find and understand what I needed.

Most of the wisdom and understanding of this planet was acquired orally, through conversation with remarkable people. Great artists can write or talk simply about profound subjects. Academics may think books are the only source of information. They are not. *Textbooks are not sacred.*

5. *A good reader reads well no matter what the subject?*

"Reading well" does not mean reading everything at the same pace and with the same technique. A good reader does not always begin with paragraph one, does not always look at the table of contents and index first, and so on. A book of poetry calls for a different kind of reading from that used to understand a computer manual. A physicist may find a physics book a breeze but will be bogged down in a social science text. And no two physicists will approach a new text in the same way. No one is equally good at all types of printed matter. Because of experience, background and interest, it is natural for each reader to be good at some subjects and not others. Nonetheless, with confidence and self-esteem, any motivated reader can gain access to the ideas in any book efficiently and with pleasure. *A good reader is a problem solver.*

We hear people say, "Oh, I read 250 words per minute," or "I read 400 words per minute," and so on. But reading everything at the same pace is the opposite of good reading. Hardly anyone thinks to ask, *What* do you read at that speed? James Joyce? Your chemistry text? The newspaper? The want ads? A computer manual? Familiar material? Strange material? Clearly, the reading has to be paced to the material and to the reasons one is reading it is in the first place. A reader needs a variety of speeds and approaches.

It makes sense to check out the job first. Browsing or messing around reveals what needs to be done. When your purpose has been achieved, it is intelligent to quit.

6. *Poor readers plunge in anywhere?*

Conventional wisdom would think it is terrible to start anywhere. But just about any approach that breaks free of word-for-word, beginning-to-end, unformatted reading is better. Starting at the back could actually be more efficient. Halfway toward the front, a reader will have grasped all the essentials. One never knows in advance, but browsing will reveal whether this result is likely. At the least, the reader would be active.

7. *Good readers read and understand every word of a chapter or book?*

Oh, sure! Most teachers seem to think so. Many reading teachers—who should know better—think so, too. But ordinary mortals write textbooks, and their message did not come down from the mountain. Even a well-written text may contain only a few pages that are relevant for a particular reader. Thirty readers of an assigned text will have thirty different interactions with it. Your own purpose is what governs the intensity and thoroughness of the encounter.

Unnecessary thorough reading is poor reading and even fosters counterproductive habits. There is nothing admirable in running one's eyes over black squiggles on flattened wood pulp.

Get in and get out. Eat what is nourishing. Save the forests.

8. *The best readers begin at the beginning and work through each sentence to the end?*

Imagine reading a newspaper in that straightforward way—or a love letter. There is hardly ever a good reason to read word-for-word; moreover, there are plenty of good reasons not to. To start in at the first word is like walking blindly into the wilderness without a map, equipment or a destination.

Reading is series of passes through print that culminate in a desired result.

9. *Textbooks encourage good reading habits?*

More often, they contribute to *poor* reading habits. People who can proficiently read self-selected books are often "stupid" when it comes to schoolbooks. Reading such books can indeed be stupefying. Passive reading leads to inattention, impatience, somnolence, regressions, befuddlement, little or no absorption and general resentment. The wise, self-educating student shifts from *having to read* a text to *choosing to read it,* and decides his or her own agenda.

It is natural to read well, and motivated readers have few bad habits. When we ourselves control what we learn, our behavior is intelligent. But when students feel forced to read, trouble starts. If they apply their natural skills to textbooks, however, they will have good results. Apply the principles of the sandbox, and reading a textbook is a cinch.

10. Good reading is a talent of gifted human beings?

Without interference in a supportive environment, anyone will read pertinent topics as well as necessary. Reading is part of the equipment acquired in a literate culture. Need and desire and *joie de vivre* educate.

Once you've cracked the code, further skill depends on background, need or desire, and habits. Self-concept and emotion are major influences. Accomplished reading teachers spend more time on mental health than on technique. Good reading, like the use of language, is directed by the nonconscious right hemisphere, not in the conscious mind. It is something that goes on while we attend to other things. Thinking about reading *while reading* cripples.

Aptitude is not essential for accomplishing any task, including reading. So even if some people do have aptitude for reading, as some do for learning languages, talent is not essential. Anyone can manage college textbooks. In fact, a resourceful student may figure out how to conquer a subject without reading the worst stuff at all.

A Problem-Solving Approach to Reading

The same approach works for extracting meaning from print as for solving any problem—fixing a motor, taking tests, memorizing, backpacking:

> *Look the job over first. Do it. Afterward, check the results and tidy up.*

A self-directed reader approaches a government document or a Shakespeare play in the same way. Of course, he or she may scarcely pause over complete sections of the newspaper but will happily dwell at length on a few lines of Robert Frost. In either case, nothing is to be gained from spending one second on the reading itself. *It is the ideas that count.*

An alert problem solver, reading some new material, will realize there is a special set of words (usually only a few) for a special context for familiar words, and some simple relationship holding those key words together. The job is to identify these words and this pattern.

Problem solving usually starts by fooling around with The Idea rather lightly and playfully. Of course, in the midst of the task one loses all sense of time; the process is automatic. Even for an arduous task, such as scaling Everest, the commitment is irreversible and psychologically effortless. Whether you're making a sand castle, taking a trip, or reading a biology chapter—use the same general approach:

1. Get the feel of the problem. Look it over. Touch the parts.
2. Make a first guess, a tentative plan, a flexible opener.
3. Try it out and adapt as needed. More salt, less flour.
4. Check it out. How did you do? What fine-tuning is needed?

Reading as Problem Solving

Plan a little in advance.
Afterward, check the results and reinforce.

BFAR: A Method for Reading Anything

Reading schoolbooks is called *studying*. The word has a serious ring to it, but is nothing more than applying natural problem-solving techniques to printed matter. Everyone already knows how to master problems of ordinary life and has succeeded innumerable times—tying shoes, driving a car, getting to the post office. BFAR simply applies that process to reading texts. After a few sessions, BFAR will be as effortless for you as any other habit.

BFAR: A Study-Reading Method

- **Browse**

  Play around with the assignment until what needs to be done, what *your* purpose is, becomes clear.

- **Focus**

  Get the picture. Adjust your lens until the picture (the general idea) is clear. Zip through for an overview—or whatever you have decided you want to do with this stuff—*without intense reading or taking notes.*

- **Absorb**

  Once you "get it," whatever it takes to do that, go back and *mark the key ideas.* Clear up any confusion, but only if that's necessary to fulfill your purpose. Things you don't really need to know can remain totally confusing. No one has time to master every single thing he or she runs across.

- **Reinforce**

  Write out what you now understand *in your own words,* as briefly as possible, or tell it to someone.

Applying BFAR

Most students read adequately for themselves. But they don't transfer these habits to reading school books. None would argue the foolishness of starting in on new material at line one and plodding along, half asleep, looking up words along the way, committing each paragraph to memory, dwelling on trivia. But that is the way many people think textbooks must be read. The results are dismal.

Try the BFAR method a few times and see what happens. If you are worried that you will miss something, you can always follow up with your old approach. But BFAR will soon become your preferred way and will be automatic. Let's look at BFAR in detail.

Browse

The sensible way to start is to look a new chapter over just to see the territory. It is the same as opening the morning paper or checking out this week's *Rolling Stone.* Get the feel by noticing headings (headlines), interesting topics (articles and stories), pictures, graphs. If it seems appropriate to your needs, skim any summaries and the table of contents. Decide how much time will be needed to accomplish *your* purpose and how hard or easy it will be to interface with the new ideas.

Break the chapter (or book) into manageable lumps.

Set a time limit for each lump (the work you will do in one sitting). This includes time for browsing, focusing, absorbing and reinforcing.

Always allow a little less time than you think you need.

If you give yourself plenty of time, you will probably waste it. A time limit will help keep you on track. This part of BFAR is like planning for a backpacking trip. Decide exactly what you will be looking for when you go back through the material. The clearer you are, the easier it will be to find what you want.

Always have a purpose.

Focus

Focusing is not a new step. Rather, it is something that happens, *while* you are browsing. The fog lifts and the terrain becomes evident. Now you can pass through the material quickly with a clear awareness of what the author wants you to understand. Be alert and responsive to the writer's ideas, as though you were having a conversation. Question whenever it feels right, but act as though someone wants you to understand something. Be open to it.

Get the general idea, the main points and the reasoning.

In a typical chapter, there are usually not more than three to five main points, and these are usually identified by headings (headlines).

Skip or skim anything you don't need.

Don't take notes or mark the chapter—yet. That comes in the next pass.

Absorb

The BFAR process is seamless, and you will feel yourself gradually absorbing the material right from the first. Absorbing is something that you have been doing all along. The next step is a natural progression:

Go back through the chapter and find the main idea.

Highlight or <u>underline</u> it, the key words only. Put some sort of outline notation in the margin (I, II, III or ***, **, *, and so on). Underline supporting ideas only if they really seem important or might help you brush up for quizzes. Don't get carried away. I have seen textbooks with every single line underlined—with a ruler. No doubt by someone with a pocket liner. . . .

Mark just enough to trigger your memory when you review for tests. Too many notes will only confuse you.

Reinforce

The process so far will leave a cache of data stored temporarily in your mental wetware. But if you don't *save* your work—even if you have done a good job—the vivid picture will fade as quickly as a dream. Therapists encourage clients to jot down their dreams immediately—this "saves" the dream, and it becomes part of the person's waking awareness.

The same mechanism operates in transferring a reading session from short-term memory to long-term memory. So always take one final step:

Write it down or tell it to someone.

Get it on paper *from memory* and *in your own words.* Write quickly and briefly. Abbreviate. The purpose is to check out your understanding. Can you remember the gist of what you just read? Is it clear?

Skim back over any material that is still fuzzy. Some students write the gist in the bottom margin. Having all your notes and your own emphasis in the text itself eliminates the need for a separate notebook. Everything of importance stands out and is easy to review. Your own outline in the margin reflects the thinking that put it there. The results is a geometric reduction in study time.

Tell it to someone. Anyone—even a little kid or your dog. You will know immediately, as you talk, how well you grasped what you read. I have heard more than one teacher say, "I never really understood my subject until I tried to teach it." Of course. Until such *interfacing* occurs (translating from the language of the book to the language of the reader) there is no real understanding.

Once you can say it in your own words, it is truly yours. And you can take a break. But don't leave out this step! *If you don't reinforce, you will forget most of what you read and will have to do it all over again.* When you do reinforce before stopping, you only need brief brush-ups later.

Questions About BFAR

Won't I miss a lot using BFAR?

No—you will get far more. Conventional study methods are too mechanical and too passive. It is almost impossible to use BFAR passively. Remember, you can read as thoroughly as you choose. Simply continue the process until *your* purposes are met. Wherever you decide to stop, every step will have had maximum value.

Need a security blanket? Experiment with BFAR. Apply it just as recommended. But then, just to ease your conscience, study the material the way you usually do. See for yourself if you lost anything of value. Experiment. At some point you will develop your own system of BFAR modified by productive techniques you have used in the past.

Isn't BFAR more time-consuming?

Every bit of time spent applying BFAR is productive time. Every assignment gets a custom fit. Once you get used to BFAR, your overall study time will be four or five times faster. Your pace will vary. You may dwell on something intriguing or unfamiliar and pause scarcely at all on the obvious, redundant, or irrelevant stuff.

BFAR is *efficient*. Its purpose is to provide a map of the best route through the assignment. Most students can't afford the scenic route.

Most teachers test for trivia. Where does BFAR come in?

BFAR is an essential first step. Bits and pieces of random data float chaotically in the memory banks. BFAR provides a structure on which to hang these baubles.

So once you know what the chapter is all about and where the emphasis is, work on gathering and memorizing facts. Use your hand as a guide and go through the text, picking out test items. As you know, some teachers even test on footnotes, by-lines, dates, the color of the hero's shoes. After the first quiz, you will know what things will probably be on your teacher's test. Make your own list. Sort the details into related bunches and use a suitable memory technique to get you through the test. When the course is over, press the delete button.

What about poems, stories, novels?

Works of art require getting used to. Until a "reader" interfaces with the unique language of the artist—be it a Cézanne painting, the Arc de Triomphe, a Liz Claiborne design, or *Ulysses*, there is no escape from messing around a little first. It is the same problem a novice scientist encounters with differential equations or subatomic physics. You fiddle around until you get on the artist's wavelength.

A sonnet can be read in less than a minute, but you'll need to take several passes through before it clicks. In other words, *browsing, focusing, absorbing, and reinforcing.* If it is a really good poem for you, you will end up knowing it by heart, *in* your heart, and BFAR will be effortless and natural. You will not have wasted a minute, even though the 14 lines have taken an hour to learn. You will even feel refreshed. Perhaps a Frost poem doesn't at first come across, but then you read two or three others and come back, and the first one is suddenly clear.

A good novel is the same. Sometimes you catch on only after a couple chapters. Then you start in at the beginning and say, "Oh! Ah!" and so forth. Sometimes you open the book in the middle, just to get the feel of the writing or its quality. You'll want to put lots of books back on the shelf at this point. If you have read a couple of novels by Kurt Vonnegut, you are formatted for the next one—but you do have to be on your toes. Passive reading won't cut it.

To be guided through an example of the BFAR method, see Appendix A.

Tactics for Reading

BFAR, problem solving, using a computer, these are all different terms for the same thing: Dealing efficiently with the environment. In the broadest sense, it is always the same process. Following are some applications.

Read backward.

As mentioned in this chapter's Commentary section, reading backward is more productive than reading forward. Just about anything would be. It is not all that crazy. The gist is sometimes bunched in a summary, and if that isn't clear, one browses backward until it is. Often less than halfway to the front, the idea make sense and one can quit.

Reading backward simply forces one to *pay attention, put the material in one's own words, and connect new ideas with what one already knows.* In other words, BFAR—but from the back.

This approach requires *active processing of information.* As always, it works better to have a system. Not being dominated by the authority of the writer enables readers to use their own intelligence and to direct and control their own education.

We are free to get meaning from print in any way we can dream up.

Read the bold print. Look at pictures.

This is what we do with a newspaper. If the headlines and pictures contain all that we want, why waste time going further? Getting an overview is the first step in BFAR anyway, and some books don't deserve any more attention than that. In an emergency, this approach may salvage your grade.

Getting the surface features reveals the pattern of the chapter and the author's main points. If you happen to know something about the subject, your background may provide your own supporting evidence. Or the ideas may be simple enough that no explanation is necessary. But when you want to commit new stuff to memory, you have to find the pattern. Your mental computer doesn't like to store random data.

While browsing and skimming, you also get a chance to fit in the new ideas with what you already know. Once you see the overall pattern, you can come back and examine fuzzy parts more carefully—but in a more meaningful context. You may want to read a paragraph here and there and think about it a while. But your own needs will determine where to pause and when to press on.

Figure out the assignment.

If what the teacher expects isn't clear, a student can spend hours studying the wrong thing. So the assignment itself is a reading problem or an opportunity for problem solving. What does the teacher really mean by saying, "Read Chapter 2"? In life, you read for yourself, but in the school game, there is also the teacher to satisfy. Educate yourself, of course. But also recognize that teachers make tests.

"Read Chapter 2" could mean any of these things:

- Get the general idea.
- Be able to give the main idea and its supporting details in the author's words.
- Put the main idea into your own words and supply your own examples.
- Memorize the main and supporting ideas word for word.
- Be ready to play Trivia.
- Use the book as a door stop.

Or whatever. Clear that up first—if possible, before leaving the classroom. The teacher may cover the very same chapter material in class, and so a general overview is all you will need from the book. Fortunately, after the first assignment, it should be fairly easy to guess what kind of reading the teacher expects. No matter what the teacher wants, to get familiar with the territory and to get formatted, you will need to do some browsing.

The remaining study time is free for your own purposes. BFAR will reveal how much time you will want to allot to the chapter.

Devise a plan.

When you hit a snag, figure a way through or around it. For instance, the material may contain some problem that browsing and skimming can't solve. You will need to come up with a plan of some sort. Keep in mind that any difficulty can be overcome.

There are always alternatives. Make that your cardinal rule. Once you take a look at a chapter, you will have to figure out what is in the way and remove it. The problem could be almost anything. If you are falling asleep, you could stand up to read, read twice as fast, read backward, or force your attention by moving your hand along the page as a pacer. If the text is impossibly difficult, you might get someone else to read it and explain it to you or work through it with you. Just be alert to the stumbling blocks and use your imagination.

How to identify the trouble? Just ask, "What's stopping me here?" Is it the whole chapter, just a few passages or some concept? Is it the style—too commonplace to keep you curious, too pretentious, too distant from your experience, the layout? Some readers will close a book just because they don't like the print style. If you can identify what is really causing the trouble, the solution is close. Solve it just like any other problem.

Using problem-solving questions (see the upcoming box), decide on a plan. Then try it out. If a better approach emerges, feel free to try it. If your approach is successful, browse through the material and see if it has become clear.

Devising a plan may seem time-consuming, but in practice it can be done in a few seconds. It is just a matter of getting clear, of "grokking," as Robert Heinlein once labeled it.

Questions to Ask in Problem-Solving

- *Have I had the same problem before or one somewhat like it?*

  It doesn't have to be in reading. A situation such as fixing a motor or a carpentry problem or a weakness in your tennis game might also suggest what to do next. Would a solution like that work here?

- *Can I turn the problem upside down, or say it, or see it a different way?*

- *Can I work on other parts of it?*

  If so, gradually work backward to the difficulty. This will give your nonconscious mind a chance to figure out what to do.

- *Can I at least solve just part of it?*

  There is usually something familiar to start on. More often than not, difficulties disappear on their own.

- *Can I say it more narrowly? More broadly?*

  The trick is to find different angles from which to view the situation.

- *What things do I already know that could help me here?*

  Try things from any field, not just reading. Get formatted any way you can. Then use BFAR.

- *Can I state the problem in different words?*

  Does that reveal possibilities I didn't see before?

Typical Reading Problems and Solutions

Here are a few solutions to reading difficulties that may work for you. As you develop a bag of tricks for getting meaning out of print, make conscious note of what works.

It's Too Hard

Narrow it down. Is the problem vocabulary, style, complexity, lack of experience with the subject?

Unfamiliar Vocabulary

If just a few words are causing the problem, (skimming and browsing will reveal this) they will usually be explained in the context, as you read along. Don't dwell on individual words at first, and don't fragment your attention by looking them up in a dictionary. Just get the general idea. If the words actually do prevent understanding, then look them up—but only after you have passed through the material a couple of times.

Too Many New Words

- **Divide and conquer.**

  Don't try to master them all. *Only a few of the new terms will be key words.* Get the overview; look at pictures and bold print. Then, if necessary for understanding, play with the troubling words. Break a word into its parts—the root, the affixes. Words from Latin and Greek so often found in school books use the same parts over and over, and you probably already know many of these. Whole paragraphs of pretentious language can be translated into ordinary English.

- **Read a different, clearer writer on the same subject.**

  Often the problem will be with the author, not with the subject itself. If so, find a writer you can understand (some teachers are willing to lend students texts by others authors. Or get books from the library or from used-book stores.) New subjects are confusing enough without having to figure out the author, too.

- **Use the book's index as a word list.**

  There is no quicker way to discover what the author thinks is important. Usually, the more references to a word, the more important it is. How often does it crop up; how many page numbers are listed? Also, how many of the words in the index are unfamiliar? If most of the index is familiar, you may not learn much from the book.

- **Let your vocabulary develop naturally.**

  Drudges look up every new word in a chapter as they go along. It is counterproductive and somewhat insane. Normally, we acquire vocabulary while doing other things. Work for understanding, instead. Study vocabulary only when absolutely necessary (or when you have nothing else to do). Few students have the time to look up every new word. You will learn thousands while in college—*without* this agony. As you learn new ideas, the vocabulary follows.

Ideas Too Strange

A college education *should* take a student into strange worlds; the stranger the better. Otherwise, what is the point? An easy course may be comforting, but it will not do much for your education. So if you have never studied anatomy or chemistry or literature, they will indeed be difficult—at first. With some conscious help, the right hemisphere will happily decode the new "language." Format your disk, and the interfacing will be effortless.

- **Make it familiar.**

  Chemistry is *like* something you already do know and understand. Find an analogy or a connection, and chemistry will make sense. Ideas have to fit in with the rest of one's reality picture. So play with possible connections. Ask yourself, "What is it like?"

  It may not be the entire chapter that is confusing, but only one aspect. Identify the obstacle. Is this part like baseball? Fishing? Reading music? How did you master that? Try a similar approach. Or *see* it the same way. We understand the universe by analogy, by comparison, by seeing one thing as though it were another. Visualize.

- **Try a book for kids.**

  There are beautifully written books for kids covering almost any college subject. They are clear, and they use simple, direct language. (Some textbook writers could take lessons from them!) Get the general idea from the kid's book—*get formatted*—and then fill in necessary details from your text. You will find it has mysteriously become more comprehensible. (Tell the children's librarian the book is for your little sister.)

- **Try classic comics.**

  Try *Cliff's Notes,* videos, and film.

- **Explain it to someone else, even to the refrigerator.**

  At least put in your own words. Snags often come loose this way.

Get formatted any way you can. Then use BFAR.

It's Too Complicated

When you look in the box holding the new barbecue grill, the "easy" assembly may look hopelessly difficult. But the more boxes you opened in the past, the more instruction manuals you worked your way through—the more certain you became that you could do it. So a new concept in accounting or in creating macros for your word processor is just one more box of parts to assemble. Lots of strategies are available.

- **Look at the finished picture.**

  A video or even a photo of someone doing what you have to do will provide an overview. Pictures and diagrams in the text may be the map you need. Work back and forth between the words and the pictures.

- **Handle the parts.**

  Look at the pieces. How many of each? What appears to fit into what? When? Some will fit in nicely. Some will need to be played with, and some set aside temporarily. Sometimes just laying out the parts reveals a pattern. Some of the bells and whistles will never be needed.

- **Work from the known to the unknown.**

  Browse until you find something you can grasp. Work your way out from there, filling in the picture with more and more details until the concept makes sense.

- **Talk it out.**

  Discuss it with someone—a friend, a tutor, your teacher. Trade phone numbers with several other students.

- **Look for structure in the table of contents or in the layout of the headings.**

  You will find relationships there. You can see what the author considers important and what less. You may have let yourself get bogged down on a trivial point. Look at the overall pattern to rule out this possibility.

- **Draw a picture, make a diagram, draw a map.**

  This will reveal relationships and keep things straight.

- **First, work the problem or read some examples.**

  Sometimes hands-on experience can clear up confusing explanations or directions. Once you have been there, directions are easier to follow. You have something to hang on to.

The Style Is Unfamiliar

Chaucer's English is 600 years old; Shakespeare's is 400. That takes getting used to. Modern English has all sorts of varieties. If an author does not write in a familiar dialect, your wetware will have to *interface* with the writer's. Expect to play with unusual or complicated phrasing, old-fashioned sentence structure, or strange dialect until it feels comfortable. *Anyone else's language is a foreign language.*

- **Begin with the familiar.**

  Find something in the passage that *does* make some sense, and play with the context, the surrounding language, until things come into focus. Squinting or drudgery will only interfere. Be attentive but relaxed. The nonconscious mind will do the formatting for you.

- **Rearrange the sentence.**

  Move phrases around or leave them out temporarily until the sentence is simple and direct. That often solves the problem. Play with a messy sentence until it comes out in your own language. Then reread it; it will probably make sense.

- **Compare the troublesome passage with something you do know.**

- **Try a hunch. Guess.** ***Maybe it's like . . .***

- **Try a different author or a different translation.**

  Different translators can make Aristotle either dreary or stimulating. Writers can either kill physics or make it beautiful. Pick a style you like.

  Read a biography to see the environment from which the person's work emerged. There are good books for laymen—even on subatomic physics or economics or the Japanese language (or English!). Then go back to the text and be amazed how much easier it has become.

- **Watch a video or see a film about the author or about the subject.**

  Your AV library may have just what you need. The whole idea is to make the strange familiar.

- **Read the critics first.**

  Magazine articles on your book, your subject, your author often clear things up. Articles on Mars or Jupiter, Beethoven, or Richard Nixon can provide discussions on complex issues in laymen's terms.

  Try short, critical articles in encyclopedias. Go to the section in the stacks and browse the books there. Magazines like *Popular Science, Popular Mechanics, Psychology Today, Time, National Geographic,* and *Scientific American* often contain readable versions. They can provide the first *browsing* step of BFAR.

It's Too Easy, Too Boring

Uninteresting stuff is hard to read. Do anything to avert boredom. Bored readers develop bad reading habits. Recipients of love letters don't.

- **Browse, skip, skim.**

  Shoot for the *framework* and *key ideas.* See if you need to read any further. If one example is enough, don't fall asleep over six. Do you really need the explanation? Do you really need the footnotes?

- **Check the table of contents and index for organization and vocabulary.**

  You may not need to read any further than that. Or maybe you can narrow down your work.

- **Read backward.**

  Social science and psychology texts tend to save the punch line for the last. So start there. Then, if you really want to read the history and conditions of the experiment, you know where it all leads. Otherwise, you can skip the preliminaries.

- **Read a book that is better written.**

  A lousy, repetitious style can kill a subject. Shop around.

- **Read twice as fast.**

  It will keep you on your toes.

- **Take frequent breaks.**

  Plan in advance how much you can tolerate in one session. Time yourself.

- **Turn it upside-down. Make it unfamiliar. Convert dry reading into something more juicy.**

  You can always make the commonplace sparkle. Take a different route to work or walk; the world changes. Its the same with textbooks. A boring schoolbook becomes fascinating if you explore *why* it is so stultifying. *How can I stretch this dry chapter out of shape and regain interest in it?*

What *else* is this technical subject like? Converting those multisyllable explanations into ordinary language can do the trick. In *The Games People Play,* Eric Berne pointed out that clients soon created their own expressions to replace technical terms: *wooden leg, rapo, now-I've-got-you, you-son-of-a-bitch, look-what-you-made-me-do.*

Have Lots of Alternatives.

No two writers are the same. As you encounter new snags, combine some strategies and vary your approaches. Something will always work.

Keep track of your successes and use variations of them.

Gradually you will develop dozens of strategies and use them automatically. Getting what you want from print is problem solving. When we are passive, reading seems difficult and we may develop a habit of helplessness. Defeatism develops, apparently, from being assigned things we don't care to do. So school assignments can actually contribute to poor reading. But we all know that strong need or desire can enable an ordinary reader to understand complex, difficult material.

A few successes will generate the confidence that makes you persist long enough for the payoff. So persist!

Don't Forget to Save Your Work

It is one thing to liberate ideas from print; it is quite another thing to hang on to them. New ideas fade fast from short-term memory. Save them. Why do the job twice? *Use those memory techniques (mnemonics).*

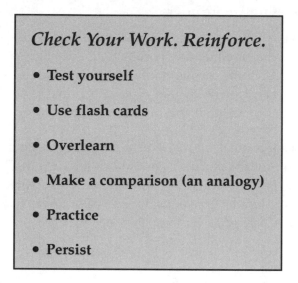

> ***Check Your Work. Reinforce.***
>
> - **Test yourself**
> - **Use flash cards**
> - **Overlearn**
> - **Make a comparison (an analogy)**
> - **Practice**
> - **Persist**

Having to do good work over again is painful, so *reinforcing* is a vital step in the reading process. No matter how short or long your study session,

Always reinforce before taking a break.

Don't Fail to Practice

Ideas cannot be transferred whole. They have to be chewed and digested to become flesh and bones. Once an idea is *absorbed* from the printed page, neither it nor the reader will ever be the same. Reading is thinking. Decoding the print itself is just the start. It is a natural process cultivated by practice.

Most people's reading is inflexible. If they don't get it right away, C students throw up their hands and quit. *But the only thing we can understand the first time through is something we already know.* On the other hand, new ideas need a quick read-through, then a more careful reading, then a checkup afterward—with lots of pondering in between. An active reader can catch on much more quickly than someone reading passively.

So relax a bit, play around with troublesome passages, and try putting it in your own words. Be flexible. In your first experiments with BFAR, allow a little time for getting used to the approach. You will get faster as you gain experience.

Sample passages for practice are provided in Appendix B.

Textbooks into Love Letters

The man that hath no music in himself,
Nor is not mov'd with concord of sweet sounds,
Is fit for treason, stratagems and spoils.

—Shakespeare

In reading, the first thing we must do with anything new is find a way to love it. A chemistry or economics textbook, John Milton, the writings of your political opponent—all must become love letters, if they are to be read well. The sages know: The love is not in the print but in the heart of the reader. Loveless reading is ashes in the mouth. But loving *anything* new is not difficult, once you catch on to how lovable *everything* is.

To find out how lovable everything is, *mess around.* In a playful, hummy sort of way, as Pooh would say. Any lover will tell you that. The poet says the first thing to do in the morning is take down a musical instrument. Tune yourself up. Get in harmony. Brushing your teeth becomes full of wonder. That B movie becomes fascinating; a C movie is even better.

Why, who makes much of a miracle?
As for myself, I know of nothing but miracles.

—Walt Whitman

If we look at the world with the wonder of a three-year-old plus the illumination of our adult minds, college and college reading become what they should be: a chance to see the universe with open responsive eyes.

Read assignments *as if* they were love letters, and soon they *will* be.

Marking and Making Notes in Books

Get all your notes in one place, if possible. Make the fewest notes you can get by with. "Simplify, simplify."

Compress and combine.

The less junk in your notes, the clearer and freer your mind will be. Too many notes are confusing. Don't let them become such a mess that you end up having to do your original work all over again.

There are two purposes for marking texts:

1. *To see how the chapter is put together, to discover its structure, to get a blueprint.* You will see immediately what the main points and supporting points are. You will also see what is mere repetition and what is padding. If you are alert, you can skip all that.

   Mark these key ideas in the Absorb step of BFAR.

2. *For review, to have the key ideas clearly marked and in the right place for brushing up later on.*

   Make your notes stand out.

Mark just enough to trigger your memory of the pattern and the situation. Two words where one will do is 50 percent inefficient.

For example, if you were to be tested next week on the ideas on this page, what is the least you could mark so that next Thursday you could take a quick look and trigger all you would need for the quiz? How you do this is up to you. It is for your own use. Notetaking is personal and private.

Following is one, *only one*, possibility. It's designed to make it easy to see key ideas—but marking your own emphasis will help fix the ideas in long term memory and aid more efficient review.

Example

Get all your notes in one place, if possible. Make the fewest notes you can get by with. "Simplify, simplify."

Compress and combine.

The less junk in your notes, the clearer and freer your mind will be. Too many notes are confusing. Don't let them become such a mess that you end up having to do your original work all over again.

There are two purposes for marking texts:

I. *To see how the chapter is put together, to discover its structure, to get a blueprint*. You will see immediately what the main points and supporting points are. You will also see what is mere repetition and what is padding. If you are alert, you can skip all that.

Mark these key ideas in the Absorb step of BFAR.

II. *For review, to have the key ideas clearly marked and in the right place for brushing up later on.*

Make your notes stand out.

Mark just enough to trigger your memory of the pattern and the situation. Two words where one will do is 50 percent inefficient.

Notice that the marked phrases stand out, and the rest fade back.

> *Mark in pencil. While reviewing, if you see that even fewer words will serve, erase the extra ones.*

Reviewing with the book open, you notice "Marking purposes" and see the I and the II. You try to remember. If you can't, you glance to the right. Oh, yes: *Structure* and *review.* If you still feel shaky, the information is right there where you need it. You may browse or mull over anything that has faded.

The same procedure can be used for a whole chapter. First, see just how much has to be remembered or mastered to satisfy the teacher's requirements. Then, in the Absorb step, try to remember without help. "What's the writer getting at? How many subpoints? What are they?" Underline or highlight phrases you need, and key them to indicators you put in the margin (I, II, III, A, B, C, ***, **, *). Browse or play with any point still unclear and then mark its key phrase. This approach emphasizes key points and shows their relationships. At the same time, it stores data in permanent memory.

Refining Your Notetaking

Here are ways to make your notes even more helpful.

Making Margin Notes

To make margin cues more useful, write key words or phrases in the margin (as we did in the above example).

There are usually three to five key words or phrases in a chapter, and usually they are in headings or in **bold print** or *italic.* But remember, the fewer things marked, the better. The skeleton should stand out plainly.

Or substitute a figure of speech, something you can see that grabs the mind and sticks. What is it like? Marking is like mapping a route on a road atlas. So if you want to think of the right way to mark a chapter, just think of it as "mapping your way through the territory." Use what works—any good memory device you like.

For your own use, anything else you feel like jotting down is up to you. It is common for thinkers to "talk back" to an author in the margin, or extend the idea there. But, of course, *that* is education—something you do out of the joy of using your mind. Once the assignment is knocked off, you are free to think. In most cases, assignments want only the facts.

You can put compressed class notes in the margin, too, alongside the appropriate passage. When you review, everything will be where you need it and easily accessible.

Rewriting

Once you are sure you know the essence of a section and have marked it, rewrite the gists in your own words in the bottom margin. Use a pencil and eraser.

When you review, rewrite your rewrite in still fewer words. Remember, putting the key ideas in your own words at the end of a study session is crucial. If neglected, memory fades rapidly. Active restructuring in your own words dramatically improves retention. Only brief touch-ups are needed thereafter.

Make it a fixed habit to go back and map or mark the assignment, and never take a break until you sum up in your own words. After a few tries, you will enjoy remarkable improvement in understanding and retention.

Mapping

Visualizing is a powerful memory aid. To see the pattern of a messy assignment, try sketching a map on scratch paper during the Absorb step of BFAR. Any kind of a picture is okay. This chapter might look something like this:

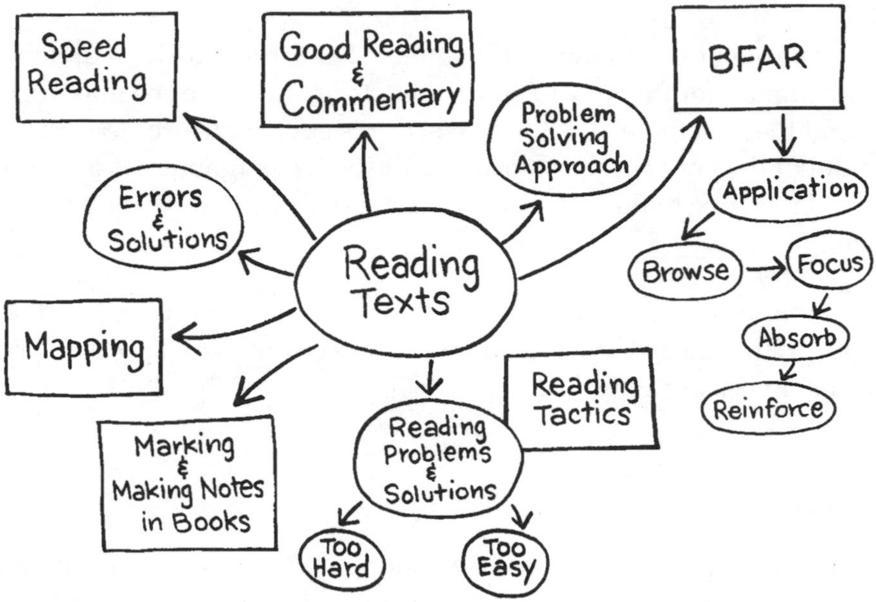

For a section of a chapter, such as the BFAR method in this one, you can use this same mapping approach. And if you prefer, you can put in a map instead of a summary at the end.

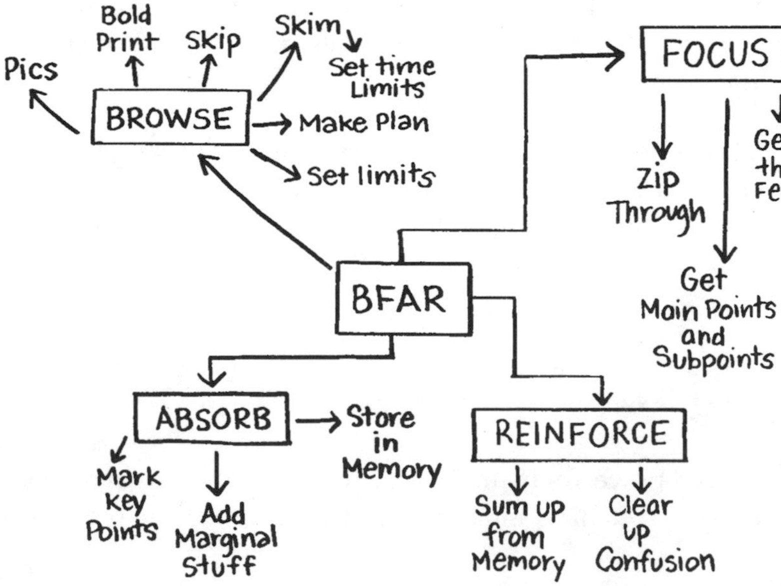

Errors and Solutions

Some reading problems are not in the print but rather in our approach. Here are some common mistakes and ways to avoid them. In general,

Always read for meaning. Always fit new material into patterns already in your mind.

Incomplete or Weak Understanding

A quick once-through on how to do something may make things clear enough. But when it's time to perform, we can't. How can we make sure we really do know it?

Solution: Explain it is your own words to someone else. Preferably, choose someone who doesn't already know it. Have that person ask lots of questions.

Teaching someone else is one of the best ways to learn.

To teach well requires that you understand both the pattern and the details. If you can't find an audience (your cat or dog will do in a pinch, or even the TV), write it down or draw a sketch or both.

Jumping to Conclusions

Consider, for example, statement 3 in the Commentary at the beginning of this chapter: "For most students, reading is a waste of time." Some students react immediately. They have been taught that reading is a good thing and could *never* be a waste of time. Jumping to such a conclusion makes it difficult to consider other possibilities, among them the idea that most students read inefficiently.

Solution: Delay judgment. Don't draw conclusions from isolated sentences. Think of the whole context of that paragraph and the surrounding ones. Tell someone else what you think it means. Rephrase it and then review to see if it works.

"Don't bother me with the facts, my mind's made up" is a general communication problem. In reading, prejudging can dominate the entire interpretation.

> *The only way to avoid prejudging is to be conscious of this natural tendency and refuse to agree or disagree until you are sure of what the writer really has said.*

See the material from the author's point of view first. Then judge, if it is really necessary.

Inferring Too Much

"Daddy's outside shaving the windows." The child thinking this has broadened *shave* beyond the context. (Poets do this on purpose.) Or the child calls any male Daddy.

Solution: Take only as broad a meaning of the passage as the writer intended.

Draw the meaning from the whole, not an aspect.

The poet may intend a broader meaning. The clinical psychologist may limit a definition. Check out the context.

Inferring Too Little

We all acquire meaning from our experience. Typically, college students bring a narrower meaning to many words than is intended in their books and classes. (Senior citizen at the vet's with Fifi: "Well! I never heard her called *that* before!") A limited meaning may have worked well enough at home, but not now. For example, many people think *to criticize* means *to find fault with,* but the academic world usually takes it to mean the examination of both good and bad aspects.

Solution: The full context will reveal whether a broader meaning is intended. Stay open to possibilities.

Education is learning that additional possibilities still exist for all concepts.

Too Rigid in Your Viewpoint

If we *know* we are right, it is impossible to read clearly. We effectively block or twist whatever the writer says. Certainty can stop a conversation cold and prevent us from learning anything new.

Solution: Develop the habit of seeking out other viewpoints, other aspects, other possibilities. Knowledge is what we know so far. It is always limited to the facts available. If paying close attention to someone else's views threatens your reality blanket, make a game of it at first. You can always run back in the house if it gets too scary.

Education means learning to tolerate and appreciate a variety of views.

Taking the Wrong Slant

Picking up the wrong cues can lead you to misread an entire passage. For example, students in an English class were missing the point of a passage about how well views of right and wrong survive if viewed from a distant star. Why were they missing the point? Finally the teacher noticed in the first sentence the words *Zen* and *Christianity*. The students were sidetracked by these interesting words and were missing the main idea entirely.

Solution: BFAR. It usually eliminates the danger of misreading. It requires an active, deliberate search for meaning and includes the safeguards of marking and rephrasing. "In my own words, this is what I think the writer is saying." Then check it out to see if you are right. Compare your understanding with other students, too. That usually reveals where you may have gone astray.

Missing the Pattern

When we read passively, we don't discover the map, and the territory then becomes a confusing maze. Since learning is actually restructuring one's reality picture, casual reading is counterproductive. Unstructured data will not stick.

Solution: Browse, browse, browse before diving in. Get an overview. Mark and rephrase after you do.

Rules and Directions Are Too Hard

If you can't make heads or tails of explanations, it may be that the wording is too general or too abstract. There may be no familiar images, nothing to *see,* nothing concrete to hang on to. In ordinary life, rules usually come *after* experiences. We plunge in, and afterward the description of where we have been is perfectly clear and easy to remember.

Solution: Work backward. If directions or an explanation are not clear, go immediately to an example, anecdote, picture, diagram, or problem. Even if you don't quite understand, the explanation will make much more sense once you have glimpsed the territory. There will be something concrete to look at as you work through the rule or instruction.

When you have a bicycle to assemble, look at the picture of the finished bike, play with parts, lay them out in bunches. What goes with what? Figure out roughly where things go and when. Parts only slightly different require closer scrutiny.

Mess around. Then *read the instructions.*

Passage or Instructions Not Clear

A passage may become so involved and complicated that you get lost.

Solution: Work your way through, *out loud.* Visualize the steps as you go. While he worked, lying on his back behind our new gas clothes-dryer, the installer had my wife read directions to him out loud. And he made her *go slow.*

Writing instructions or directions or manuals is an art. Not everyone is good at it. Your teacher may have botched it. In that case, try to get a clarification before attempting the assignment.

Speed-Reading

Efficient reading is speed-reading. BFAR gets the job done in the fastest possible time. After even a little practice, you will see a remarkable reduction in time spent getting what you need from print. Speed, of course, varies with purpose and material, but BFAR allows for that.

Most people read 250 to 300 words a minute (WPM). But they read everything at the same rate and read every word. You can see that is not a bright thing to do. We talk at about 150 to 180 wpm. So the reading average isn't much faster than talking. Your rate ought to vary from about 120 wpm, when you have to think as you go, to 800 or better, when you are skipping and skimming familiar stuff. Your average can be over 450 with practice. If you want, you can very likely learn to read comfortably every word of material that is just right for you at about 400 words per minute. You could easily reach that speed with a couple of weeks of short daily practice.

A Simple Technique

1. Use BFAR. Once BFAR is a habit, it will come easily.

2. Every day read for 15 to 20 minutes, at a rate a little faster than is comfortable.

Select a novel or anything comfortable for you and of high interest. Figure out how long it takes you to read a page of that material at your present rate. Then keep an eye on the clock or use a timer to pace yourself—a little faster each day. (Words per minute is the number of words you read, divided by the number of minutes it took you.)

> *Pace yourself by moving your hand across the page just under the line you are on.*

That is all there is to it. Speed-reading is a habit, and you get faster by getting in shape. Slower speeds invite bad practices: reading word-by-word and missing the main idea: passive fooling around; skittering back over material you could have absorbed the first time (called *regressions*); dwelling on words you could grab at a glance. But just by speeding up, you can get rid of most of these faults or greatly reduce their effect.

BFAR shows you what to skip and skim, so you can actually get meaning from some material three or four times as fast. You won't be reading every word, but you should only do that when every word is important.

Vocabulary and Speed

It is true that a limited vocabulary can slow a reader down. But does that mean you should take a crash course in vocabulary? Not necessarily. *Vocabulary usually takes care of itself.*

Most adults know about 50,000 words. But college sophomores recognize three to four times that many. How do they learn so many words in two years? It is not from poring over dictionaries and underlining every new word in their texts. Their new environment is so full of experiences and ideas never before encountered that words to describe them naturally follow—thousands and thousands of them. Most students hardly notice it happening. Going to college is like going to a foreign country. If you allow yourself to go native, you will soon be speaking the language.

Don't be alarmed if college texts seems foreign at first. They *are.* Gradually they will begin to make sense. Meanwhile,

Read for meaning and pattern; look for ideas.

Usually you will get what you need, and bit by bit, the vocabulary will clear up. Fall in love with ideas and the vocabulary will follow.

Building Vocabulary

Of course, the larger your vocabulary, the smoother your reading will be. So, if you do have spare time, deliberately acquiring a larger vocabulary can pay off. It is quite true that people who know lots of words have an easier time of it in life. Norman Lewis's *Word Power Made Easy* makes vocabulary study stimulating.

But a vigorous curiosity is all you really need. In your spare time, for the fun of it, notice the origins of words, their root meanings and their affixes. Browse your dictionary. My grandchildren have me going back to the dictionary to see where words I have used all my life come from. Notice *etymology* (the origin and history of words). See how words are related. Everyday words are likely to originate from Anglo-Saxon or Middle English. *Daisy,* for example, is from the Middle English *daies ie* (day's eye), the sun. Textbooks have a high concentration of words from Latin and Greek. Broken down, they are not formidable.

Every time you look up a word, put a check (✓) in the margin.

Rarely will an item end up with more than three checks.

So, the natural way is best. Be open to new ideas and the words will follow. Develop curiosity about words and have fun with them in your spare time. Little children love words—that's how they learn them so easily. The more words you do recognize, the more easily and quickly you can get through the print, and the easier it will be to understand the ideas.

Demystifying College Reading

Anyone who can read at sixth- or seventh-grade level can get necessary meaning from college texts. Once we know how to decode print, success owes more to problem-solving experience than to reading skill. Reading *is* problem solving. Consciously noticing our own processes will gradually build a background of alternatives. Awareness of these alternatives gives us the confidence to persist.

Confidence, persistence, and knowledge of alternatives are basic to success.

Since most people have been good problem-solvers in some area of their lives—music, carpentry, tennis, mechanics, keeping house—they already know how to solve reading problems. Getting meaning from print depends on realizing the similarity of reading to problem solving, and on applying the same techniques.

So focus. Gather more information. Reconsider. Set and change goals. Use possibilities, probabilities, pay-offs and penalties.

BFAR (Browse, Focus, Absorb, Reinforce) is another way of saying it. Each step has its own obvious substeps and reminds you to use problem-solving knowledge.

The secret of a joyful college experience and a happy life is to become a passionate problem-solver.

C H A P T E R

5

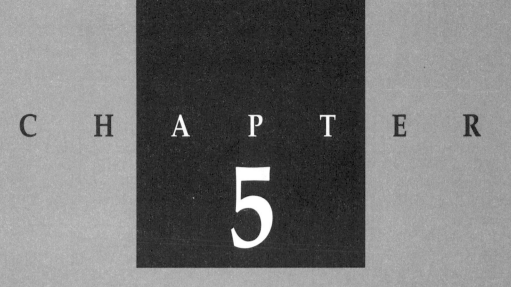

Taking Classes and Doing Assignments

Applying Natural Learning Techniques in Counterproductive Classrooms and Study Environments

". . . for the eye sees not itself
But by reflection, by some other things."
—Shakespeare

To take classes, apply BFAR:

- **Get ready beforehand. Anticipate what will be discussed. (*Browse* text and notes.)**
- **Watch for the key idea and supporting points (*Focus. Absorb.*)**
- **Write down the gist—*before* leaving the class or study session. (*Reinforce.*)**

School Daze

Mark only the ideas you agree with. Then read the commentary that follows.

☐ **1.** Lecturing is the best teaching method.

☐ **2.** The purpose of the classroom is to provide information.

☐ **3.** The better the student, the fuller the notebook.

☐ **4.** Environment controls learning.

☐ **5.** The more time and effort spent, the higher the grade.

Commentary: What Really Happens in the Classroom

1. Lecturing is the best teaching method?

Even though research shows lecturing to be one of the *least* effective teaching methods, most classes are still conducted with students seated passively in rows and the teacher in front doing all the talking. Lecturing as a teaching mechanism is so ingrained we have actually seen a teacher droning on at only four silent and polite students seated in front of him. Another instructor arranged the seats in a circle but lectured all the same.

Most college teachers know little about the findings of educational research. Most institutions accept knowledge of subject as sufficient qualification for teaching. The old, counterproductive methods persist. Fear ("You'll be tested on this") is still used to motivate students, even though positive reinforcement is known to result in better learning with fewer neuroses.

2. *The purpose of the classroom is to provide information?*

We live in an information-rich environment. But teachers still try to transmit information that can be acquired better and easier elsewhere. Their crude packaging leads to passivity and absenteeism. The conventional classroom structure is antiquated and ineffectual.

Unfortunately, traditional classroom practices promote dullness and passivity. Passive mental habits lead to C's or worse for the majority of students. But we know from Benjamin Bloom and others that 95% of these same students succeed in other settings.

3. *The better the student, the fuller the notebook?*

The 5% of students who get top grades despite the traditional structure do not necessarily work harder. Often, they work and worry far less than C students. Any normal person, recognizing the structure and using it to advantage, can get top grades in less time and with less work. Notes taken are fewer but more meaningful. New habits may be needed; some are easy to acquire and some taking practice and planning.

The real key to success in class and in doing assignments is habit.

4. *Environment controls learning?*

The setting in which we learn does exert a powerful influence. Classroom experience can imprint a self-image that persists throughout adult life. Fortunately, rather that accept the situation and be its willing accomplice, an aware student can actually control his or her relation to it and even enjoy it.

If you want to see what you are really learning, observe what you are actually doing. Are you sitting passively? Are you unquestioning? Are you letting others decide how much work you will do, where, when, and how? If so, you are learning how to be a passive, other-directed adult.

You do have alternatives. You could just as easily become the sort of person who considers a negative environment a challenge and an opportunity to develop problem-solving skills. You will be learning how to wake up in the morning and think, "I wonder what is going to happen today."

5. *The more time and effort, the higher the grade?*

Drudgery is not admirable and is almost never rewarded. Time and effort spent are irrelevant; results are what matter. If you can accomplish your goal in 10% or even 1% of the time, why spend one second more? The time could be spent furnishing your mind and spirit with wonderful ideas and experiences. You do have that choice.

How To Take Classes

> *For an almost certain C grade or better, pay attention, attend every class, and be sure to take every quiz and test—even if you do nothing else outside of class.*

Most teachers still see themselves as transmitters of information and feel guilty if they don't "cover" in class everything they think is important. For them, the text is back-up material. And you can be pretty sure their tests will focus on what they talk about. So, if you don't intend to study at all, make sure to select teachers like this and apply good techniques *during class.*

On the other hand, if you love the subject and want to master it, these same techniques will yield the basic information with the least wasted time. And that will free you to go after your education.

But don't try to change twelve years of habits overnight. *Build new habits one step at a time.* Enjoy the challenge, and don't take yourself or the subject too seriously. It is pitiful to see the inevitable collapse of a student's massive self-improvement program, usually about one week after it starts. Absorb tactics you like gradually and at your own pace. Some ideas you will be able to use immediately. The rest you can add as you go along. Let your own temperament be your guide.

The right strategy will enable you to complete most of your work right in class. That could be a godsend if your time is severely limited. With occasional review, this could be enough for you to get by.

How to Pay Attention: BFAR

With minor adjustments, BFAR works just as well for a lecture as it does for a text. You don't have to master a new system, but you do have to have *some* system. Most students just let the 50 minutes happen *to* them. Using BFAR puts you in control and makes paying attention automatic and effortless.

Think of a lecture as an audio book.

So if you let the B in BFAR stand for Before instead of Browse, the rest—Focus, Absorb, and Reinforce—will do fine just the way they are. Just make the necessary allowances for the message being spoken instead of printed.

1. Anticipate the lecture pattern.

2. Then find the teacher's point, and listen for subpoints and supporting details as you go.

3. Immediately afterward, while still in your seat, write the gist in your own words, *before* you leave the room.

Paying Attention: BFAR in the Classroom

Before

As you know, most students take a while to get settled (if they ever do at all), and by then the teacher has already said what he or she will be talking about and will have announced assignments, test dates, and so forth. By the time most students are ready, the teacher will be well into the first point and the game is almost lost. This lag is natural but costly. The solution is to develop a new habit.

Get ready before *the teacher starts in.*

To get formatted for the onslaught of new information, browse your notes from a previous session, browse the gist of your most recent study session, and glance at the chapter or material you know will be lectured on. That may appear to be a lot of work, but in actual practice it can be done in a couple of minutes, even in class before the lecture begins. The object is to get an overview, a map, to keep you on track.

- **Avoid taking classes with friends.**

  Be ruthless. Your pals will expect you to exhibit your old behavior. They will distract you; you will perform for them. A boyfriend or girlfriend is an even worse nuisance: whispering, note passing, casting eyes back and forth, erotic daydreams, showing off. Five years from now, your audience will have disappeared, and you will be left holding your lousy grade card.

  If you want a study partner, find someone new in the class.

- **Sit in a conspicuous place as close as you can to the teacher.**

  Students who sit close to the teacher tend to get higher grades. Obviously, if the teacher can *see* you, it will be harder to fall asleep. The more monotonous the lecture, the closer you should sit—on the teacher's lap, if possible. Shun windows and attractive fellow students, too. Closer up, you will be more attentive and there will be fewer distractions.

- **Get ready *before* the lecture starts.**

  Go to the toilet. Don't stuff yourself with lunch and then fall asleep; don't skip a meal and starve so that your stomach growls, either. Get there a little early to allow time to get a bead on things. Lay out your stuff. (Bring only what you need; put everything you are not using immediately off your desk.) While waiting, use the time to review your notes and get formatted for the lecture.

- **Put your personal problems on hold.**

  You can't do a thing about them during the next 50 minutes, anyway. Make a note for action later. Keep a reminder list.

- **Work on these habits until they are automatic.**

Focus

- **Find the structure.**

  The sooner the better. You can probably anticipate the teacher's outline from your notes or from a preview of an upcoming chapter. Just check out the headlines (headings), bold print, pictures and graphs. Get an overview. If you can see the structure, you will know what to focus on. Otherwise, the lecture will look like a hopeless hodgepodge. Find some sort of skeleton to flesh out. Even a really bad lecturer hopes to make some point, though you may have to be very alert to find it.

  Remember, *a lecture is an audio book.* But since you can't reread a lecture, you will have to adjust your guesses about the point of the lecture and the key subpoints—as you go along.

  Watch for the plan. Only by centering on an overview can a listener distinguish what a speaker thinks is important. Otherwise, it will sound like a laundry list, just a long list of assertions.

- **Don't prejudge.**

  First, see the lecture from the teacher's point of view. Listen sympathetically, not because you are nice but because you can't get the real message any other way. If you can't see it the way he or she does, you have not understood at all. Treat a lecture as you would a conversation with a friend. If you make a snap judgment right off, that prejudice can color the entire lecture.

  If you insist on evaluating, save the hatchet job for later. Of course, your brilliance will usually result in a lower grade. "Don't bother me with your thinking. Just remember this—as I present it to you—for the test." The lecture is to be remembered, not thought about. Top grade getters meet the *teacher's* goals.

  Avoid emotional involvement. Most teachers resent smart-alecky students, especially those who challenge their ideas in class. So if you care about your grade, save reflective thought for later. Unless you are sure the teacher values individuality, use your own time to mull over, restructure and sort out ideas. Of course, a well-oiled mind is what education is all about, but grades are rarely based on thoughtful response. When they are, you and everyone else will know it.

Absorb

Just as a text does, a speaker usually has one topic to present and about three to five supporting points. At first, watching for the structure is difficult, but with practice you will recognize cues and will even learn tricks for staying awake—not because it is virtuous, but because you don't want to slog through the whole thing again (because you won't get the chance, anyway. Most courses center on class lectures. So get it and keep it.

Being passive in class is self-defeating. Passivity is addictive. Your brain will start treating class time as nap time. As a countermeasure, make a game of finding structure anywhere. Practice on something boring—sermons, TV documentaries, your neighbor's rambling discourse. After a few tries, you will see it is more fun than dozing.

You can even turn a one-way lecture into a dialogue. Mentally connecting it to your own experience keeps you involved. You can always find ways to relate the ideas to your own background and translate what you hear into your own language. If you can say it in your own words, it will make more sense, and you will remember it.

- **To stay awake, say something.**

  If you have ever offered a comment, asked or answered a question, you know that for a while your attention is sharply heightened, even after the laser moves on to someone else. So, to keep alert, deliberately get your voice into the arena. Every time your mind begins to wander, ask a question or offer a comment. *Use this tactic sparingly, however. Don't make a pest of yourself.*

  There is usually plenty of room for legitimate questioning and commentary. Often the question you ask is the one someone else was thinking but was afraid to ask. Use the technique just enough to make yourself feel a part of the dialog and not a bystander.

- **Reduce fear in steps.**

  To overcome fear of talking in class, start with nonthreatening opportunities. If the teacher asks the date or where he or she left off, you can at least answer those questions safely. That way you get to hear your voice in the room. Do that every chance you get. Speaking up will begin to feel okay. Do whatever you can to get comfortable. Get used to the teacher. Drop by his or her office. Shocking as it may seem, by such a simple act you can often turn a teacher into a human being. That in itself will make going to class a lot less stressful.

  There are lots of solutions to school anxiety. Counselors can suggest some, but mainly just think about ways to make yourself feel at home. And Chapter 6 tells you about handling stress in school.

- **Be noticed.**

  Take every advantage you can get. Students who hide, keep their heads down, and avoid the teacher are begging for a lower grade. The front office starts wondering about a teacher who gives lots of high grades, so most teachers try to make their grade sheets have a range. Guess what happens to borderline students they don't know. Guess where the C students usually sit.

- **Show an interest.**

  Make eye contact, but don't stare. Just let the teacher see you are responsive. Use your body language just as you would in a conversation. Let your face be expressive. A room full of poker-faced students is pure hell for a teacher. You want the person who gives the grades to feel friendly and helpful. Like any other animal, teachers can be conditioned to behave well or poorly. Students have tremendous power to affect class atmosphere. So lean forward, ask enough questions and make enough comments to keep your hand in. But don't hog the show.

- **Make sure the teacher knows you and knows your name.**

  When you meet out of class, say, "I'm Tony Archdeacon in your 10:00 class." Be sure to visit the instructor's office within a few days after classes start—for any reason. Your real purpose is to make sure the teacher knows who you are ("I'm Emily Heilman in your 2:00 class") and to find out more about the teacher.

  Anonymity and low grades go together. So make sure you are not forgotten. You can just go through the motions, but you will feel much more alive if you really do get curious. If you simply can't, at least don't be obvious about it. ("I had an hour to kill, so I came to see you.")

- **Take notes.**

  Taking notes won't necessarily help you remember better, but it can help you pay attention while you absorb the pattern and key ideas. You stay on track more easily. Notes can also provide safe storage for later memorization.

The fewer notes the better, however. Since you can't listen well at the same time, just get down a word or phrase to trigger the context later. Figures of speech work better than technical jargon. Make the lecture yours by using your own marking system—indentations, spacing, a map.

Abbreviate. You are not a stenographer. If you try to copy everything, you might as well stay home and send a tape recorder instead. You won't be able to think about what is being said and you will have to go over the whole, dull, boring thing again at home. Not a pretty prospect.

Instead, get the gist down in the fewest possible words: key ideas, important details, any graphic idea to help you remember. Brevity, brevity, brevity.

Leave space so you can fill in later as needed.

Reinforce

Memory fades, so take one or two minutes to reinforce your understanding—before you leave the classroom. Otherwise, stimuli outside the door will wash out most of your work and you will have forgotten even an interesting lecture by bedtime. Most people ignore this step, but it is a bad investment to waste 50 minutes just to gain two.

- **While still in your seat, write from memory in your own words the gist of what you just learned.**

  Check over your notes to resolve any confusion, or grab the teacher before he or she makes a getaway.

- **Within 24 hours, review again by rewriting your notes in even shorter form.**

  Use memory devices, if needed. Convert material into "test" questions.

- **When possible, transfer notes to the margins of text chapters, if the chapters discuss the same material.**

  Your book will then contain in one place everything you will need for review.

Common Problems in the Classroom

Here's what to do when your classroom time is especially difficult.

Vocabulary Issues

It Sounds Like Greek

It could be that the teacher is showing off, or you are not used to the way academics talk, or the subject itself simply involves lots of new words.

Use BFAR to get the main ideas—despite the fog factor.

If the class is tolerable otherwise, you might as well stick around and pick up some new words.

Technical Jargon

Translate it into your own language.

Most school subjects involve a few new words undergraduates need to know. You'll usually picked them up indirectly, while talking about ideas. Majors in the field will acquire thousands more, just by being involved in the discipline.

But a down-to-earth teacher *can* talk sensibly about highly complicated matters, without having to resort to jargon. So, scout out a teacher who loves the subject and can talk about it in English. Start networking early to find the best teacher *for you.*

If you get stuck with a pompous or pretentious teacher, *find a fellow student who can be your interpreter.* Somehow, you must get the main ideas into our own language. You can be certain words you must know will be manageable. Memory devices will store them for you.

Also, ask occasional questions about key terms or concepts. That will provide some breathing space for formatting.

Language Readiness

> *If the language of the course is too confusing, get used to college first. Then take the course later.*

After a semester or two your college skills will have improved. You can bank on it. You will know the ropes and will be used to academic language. You won't be the new kid on the block anymore. Without even trying, you will understand lectures that would have been impossible earlier.

Strange Meanings for Familiar Words

Get used to it. Education expands or restricts the meanings of words. As you broaden your experience of the world, just about every word you ever knew will expand its possible meanings. There is no such thing as *the* meaning of a word, only *a* meaning. Discovery is one of the joys of academic life. So welcome it.

> *Let the context show how the word is being defined.*

The conversation or the lecture will reveal that a special, more general, more precise or altogether different meaning is being used for words such as *disinterested, uninterested, catholic, ignorant,* and so forth.

Teacher Problems

Irreconcilable Differences

If it is really necessary, drop or transfer. But use this option as a last resort. Lots of students chicken out too soon. Those who do tough it out and prevail often consider the experience strengthening. So analyze the situation with a cool head.

If it is clear things are not going to work out, decide if it makes better sense to drop or transfer. Check the college catalog for deadlines. If you try to transfer, use tact. It is considered okay to change sections because of a job conflict, but not because the teacher is a jerk.

Night of the Living Dead

If the teacher is inescapably boring, use BFAR. BFAR should keep you awake. You can use dead space to polish your map. Try occasionally offering comments and questions. It will keep you mentally active and help keep the teacher focused.

Revolting

We have all had a few awful teachers—disgusting, loathsome, nauseating, repulsive. Don't be too hasty. How many of your snap judgments have proven wrong? I remember a high-school algebra teacher I thought was homely. She got more and more lovely as the course progressed, and she turned out to be one of the best teachers I ever had.

If the problem is tolerable, stick it out. So what if the teacher wears the same outfit all semester, has strange habits, twitches, lisps, or in some other way is human?

We learn the most from people who are not like ourselves.

Thousands of students have started out hating a teacher and ended up having great respect—even affection. And *vice versa*, of course. So don't bolt too soon. Sometimes a few office visits help. Strange to say, teachers are just people, like you and your friends. Drop or transfer only if it does turn out the situation is impossible.

Class Subject Issues

Boring Subject

Get it all done in class. Use BFAR.

The danger is daydreaming. Not only does your work get sloppy and you miss the few worthwhile ideas, you also develop a bad habit that can affect your attention in good classes. So watch for main ideas. Make a game out of the experience. Watch for body language that will reveal a main idea in the offing.

If it is a required subject, coolly aim for the grade. Otherwise, consider dropping. *At all costs, don't let boredom ruin good class habits.*

Square Peg, Round Hole

"I'm no good at chemistry." "I've always hated math." "You have to have talent for oil painting." Do you and the subject you are required to take seem to have a personality conflict? Lack of talent or aptitude, emotional blocks—research shows none of these inevitably leads to failure.

You don't have to be good at something to do well in it.

You *can* do subatomic physics, sing at Carnegie Hall, walk a tightwire, apply oils with a sledge hammer, and have your work displayed at the Museum of Modern Art. It is a matter of need, desire, and a sense of available alternatives. You can do just about anything. Just figure out alternate routes to success.

On the other hand, you don't have to do anything you *really* don't want to do. You will not burn in hell because you never made sense of chemistry or because the metaphoric language of poetry drives you crazy. When you think of all there is to be known, no one knows very much. Human knowledge is a thin layer of dust in a vast universe, and nothing is dead certain. So enjoy what direction your own nature takes.

If you don't want to take an elective course, don't. But if you have to take a course, find alternatives that work for you. There will always be a way to deal successfully with any problem.

Here are some other tips for handling difficult classes and teachers:

- Consider alternative texts. Keep a couple of alternative sources for cross-referencing—children's books, tutors, conferences with the teachers, plea bargaining, a different teacher, test analysis, chicken soup, some, all or none of the above. When you're in a foreign country, get a good native guide.

- Consider auditing the course. That will get you formatted. It can work wonders.
- Take the course again. Some schools allow you to try for a higher grade. Check the college catalog or ask your registrar.

Take Charge of Your Own Schooling

You are the final authority on what happens to your intellectual life. No one else knows more about what you should be doing than you. The saddest people are those living lives planned by others.

Course Requirements Are Extra Tough

A reasonable teacher requires no more than two hours of preparation for each one-hour class session. Five, three-hour courses would mean a 45-hour week. That would be sensible and fair. If necessary, an efficient student should be able to master the work in half that time or even less.

A course description that lists far more work than is humanly possible should be taken with a grain of salt. These teachers are on an ego trip and are more interested in looking in a mirror than into your work. There is no way the teacher could actually verify that all that busywork was actually done. So if you have to take the course, use your intelligence to plan out your survival. It will be far easier than you may think.

The more gigantic the reading list, the less the surveillance from the teacher.

- **Find out what the teacher *really* wants, and give it.**

  Rarely will you have to read more than one extra book. Skimming and browsing are often enough to fill you in on other "required" books. Meet the requirements, of course, but don't be the only one in the class to do all the work and end up with a C.

  On the other hand, as you know, the workload per course can vary wildly. So,

- **Preplan. Use BFAR.**

- **Don't take more than one time-consuming course per semester.**

  Mix in some mickey-mouse courses, too, so that your load each semester is balanced. I knew a student who had a full-time job and made straight A's in 28 units of work. I would not recommend many of his shortcuts, but his experience does bear out the fact that a well-organized student can accomplish far more than most would dream possible.

Your Job Interferes

A full-time student can usually handle a part-time job for as many as 20 hours a week. Normally, unless one is very good at the school game, the results fall off after that. But there are lots of ways to maintain a good GPA.

- **If you must work, consider taking fewer courses.**

  What's the hurry? If you spend an extra year in college, will it make any difference 20 years from now? Why torture yourself?

- **Try for a grant or a scholarship.**

  Cases are on record of resourceful, ordinary students having their entire college work paid for by beneficent funds. Millions of dollars go unclaimed because students like you don't apply. Librarians and counselors can help you find books and services tailored just for you.

- **Consider time, place and circumstances as variables, not restrictions.**

  You have as much right to a good education as anyone else. Have the self-esteem to insist on it.

General Boredom

- **Take only interesting courses for a semester or so until your enthusiasm perks up.**

  If it doesn't, college may not be your cup of tea. Contrary to your parents' wishes and despite their crushed hopes, that is not a character defect. Lots of accomplished human beings never went to college.

- **Take a year or two off.**

  After that, either you will be eager for what college has to offer, or you will know it is not for your. Many people come back to college 10, 20, even 30 or more years later—when they are hungry for it. They are almost invariably excellent students.

  If you do drop out, your parents may be disappointed, but most survive the trauma. Some even remember drop-out students in their wills.

The Old College Try

In a "Calvin and Hobbes" cartoon, Dad explains that the Old College Try means, "You join your friends, get some cheap beer, order a pizza, and forget about tomorrow." It *is* an awful lot of fun, as many of your friends on skid row can attest. But what's so bad about a good 40-hour work week and *then* a thoroughly good time? Or a schedule that provides for *both* work (which could be treated as play) and play?

After they flunk a few classes, students who wake up realize regular attendance is insurance. They can be almost certain of a least a C grade, even if their work outside is rather sloppy. The reason is that they are able to keep track of the structure of the course. They know what the teacher emphasizes, when the test dates are, and what will be covered.

Regular attendance has a quieting effect. It is a stabilizing center around which to structure other activities. At least you will know where you will be 15 hours a week. Routine is a good antidote to school anxiety. And once the habit is in place, the mind is released for more creative pursuits. If school success is important to you, this simple habit will carry you a long way toward that goal.

Some students seem to think a sheepskin will transform their lives. The truth is that whatever habits you develop now will be the ones you will live with later. What we are now points to what we will become. Check it out.

Rigidity

A single, unbending approach to all classes is disastrous. Every subject and every teacher calls for a unique response.

Interface. Format.

Figure out what behavior changes you will need for each situation. Make a plan of attack and change it if necessary. Use BFAR.

Schedule Conflicts

Everyone has different needs. Some students hate early morning classes or have to be at work in the afternoon or have to miss a class every Wednesday, and so on. There are dozens of complications. Solution?

Develop a sense of alternatives. There is always some ways to resolve conflicts. And experiment until something works. Sometimes the answer is the opposite of what you thought. For example, some students consider a difficult teacher or subject an opportunity to develop problem-solving skills. The more often you accept a challenge and persevere, even if you lose the game, the stronger your character becomes. Taking action and making decisions is what life *is,* isn't it?

So, maybe a morning class would help you get over a self-indulgent sleep habit. If not, ask the teacher if you can attend a later section—but keep your records in the earlier one. (Sometimes teachers need names on a roster to keep a class from being canceled. So you both benefit.) If you have to babysit every Wednesday, or whatever, see if you can pick up the missed session in another section. Or work with another student who can help you with the missed class. See if the teacher can help you figure out a way to meet course requirements some other way: library work, assisting the teacher in another section, even a different course. If you work swing shift, maybe the teacher will let you checkerboard your attendance among several sections. And so on. Just about any arrangement you can imagine has been tried.

Students have innumerable legitimate problems. But if you are serious about your education, there is almost always a way.

Avoid Ragging the Teacher

It is not the most brilliant idea to fool around in class or try to get the teacher's goat. Don't forget: *Victimized teachers still assign grades.*

The school game is about all about grades, isn't it? It may be fun to frustrate a teacher or challenge his or her authority, but to what end? A wise group of students would serve their interests better by making the teacher feel comfortable. Teachers, like the rest of us, give their best when they feel appreciated. If you want an education, fostering cheer and helpful response from your teacher is in your best interests.

Try some behavior modification. Turn the teacher into a pussycat.

Culture Shock

Most entering freshmen find their values threatened—one way or another, in or out of class. New teachers and new students may talk, eat and dress weird (that is, weird to *you*). College can be like a foreign country—that is how it should be.

The purpose of education is to disturb all settled ideas. If you want to keep all your old ideas and values, stay home. Stick around, and you can expect a satisfying restructuring of your world view toward the end of your junior year. By the end of your senior year, most likely you will become committed again—not necessarily to your old ideas—but with more openness and responsiveness.

If a course or teacher steps on your toes, relax. Things will sort themselves out. Remember, you don't have to believe alien ideas—just understand them. Before jumping to conclusions, keep in mind therapist Carl Rogers's advice:

First, see the idea from the other person's point of view.

Getting the Jump on Assignments

- Carry a pocket-sized notepad. How frustrating to spend two hours on a misunderstood assignment. Be sure of exactly what is wanted.

- Write down instructions word for word. A turn of phrase can make all the difference. Use that notepad and make it a habit. Date your entries.

- Include due dates. While still in class, make sure you know what is expected. Clear up any confusion then and there, with your teacher or with another student.

- Do assignments as soon after class as possible. The purpose of the work will be fresh in your mind. Math students find it helps noticeably to do problems right after class, so they deliberately provide an open period for that purpose. That way, the examples from class are still fresh in their minds.

Read on for more specific help in the assignments part of the school game.

How to Do Assignments

- **Plan ahead. Make a schedule.**

  Decide exactly what the teacher wants.

  Allow a little less time than you need.

  Have a place for nothing but study.

  Study at the same time or times.

- **Use BFAR.**

Study-Time Check List

Mark only the items that match your study habits.

☐ **1.** I am almost never free of anxiety about assignments, things to remember, and tests.

☐ **2.** No matter what the assignment, it always expands to fill whatever time I set aside.

☐ **3.** I spend too much time on some subjects, and then I don't have time to do the rest properly.

☐ **4.** I have a hard time getting started. I put off subjects I don't like and spend a lot of time getting ready.

☐ **5.** I daydream a lot during study time.

☐ **6.** I have never planned out my study time. I have never made a schedule, much less stuck to it.

☐ **7.** I have no idea how long a math assignment should take or if it should take less or more time than some other subject.

☐ **8.** I don't have a study plan. I just sit there until the job is done or until I run out of time.

☐ **9.** I study wherever I happen to be: in the kitchen, on the couch, in bed, in my car.

☐ **10.** I don't have a set time for study. I study any time of the day or evening.

☐ **11.** During study, personal problems keep distracting me.

☐ **12.** People keep interrupting me during my study time.

Wasting Time on School Work: The Solution

Most students have never learned how to handle assignments efficiently. They spend *all* their time out of class doing schoolwork or worrying about it. The work expands to fill whatever time they set aside and slops over into everything else, too. They waste time on some subjects and have to skimp on others. Or they sit staring at the books, doing anything they can to avoid getting started. They have no idea how long it takes to master a history chapter or how fast they can read a page of *Journey to Ixtlan*. They have never made a schedule for themselves in their lives. Their feelings about studying vary from mild anxiety to hysteria. They wonder why other people get the grades. Yet,

> *Spending the least possible time and emotion on assignments is a simple skill to acquire. To keep assignments in their place, you need to plan your work and build productive habits.*

Other chapters of this book cover some aspects of schoolwork—memorizing, mastering textbook chapters, getting ready for tests. This section shows how to square away study time so that you will have some left over for yourself. With a full course load, you should be able to have a normal work week of 40 hours or less. With brutal efficiency, you can reduce the time even more—usually with better results. No doubt you do have better things to do than to stare dolefully at a schoolbook.

Make a Schedule

Unless you enjoy living chaotically, sooner or later you will have to get your act together. Messy habits will not go away all on their own.

Things that recur regularly, such as assignments, must be done so automatically that no thought or effort is needed to get you going. Routines are life-savers. They free the spirit and your time. *It is a matter of habit.* If behavior modification can teach a pigeon ping pong, you can try a little on your own sweet self. It's simple:

Find out what needs to be done. Do it for a while and keep track. Watch the desired behavior become a habit.

1. To start, just observe what you are doing and how you spend your time. Write it down: What. When. Where. How long.
2. Then, based on what you find out, make a schedule.
3. Try it.
4. Fix it up until you get a plan that works.
5. Stick to it. One day you will wake up and find it is a habit.
6. Enjoy the bliss.

First Week

Keep track of how you spend your time.

Do things as usual, but try some kitten-watching. That is, just watch yourself in action, as if you were a kitten playing. It is perfectly possible to stand off to the side, so to speak, and observe this person—yourself—going about his or her business. Know then thyself, as Socrates advised. Some people have lived out their entire lives without ever taking an objective look at the pattern of those lives. Things keep happening *to* them; they never *make* things happen. That is not the way of a successful human being.

Take charge of your own life; first get a clear picture of what is going on. You will need some sort of chart, possibly like the one that follows. If it suits you, there are several provided in this back of this book. Or create your own.

Time Use Chart			
	SUNDAY	MONDAY	TUESDAY
8			
9			
10			

Keep the following information on your chart. Abbreviate everything as much as possible.

- The exact amount of time for each study session
- Where you study
- When you study
- Which book or how many pages or how many problems done
- Highlight the time you could have used but didn't.
- Analyze your chart.

After a week, examine your chart and see what changes you want to make. Maybe you will want to change *where* you study for your history class or *when* or *how long at one time.* Maybe you want to study in your room at your study desk instead of in the library, or maybe in the morning instead of at night.

You must find out how long it takes to do things. How many pages of history can you master in a given time slot? When do you do your best work in history? Where?

You will need the same kind of information for each subject. If it is hard for you concentrate on art history in the evening, how about early morning? Maybe mechanical drawing or computer programming would be better for evening study.

Second Week

Follow a preplanned tentative schedule.

How would you like your work week to go? Block out a plan that suits you, on another chart. Use what you learned from analyzing your first chart. This time, provide in advance for priority items. Slot in a reasonable time-frame for each task and what will probably be the best time of day and the best place.

> *Allow a little less time than you think you need. Build in just enough pressure to keep you alert.*

How much can you do in a given time? Try for a little more at each study session. How long is your attention span? How soon do you start to daydream or get sleepy? Figure it out and create a session just long enough. If necessary, distribute the work over several separate sessions. Or build in regular short breaks.

Lay out the week's plan on your chart. Then try it out, step by step.

As the week progresses, you will need to make some adjustments. You may have been overenthusiastic, or you may run into snags. But by the week's end, you should have a good idea of what works best for you. You will know what, when, where to study and how much you can get done in one session. Your third week should be just about right.

Be sure to leave some free time for emergencies—and for fun.

Third Week

Lay out a workable schedule. Try it out. You will need only slight adjustments.

Fourth Week and Thereafter

Follow a preplanned schedule each week. Shortly, your routine will be part of you, like flossing your teeth or driving a car, and you won't need a chart. Regular habits free the nervous system to attend to the work itself. You will experience an exhilarating productivity. Thomas Jefferson biographer Dumas Malone said of his 35 years on the project, "My policy has always been in accord with my temperament: I don't press, but I keep eternally at it." He was in his mid-eighties and had completed five award-winning volumes. Fiction writer Richard Ford writes for three hours every day, 365 days a year.

Habit is a way of trying without trying, effortless effort.

The Assignment Itself: BFAR

Now for some strategy on actually getting the work done.

Make a Plan and Stick to It

Never, never just wade in. Use BFAR (Browse, Focus, Absorb, Reinforce). That is the real secret for saving hours.

- Read over the assignment until you are sure what is required.
- Meet personal goals *after* the teacher's.
- Examine the whole task first. Then break it into manageable segments.
- Above all, be sure to reinforce after each segment and at the end of the whole assignment.

Remember, the idea is to get the assignment internalized as much as possible right then and there. You don't want to have to redo the work later. Thereafter, only brief, minor touch-ups should be needed.

- Write from memory the gist of each session. Then use mnemonic (memory) devices for key ideas.
- Put the material in the form of a test—just like one your teacher would make.
- Remember—if you don't reinforce, you will lose 90 percent of all you learn.

Review Periodically

Before starting a new assignment, refresh yourself on what you learned the last time. Review is a good way to get warmed up for the new work. Go over anything that has faded. *Every week or so, do a quick check-up.*

Use BFAR for a general review the night before a test.

If you run into snags, remember that you do have problem-solving tactics. Use them. You have many resources and alternatives. Every problem has many solutions.

Teach It to Someone Else

Teach a classmate, your spouse, a fifth-grader, your dog or the TV. There is no better way to learn than to try to explain something—*in your own words.* You will see immediately what you don't really understand. The process forces you to be clear.

You can use a study partner, too, but work it through as best you can on your own first. Otherwise, you may rely on the other person and get sloppy in your study habits.

Improving Concentration

When people are passionate, they concentrate effortlessly. The capacity to absorb is natural and routine—if it's not interfered with.

A good way to kill concentration is to have someone else set your agenda. It is not surprising, then, that perfectly brilliant creatures become stupefied in a school setting. Essential motivation is missing. We become passive, and when we are, we waste time. We dawdle, appear stupid and feel dull. As you know from earlier chapters, without concentration, there is no way to get concepts into our mental computers. Somehow, we have to take charge.

> *To combat inattention deliberately, apply a* method *for concentration.*

This book lists several preventive techniques for battling inattention when you're attending classes. Following are a few more ideas about concentrating better out of class.

Have a Regular Place to Study

You can have one or several study spots. Whatever spot you choose, however, *do nothing else but study in that spot.* The mind must associate only efficient study habits with this place. When you sit down, work begins.

- **Allow no distractions.**

  No picture of your favorite mountain lake or sweetheart. No ringing telephone. No visitors. (Hang a do-not-disturb sign outside your door or on the back of your chair.) No picture window.

- **Have on your desk what you need for this time slot. Nothing else.**

  Put everything else off your desk and out of sight. Get it?

Set Time Limits and Quantity Limits

- **First, plan exactly how long you will study.**

- **Decide how much you will do and what results you want.**

  Consult your schedule.

  Use BFAR to determine where you should stop for a breather. If the material will take an hour but you can tolerate only 20 minutes at a stretch, plan two short breaks. But, for reinforcement, complete BFAR on each part before each break.

Study Similar Subjects at Separate Times

- **To avoid fatigue, distribute study over several individual sessions.**

  If you must do more than one assignment at one study session, make sure they are not of the same sort. Shifting to another frame of reference will refresh you. Winston Churchill went from his work in government to bricklaying or painting. Because each activity called for different skills, he was able to be at his best almost continuously. So do your literature and math assignments together, but not literature and humanities or math and physics.

  Your mind is capable of working efficiently all the time—provided it doesn't get bored.

- **Do difficult or boring subjects first.**

  Save what you enjoy for dessert.

Reward Short-Term Goals

- **When you achieve your goal, do something you like.**

  Decide how many pages you should master or how many problems you should do in the time you provided. *Be firm. Set your clock.*

Rewards can be playing a tape you like, walking the dog, having some tea, anything you like.

But if you don't fulfill your plan, no reward.

It also helps to keep track of successes and failures. Try a chart: Each success is a plus (+), each flop is a minus (–). You will see a pattern emerge with more and more pluses and fewer minuses.

Likewise, you can keep track of how much you do from day to day. Monitor increases or decreases in the number of pages completed in a given time, or changes in the length of your attention span without tiring. Developing study skill is similar to developing facility in any other activity—sports, carpentry, auto mechanics, whatever:

- **Keep your goals modest. Work one step at a time. Practice regularly and monitor your progress.**

Settle Distractions

- **Don't get involved fixing your car, arguing with your spouse, doing your taxes before a study session.**

  Settle problems *after* you study. Use some mind-quieting techniques: a slow walk, largo movements from classical music, and so on. Come to your work with a clear, alert mind.

- **Train everyone to respect your study hour.**

  Learn not to answer the door. Or insist that guests entertain themselves. Turn off the phone. You will see people quickly adjust to your schedule. Anyone who doesn't will become a former friend.

  Remember: your grade is at stake. So be ruthless. Insistence on your study habits will pay off for all concerned. You will have peace of mind, and after a successful study session you will be free to give your full attention to other people and things. Won't that be a welcome change?

Adjust to Random Noise

When you are absorbed in what you are doing, nothing can distract you. You could study happily in a machine shop. But if you are not fully involved, the slightest sound could disrupt your thoughts. Clearly, we create our own distractions.

Distractions are always from within. We choose to be distracted, but we can also choose *not* to be. Sometimes the solution can be as simple as rearranging things. One student had been frustrated by the demands of her husband and baby on her study time. She moved her study place into the living room. She studied lying on the carpet, her husband watching TV, the baby crawling around between them. In the crib, he had cried for attention. Locked out of the study room, her husband did! Knowing that her family were contented, the student could concentrate, even though there was a lot going on around her. There is always a way to work things out.

Daydreaming

We learn what we do. If the mind is used to the study desk as a place to doze or gaze into space or gather wool, that is exactly what it will do there. It is a learned behavior; and you'll have to take deliberate action to effect a permanent change. The desired behavior has to become a habit.

- Every time your mind wanders, put a check ✓ in the margin of the book or on a tally sheet.

  Keep a record of the number for each session. If there are more checks towards the end of a session, make the next one shorter.

- If something is on your mind and you can't set it aside, stop. Take a sheet of paper and write it all out—out of your mind and onto the paper.

  The part of yourself that worries will be satisfied that something has been done and will quiet down long enough for you to complete your work.

- Keep a reminder list to reduce anxiety.
- Stand up and face the other way.

  The act is a dramatic way of saying "No!" to mind wandering. It is a sharp break. You won't have to do that very often.
- Quiet the mind.

  Use one of your mind-quieting techniques: breathing normally and counting your breaths, going through the rainbow colors, a slow walk around your room. Take just long enough to get your mind back on track. A minute or two should be plenty.
- Work standing up.

  It's pretty hard to doze standing up. Hemingway wrote his novels that way. Prop your work on your dresser, or put your chair on top of your desk and prop the text there.

Learning Environments, Natural and Artificial

Without interference, most people learn easily and quickly. If they were to examine the accomplishments they take for granted, they would feel brilliant. They should. On this planet any ordinary human being is a phenomenal animal. School should reinforce our feeling of worth and ability, but it rarely does. Indeed, it seems designed to do the opposite. It is at best a harmless bore and at worse a frightening, guilt-generating ordeal.

One reason for this contradiction is that teaching methods seldom make use of natural learning processes. They invite behavior that actually *interferes* with learning: passivity, daydreaming, timidity, lack of confidence, low self-esteem, competitiveness, procrastination.

Students have to realize the conflict between schooling and education and have the assurance to find their own approaches for taking classes and for studying. Fortunately, your own learning success elsewhere reveals excellent skills, which can be used just as effectively in school. A problem-solving approach will allow you to handle lectures and assignments easily.

BFAR is a reliable way to include the necessary steps:

- Defining the problem
- Making and carrying out a plan
- Checking over results

> *Success—in class and at home—is achieved through applying and reinforcing productive techniques often enough to establish them as habits.*

Developing these skills is the major task of any student and is the only defense against four years of chaos. Once routines are established, there will be plenty of time for pursing your own interests— without anxiety.

CHAPTER

6

Controlling School Anxiety

Nothing Is Good or Bad But Thinking Makes It So.

Whether you think you can
or whether you think you can't
you're right
—Henry Ford

The Horrors of School

People enjoy scaring themselves to death. That is what *The Texas Chainsaw Murders* and roller coasters are all about. One of the favorite pastimes of college students is dreaming up scary flunk-out scenarios. The cloud of anxiety over most colleges is almost palpable. It is true that people do flunk tests, fail courses, even bomb whole semesters. Some do flunk out of college altogether. But how many do you suppose die of it? College is a swell place for some people; it could be nice under the right conditions for almost anybody. But it is only *one* possible path of many equally attractive alternatives.

Clearly, an important principle is to trust that there is nothing to worry about in college. The whole point of this book is that ordinary people can get through college comfortably and without stress—*if they are willing to give up their insecurity blankets.* We are told that some fears, like fear of falling, are natural. But aerialists can banish that fear. So can you.

Fear of snakes, heights, space, confinement, teachers, or tests is not inevitable.

It is hard to convince students that worrying is nothing more than a bad habit—like procrastination or daydreaming. They would rather cling to the old ways than risk change, even though serendipity is obviously desirable. But if a student is ready, school anxiety can be eliminated like any other bad habit. College can truly become the time of your life.

School anxiety is nothing more than a bad habit.

Manufactured Threats and Dangers

Most teachers use fear as a motivator. Fear of punishment can make students be polite or do their homework or follow the rules. But the side effects aren't worth it. If you fall for the con, you become nervous and twitchy and can't think clearly. And of course, you always hate the person holding the club. Positive reinforcement, the rewarding of productive behavior, doesn't have negative side effects. But it takes courage to give up artificial authority, so most teachers are afraid to risk it.

Fortunately, we all have access to a much better motive than pleasing external authority. The joy of discovery, of seeing clearly, is what keeps kids in the sandbox, and it is the same for adults. *There is nothing more stimulating than the pleasure of finding things out.* In other words, the only natural incentive is reward that comes from inside, from one's own creative urge. That is what this book is all about: taking charge of one's own life, creating one's own system.

What you have learned so far in *Get Your A Out of College* shows how to organize study time, how to read a text chapter, how to listen in class, how to remember, how to take tests. Most of all, it shows how the school game really works. With this kind of awareness, it is hard to be intimidated.

> *For a person of normal intelligence, there is nothing whatsoever to fear in school.*

Sadly, most students have been trained to fear teachers, classrooms, textbooks and tests. So even though you may now understand the concepts of this book, you may have lots of deeply ingrained habits to dump. As with any other habit, you need to superimpose new, *self-enhancing* habits over the old, self-destructive ones. The following pages show how to do that.

Think of Fear as Information

There are infinite ways to look at events. Some people see the water in a glass and say, "It's half full." Some say, "It's half empty." Some might view it as three inches of water. The less-programmed minds of kids would yield many other views. But there is no such thing as *the* correct view.

There is no required, specific connection between a situation and how we feel about it. Most people think they are obliged to view events in only one way. A high grade is "good." A broken leg is "bad." Since we cannot see into the future, the most we can say about coming events is "maybe." We have all heard stories of people who thought they had suffered a disaster and later viewed it as "the best thing that ever happened to me."

Fear can be treated in the same manner. It doesn't have to be shunned.

Think of fear as information.

Perceived as messages, our feelings can pinpoint parts of our behavior that need attention, things out of balance that need to be righted. From this point of view, our fear, stress and general malaise can be considered advisories. A toothache is information; so is fear.

If we take a good look at the messages sent to us by anxiety and fear, we can be empowered by that information.

Treating Fear as an Ally

Calm Down

Otto Preminger thought the way to keep his actors from being nervous was to shout, "CALM DOWN!" It didn't work. You can't force yourself into a quiet state of mind. But you can set the stage. We don't think well under stress. We need catlike ease.

> *For the mind to be at its best, it must be fully awake but unencumbered.*

Everyone experiences this most beneficial state of mind from time to time—but usually accidentally. You can train yourself to do it on purpose. A calming ritual can become as much a habit as anxiety. Several relaxation techniques have been described earlier in this book. Just do what is most effective for you *every day in the same place, and at the same time.* Within a few weeks, the desired state of being will be automatic as soon as you start a study session. Your mind will slip immediately into its study mode. It is all a matter of conditioning.

The idea behind all of the following calming exercises is to give your conscious mind something to do long enough for it to quiet down. Instead of racing around in all directions, it is obliged to focus. Once you turn off whatever mental tape you have playing, the nonconscious and conscious hemispheres are free to communicate.

Music

- Set aside a time and place for a 15- to 20-minute daily ritual. Make yourself comfortable.

- Put on the largo (slow) movement of a classical symphony. Use instrumental music, and choose composers such as Bach, Corelli, Vivaldi, Brahms, Mozart. The beat should be about one per second—about the same pace as the alpha rhythm of the brain. Other kinds of music have proven to be less effective.

Relaxation

Use one of the following techniques or any others you have found to be effective.

The Rainbow

While sitting comfortably and with the music playing, work your way through the colors of the visual spectrum: Red, Orange, Yellow, Green, Blue, Indigo, Violet. The acronym ROY G. BIV will help you remember them.

Imagine you are floating in a rich, red cloud of warm, sensuous, romantic red. Let the color wash over your body. Absorb it. Float in this color until it is part of you. Then float effortlessly down and into the orange color.

Now float in the orange of a sunset—a pleasant, comfortable, delicious orange color. Stay here until you feel the warming orange in every pore, until you have absorbed orange into your nervous system, until you become orange. Then float down to the cloud of yellow.

Float in the luminous, lemony, morning-sunlight yellow until you feel it all over your mind and body. You are enveloped in a wonderfully yellow cloud.

Proceed through green, blue, indigo and violet in the same manner. When you reach violet, your mind will be clear and at rest. You will be in the state of mind Keats called *ardent listlessness.* You will find that you can think clearly and effortlessly and that complex matters will be surprisingly simple.

Mental Massage

Sitting comfortably, with the music playing, systematically activate your nerve endings. Focus your attention on your toes. Don't wiggle them; just notice them. When you are aware of all ten, go to the rest of each foot—soles, heels, everything. There will be a slight tingly sensation. Work your way up through the ankles, lower legs and knees, on through the whole body—thighs, stomach, buttocks, chest, back, upper arms, lower arms, hands, back up to the neck, back of the head, the top, forehead, eyes, ears, cheeks, lips, chin. Then check out the whole body by sliding your attention down to the toes again and back through every part, to make sure everything is tuned up.

Your body will feel as if you have had a massage, and your mind will be alert, quiet and clear, ready for thinking.

Take as long as necessary. The process will go faster as you become used to it. In class before a test, you can quiet your mind in just a few seconds.

Conscious Breathing

Sit comfortably, with the music playing, and pay attention to your breathing. Breath normally, but count each inhalation. That is all there is to it. If you lose track, start over. Do this as long as it takes to feel centered and quietly alert. If random thoughts float in and out, take note of them but don't fight them. Gradually, fewer and fewer will intrude and you will be able to focus quickly.

Note: If you prefer, instead of counting your breaths, you can say, "*Breathing in, I know that I am breathing in. Breathing out, I know that I am breathing out.*" Repeat the process until you feel centered.

Use any method that keeps your mind focused on the breathing and not skittering every which way. This odd job for your conscious mind will shut off your mental chatterbox and allow you to pull your selves together.

Slow Walk

Walk around at about one pace per second until you feel yourself centered and your mind is quiet. Initially, you will be self-conscious and your mind will wander, but gradually your body and the alpha rhythms in your brain will become synchronized, and you will find yourself completely in the here and now. At first it may take up to half an hour to reach the desired state of mind, but it will go faster and more smoothly each time.

During this exercise, do *everything* at this speed: talking, eating, even thinking. If anyone asks what you are up to, just say—at half speed—"It's a psychology experiment."

Ritual

To use your mind at its best, get centered. Any regular procedure for this purpose will work. *Just make it a clear ritual.* Don't confuse your mind by letting other things interfere, like phone calls or random wool-gathering. Do it the same way each time and pay attention. Make it a habit.

If you would like to work on getting a good night's sleep, for example, have a getting-ready-for-a good-night's-sleep ritual:

> I am getting ready for a good night's sleep. I am brushing my teeth with my special sleepy-time toothbrush, getting ready for a good night's sleep. I am getting into my night clothes for a good night's sleep. I am turning down the covers for a good night's sleep. Now I put my sleepy-time tea in the

> sleepy-time tea pot. Now I am putting on the sleepy-time kettle for my sleepy-time tea. I am enjoying watching the kettle begin to boil for my sleepy-time tea. I carefully pour the water into the sleepy-time tea pot. I sit quietly while the sleepy-time tea steeps. Now I carefully pour the tea into the sleepy-time cup. Now I take my time sipping the sleepy-time tea. Now I carefully rinse the sleepy-time tea pot and the sleepy-time cup and put them and the sleepy-time kettle back in their special place. Now I get into bed and turn off the light. Now I go to sleep.

Have a special place for the ritual materials. Never use these things for anything else or at any other time. Even your toothbrush is a special sleepy-time toothbrush.

Note: Fluorescent lights, even incandescent lights, are known to be distracting for many people. Try out candlelight for this ritual and see if it helps.

The purer the ritual, the firmer the desired behavior modification. You can create a ritual for any behavior you want to cultivate. Just make up a special routine and pay careful attention to the process as you go through the steps. Don't permit anything to contaminate the ritual materials and activities.

Rehearsing for Fearful Situations

Golfers who mentally rehearse their swing perform better when they are on the golf course. So try a step-by-step walk-through of the feared situation. First, go through a relaxation routine. When you are calm, imagine the steps leading up to the test, the speech, the race, whatever.

Imagine yourself back to a point where there is no anxiety. Then imagine yourself in each succeeding stage and *stay there until you feel no fear.* Since you are in a position of safety while you are imagining the situation, you can control how you feel. Gradually work through to the scary situation itself. Imagine individual parts, removing fear as you go. Take your time. Come back for another rehearsal, if necessary, until you feel no discomfort or anxiety.

The more you know ahead of time about the circumstances of the actual event, the less there will be to make you anxious. So check out the place where you will perform. Sit in the seat, stand on the platform, try out the mike, run the track. Get familiar will all the details you can know about in advance. Simulate the performance. Give the speech, take a mock test. Practice as if it were the real thing.

Reprogramming

Suppose during your mental rehearsal you come nose-to-nose with something really scary. What now? You're paralyzed. The fear seems irreversible.

Do this: Hold the fear situation on one mental screen and scan through your memory bank for a time when you were bold, brave, courageous. What did it feel like to be so strong? Bring that feeling up on your other screen and bask in it. Now go back to the troublesome situation and—while still feeling bold and brave—dispatch it.

Keep in mind you can *choose* how you feel about anything.

Change the Tape

There are all sorts of tapes available for your mental boom box. There is the talk-radio tape that chatters, chatters, chatters. Those who quiet their minds play nature's music. There are A-student tapes, D-student tapes, failure tapes. The anxiety tapes are real winners. Self-hate tapes are popular.

Is this tape familiar?

> I'm scared of talking in public. This book is too hard. I've always been a poor student. I have **all these things** to do. Everyone else gets the good stuff. I don't deserve it anyway. I'm so worried. What awful thing's going to happen now?

And on and on. We make these tapes ourselves. Thank goodness, we can make new ones. It is just as easy to run a self-esteem tape:

> I've handled lots of problems successfully. Math can't be any harder than using a computer, and I'm really good at that. I have lots of good problem-strategies. Which one would be good to use here? I'm a very nice person; I have as much right as anyone to the best life can offer. Let's take this problem one step at a time. I'll just walk my way through it.

And so on. Change to a self-esteem tape, change to a positive tape, and your life will change.

> ***Change the Tape; Change Your Life***
>
> The techniques of reprogramming and changing the inner dialogue are used with good results to help people overcome all sorts of panic: fear of elevators, sex, public speaking, and so forth. If any school situation paralyzes you, experiment with your tapes.

Other Stones on the Path of Fear

Here are some other tools for getting rid of school anxiety.

Tension

During a test—or any time—if you feel yourself tensing up, consider going along with it. That is, clench your fists as tightly as you can, and tense up your whole torso—the shoulders, jaws, neck, stomach—and then your thighs and calves, too. Then let go. You will feel an immediate release. The tension drains out. You can do this sitting at your desk. You won't be noticed. Everyone else will be occupied with his or her own anxieties.

Facing Worry Head-on

Go ahead. Indulge yourself. If you must worry yourself sick about everything—deadlines, errands, putting out the cat, tests, remembering to remember, and so on—then do a proper job of it. Throw yourself into it. Give it the attention it deserves. Instead of worrying about this or that while you are taking a test, while you are in class, while you are doing assignments, while you are on a date, save up and do it all at once.

Some part of yourself is convinced that if you don't worry, things won't get done. It is your internalized mommy trying to take care of you. So worry does came from a positive impulse. Since you can't just toss it out, you have to find a productive way to appease that impulse.

One way to face worry is to set aside 30 minutes a day, same place, same time, for worry and nothing but worry.

1. During the day, when a concern creeps in where it shouldn't, jot it down on your worry list. Promise yourself you will give it your full attention during your worry session. Then keep your word.

2. Begin your worry session with your preferred mind-quieting technique. With experience, it will take less and less time to get into the right frame of mind.

3. Take out your worry list and work your way through it. Decide exactly what you will do to dispatch each concern, when you will do it, and how.

4. Afterward, delight in crossing items off your list, one by one.

By facing your worries head-on and taking them seriously, you will soon find your worry list growing shorter. Your mind will know that you are not neglecting things and it won't need to nag you when you are concentrating on other things. As you can see, a worry session is not as nutty as it may sound. It is simply a way of attending to the details of everyday life, of organizing your day for fewer distractions.

Reframing

How we feel about something depends on how we *see* it. If you don't like a painting, try a different frame. It can make all the difference. See something you fear in a different framework and the feeling will disappear.

If you don't like how you feel about something, try different ways of seeing it until you find a frame that removes the feeling. Reframing can put a positive spin on anything. The more frames we keep in stock, the more effectively we can respond to problems. It is simply a matter of separating an event from how we feel about it. Once we grasp that distinction, we are free to reshape any aspects of our lives. We begin to create and furnish our own worlds, rather than rent from others.

Thoreau thought the flowers next door smelled just as sweet and were just as lovely as if he grew them. He reframed *ownership.* You will be safer in bear country or in certain neighborhoods if you see them not as dangerous places, but as terrains with certain characteristics to be noted. Nervously looking over your shoulder will only get you into trouble.

Likewise, look at the difference between *He gave me an A* and *I got an A.* Or, *I have to do this assignment.* A test can be a judgment of your worth as a human being, or it can be a game you *get* to play, a crossword puzzle you *get* to do. Imagine a little kid saying, "I *have* to play in the tree house."

To eliminate fear of an event, reframe it.

Loving It

The wise prefer known devils.

One way to deal with a potential danger is to get in bed with it. That is, if you know the enemy as well as you do your sweetheart, you will be better positioned for combat. Before he challenged Rommel in North Africa, General Patton had digested Rommel's book on battle. Patton did his homework. He knew Rommel's mind. He knew what Rommel would do, so *Patton had nothing to fear.*

Usually it is the monsters in our heads that scare us to death, not the events out there. And once we get a good look at what is really going on, get the feel of it, we find ourselves calming down.

A woman in a speech class said she simply could not speak in front of an audience; she was crippled by fear—fear of *what was going to happen,* not the present moment. The teacher persuaded her to stand on the stage and tell him how she was feeling right then:

"I'm terrified!"

"Describe it. How do you know you're terrified?"

"My hands are trembling. See?"

"On a scale of one to ten, how much?"

"About nine-and-a-half."

"What else?"

"My mouth is dry. I can hardly get words out."

"Yes. What else?"

"Well, my knees are shaking. Oh, they're not so bad now."

"I notice your voice is steadier now, too."

"Hmm. That's right. I'm feeling a lot better."

"Yes, I see that. What was it you were going to talk about?"

The woman went on to give her speech without any fear. By assigning her conscious mind some specific tasks, she gave it a chance to calm down. The emotion evaporated, and she could focus on sharing her ideas with her audience in the here and now. She was *in the present,* not in some imagined future. She later became a representative for a cosmetics firm and made her living giving presentations, sometimes to large audiences.

In a school situation, identify as accurately as you can whatever it is you are afraid of, and then get to know it inside and out. If it is actually the test itself, then play with the test structure beforehand. Get to love it. Chapter 3 on taking tests shows how to become an expert. When you see the actual test, it will look like an old friend.

If it is the setting that worries you, go to the room, sit in the chair, walk yourself through the process. In other words, practice taking the test the same way you practice for a track meet or for a recital.

If you find yourself starting to panic just thinking of the event, turn to the panic itself, take a pencil and actually make a list of the physiological changes you are experiencing. The conscious mind will have practical work to do and will have a chance to get out of the grip of the emotion.

To reduce fear, make the unknown familiar.

Warm Up Your Audience: You

Before a performance, musicians, speakers, and talk-show hosts do whatever it takes to make the setting a warm and friendly place: a warm-up band, or a co-host like Ed McMahon. Or the speaker will chat informally with the audience before the actual talk, even going among the people, shaking hands and talking with individuals. The idea is to get comfortable with the situation.

Keep Your Eye on the Ball

Coaches tell batters to fall in love with that sphere coming toward them. What a beautiful, whirling white orb, what a lovely arc it makes, what grace of movement. Wham! The bat meets the ball, and the batter doesn't even know the bat has swung. That works for school, too. But you do have know *what* the ball *is*. When you are up at bat, it is the ball you must be fascinated by, not your own performance, not the pitcher's. If you attend to anything else but the ball itself, you will strike out.

And you have to love it. It has to be wonderful. You have to be soft-eyed, not squinty-eyed and tense. Make love, not war. When you fear the enemy, you are vulnerable. When you love the sword coming toward your neck, your sword will meet it.

What's the ball or the sword in *your* case? For a car salesman, it's the buyer—not the car, not his or her own selling powers. For the buyer, it's the salesman—not the car or any clever buying knowledge. During a calculus test, what is the ball? Calculus? The formidable teacher? Your own preparedness? The test itself? *It is the test.* You have to find the test to be the most alluring, lovely, beautifully put-together structure you have ever encountered. You *love* it. If you can achieve that fascination, your test-taking skills will come into play automatically.

It is the same with any other interaction. When you take chemistry, what do you suppose is the ball? How well you are prepared to take it—your own performance? The subject of chemistry? The teacher? In this scenario, *the ball is the teacher.* The teacher gives the grade. If you know the teacher, if you allow your self to tune in to this absorbing entity, if you "love" this spinning orb, chemistry will take care of itself.

Change the scene: When you are reading the text for Spanish, what is the ball? Spanish? The teacher and his or her expectations? The text itself? *It is the text itself.* Learn to make love to it; make it your familiar friend, and you are in business. When you try to *speak* Spanish, the ball becomes the person you are speaking to, not how well *you* are doing. Keep your eye on the ball.

Be sure what the ball is. Then love it.

Settling Specific Fears

When we are calm, we can treat any fear as a problem-solving opportunity. It is futile to try this when we are upset. One of the methods described above will quiet the mind. You'll be able to examine the fear carefully and see what the problem really is. Sometimes all that is needed is a clear description. Often the *real* problem is something else.

For example, a student worried herself sick about getting into med school. When she calmed down and took a good look, she saw her real concern was that she might disappoint her parents. She realized she didn't really want to be a doctor, and her fear was seeing to it that she *failed.* Once that was clear, it was hard to keep up the charade.

First define the fear.

An accurate perception of the problem is usually enough. The positive function of the fearful emotion is to make the conscious mind pay attention. Once that has been done, the emotion usually evaporates. Following are a few approaches to specific fears.

Teachers

Teachers have only as much power over our lives as we grant them. Many students see teachers as rare and elevated human beings, as if a credential has suddenly transformed them into deities or ogres. *Reframe them.* Look around your classroom; some of your peers will become teachers. As you can see, there is nothing about them to fear. They have the full range of human strengths and weaknesses.

Don't hand over power to teachers that they don't really have. Reframe.

One way to humanize teachers is to get to know them off stage. Visit their offices. Don't refuse a cup of coffee in the cafeteria. Chat about other things besides school.

Take a genuine interest in teacher as a human being. A teacher who wants to enjoy teaching knows that students need to feel safe and comfortable. If you are at ease, the teacher can do a better job. The learning process flows better. Keep in mind that teachers are full of unreal fears, too. Many fear their students. Yes! One teacher in an article listed 15 things he feared in the classroom. You can imagine the atmosphere in *that* classroom. So switch your perception around. Make your teachers feel safe. They will do a better job for you.

Failure

You can bet failure itself is not the problem. You wouldn't really mind failing, would you, if it wasn't for your pride? How could you face the people back home?

But as for failure itself—my, my, my, you have failed at more than what you ever succeeded with. In fact, failure is what you do along the way to accomplishment. In order to learn to tie your shoes, you had to fail lots and lots of times. The same with potty training, riding a bike, opening your eyes under water. It's a big lie to say you fear failure. We all thrive on it. No artist ever achieves the ideal painting. Anyone who tries *at all* must get perfectly comfortable with failure.

Remember: *Failure is information.* If it's a pride problem, then solve that. But don't call it "fear of failure." It's not. If you have browsed through this book, you know already that you can get a C by just offering up your warm body a few hours a week. Any physiologically normal person can get a passing grade. Most undergraduate courses don't require expert scholars. That is one of the things you are there to learn. Teachers know it takes time to adjust. Most assignments will be within reason, more likely boring than difficult. An occasional impossible course will not ruin your career.

Lack of ability is rarely the cause of failure. After the first semester, most students see that the horrors they imagined never materialized. For some, the ordinariness of course work is even a bit of a letdown. If you would really like to fail, though, then fear the failure. It is a self-fulfilling prophecy. The emotion itself will prevent you from using your mind clearly, Sure enough, you *will* fail.

Fear of failure is a self-fulfilling prophecy. On the other hand, a few successes will show you how pleasant college can be. It is perfectly possible to go through college and graduate school with no fear whatsoever. Fear of failure is something you dreamed up. Break a leg.

To eliminate fear of failure, recognize and accept failure as a normal and natural part of the learning process.

Rejection

Fear of rejection keeps the timid in bed with covers over their heads. No one wants to be rejected. It is not like eating ice cream. But there is no way around it. As Robert Kerwin pointed out in his article. "The Art of Accepting Rejection" (*San Francisco Chronicle*), it is one of life's little paradoxes that if you want to be accepted, you have to risk rejection. If you got through the day without being rejected, odds are you haven't stuck your neck out.

You are familiar with the drill:

> I can't return this shirt to Macy's. I lost the sales slip. They'll just tell me No and I'll be embarrassed.
>
> I can't ask the produce guy to cut open this watermelon to see if it's ripe. What if he says No? He might make a remark right in front of other people.
>
> I don't have a single excuse for turning this term paper in late, so I shouldn't even try. She told us not even to think about it. She might yell at me.
>
> I would like to read my story out loud to the class, but I'd be too embarrassed. What if they laugh? What if I screw up?

Face it. If you want to be accepted, you have to get rejected. Anyone who succeeds, anyone who gets accepted, Robert Kerwin observes, has fists full of rejections.

Deliberately seek rejection. Make it a habit.

Make a list. What would you like to try today that might get you criticized or get your tender feelings hurt? You can start with easy things, like returning the leaky milk carton or not leaving a tip for poor service. But get in as many rejections as you can bear each day, and add more and more. If you get lots of acceptances, don't rest until you get a few rejections. Get used to it. *The goal is to become immune.*

No doubt you will never grow to love rejection, but you can become so used to it that it will never keep you from trying things you really want to do. As you become accustomed to being rejected, you will see that you don't die of it. It doesn't even interfere with dinner. *There is no connection whatsoever between rejection and how we feel about it.*

Keep in mind, also, that no one ever gets so good that he or she *can't* be rejected. The people who do things get rejected. John Updike still gets stories rejected. Woody Allen movies bomb. If you are trying new things, some of them will be a mess. You failed. You're a bum. You're terrible. Get used to it.

Rejection can't ruin your life; but not risking it can. One of the great pleasures of getting rejected is the surprising number of times you get accepted. People you never dreamed would say "Yes" will give you money, time, things, advice, help, even their hand in marriage.

Looking Foolish

Before class, students chat with one another and with the teacher in a perfectly natural and comfortable way. But let the teacher say, "Well, let's get started," and everything changes. All of a sudden it's *class.* Everyone benefits from a warm and friendly atmosphere, but even the best teaches have trouble making it happen. Then they say, "That's it for today," and everyone relaxes. Students who clam up in class immediately jump into animated dialogues on the very same topic.

One reason for this reluctance, no doubt, is the fear of looking foolish. Who wants to say something dumb in front of a lot of strangers? Who wants to perform in public and botch it? It could be *embarrassing.* Many students would rather die. Yet it is clear that getting into the act is the best way to learn.

> *The more a person is actively involved, the higher the rate of learning. It is self-defeating to sit on the bench.*

To eliminate fear of embarrassment, reframe it. Most people are afraid of looking foolish, but it is a costly self-indulgence. If you examine it, either you are a fool or you aren't. More accurately, everyone is a fool some of the time. So what? Anyone who is afraid of looking foolish can never learn.

It is vain to dwell on how we look to others. "What other people think of you is none of your business." Why waste your time on it? It is simply another way of giving others power over how we live our lives.

Besides, as your own experience will show, people don't spend very much time thinking about the mistakes of others. They are much more concerned about themselves. (Who is the most important person in a group photo?) An hour later they will not even remember a mistake was made or that you were the one who made it. How long do *you* remember when someone flubs it?

And keep in mind that your performance in class is almost never the main source of your grade. Any way you look at it, fear of public ridicule is exaggerated.

Rehearse yourself out of fearing foolish. If timidity is a deeply ingrained habit, try desensitizing yourself, step by step.

1. Before class, calm your body and mind with your preferred method.

2. Picture yourself getting closer and closer to the threatening situation until you see yourself asking the question or volunteering a comment. You will feel no anxiety. It is just like practicing your golf swing.

3. In class, having already talked successfully in your imagination, you are simply repeating what you have already done.

4. Speak up every chance you get when the situation is nonthreatening.

5. Volunteer the page, the time, the date—anything you can say that doesn't put your precious self-image on the line. Once you get used to hearing your own voice in class a few times, you will feel okay about it.

6. Chatting before and after class with the teacher and other students will help, too.

For true stage fright, see a counselor. If you are a basket case, many schools have programs designed to walk you through this fear. Whole books have been written on school anxiety. Considering the general atmosphere of most schools, it is not surprising that most students are afflicted to some degree. You have lots of company.

The Unknown

The future can be dangerous. One of these days it will kill you. But what is the alternative? To let fear of the unknown keep you from trying new things would be to give up on life itself. "Life *is* trouble," said Zorba the Greek. "Only death is not." The *really* scary thing is to have the same things happen today that happened yesterday. Of course, if you are paying attention, that is impossible.

Since the unknown is what happens next, the only sensible response is to embrace it. Everything wonderful you have ever experienced, happened *next.* Indeed, life is change. We really don't know what is going to happen next, but we never have known. New organisms take to it. Babies, cubs, primroses—all go recklessly into the future joyously, basking in each new moment along the way.

What happened? What makes so many people nervous about so natural and inevitable a process? Could it be the well-meaning admonition, "Be careful"? If you want to make someone fall off a cliff, just say, "Watch out." *Watch out for snakes. Watch out for muggers. This is a dangerous curve. This teacher is really tough.* Bingo. All of a sudden we take our eye off the ball—whatever that may be—and start watching our step, our swing, our performance. Sure enough, we screw up.

A young mother was driving her kids nuts keeping them out of danger. "Look," said her pediatrician, "which would you rather risk, a broken bone or a broken spirit?" She got the message. Her kids, including her three-year-old, are now the most agile tree climbers in the neighborhood.

Think of the future as what happens next.

The unknown is neither good nor bad; it is simply events. How we deal with them is entirely up to us. We can enter the next moment fearful or enthusiastic. Considering the overwhelming successes of any ordinary life, fear is an inappropriate response. Out of the mud grows the lotus.

To overcome fear of the unknown, pay attention to what you are doing. Keep your eye on the ball. Thus, a student described how he overcame his fears of heights. He was putting shingles on a steep roof and could feel himself tensing up. He was clinging to the ladder and doing a clumsy job. His attention was on falling and not on what he was doing. He told himself *Keep your eye on the ball,* the nail. As he let himself focus on this one nail, paying attention to it, not letting his mind think about anything else, his fear washed out of his nervous system.

Nailing on a roof is the same task as nailing on siding, but in a different location. It has different characteristics—which you take care of by using the roof ladder and positioning yourself in a prescribed way. The danger is all mental.

The same approach works in school. If you become fearful about your performance during a test, let yourself become fascinated with the question itself. Look at how it is put together. Start noticing its characteristics. *Keep your eye on the ball.* Hit this lovely, wonderful nail kerplunk on the head.

Anytime you feel yourself getting nervous about what is going to happen, pay attention to what you are doing *now.* Do the problem at hand. Do the next one. You will forget all about being afraid.

Appearing Ignorant

If you weren't ignorant, there would be no point in being in college. It isn't ignorance that is the bad thing. It is ignorance of one's own ignorance that prevents many people from learning.

If you think you know things, you won't bother to take a good look. "There are a lot of completely educated people," said Robert Frost, "and they are going to resent having to learn anything new." Colleges are full of people who know things. Some are quite vain about it. So to protect themselves, they just don't ask. "Everybody knows so much more than I do. Every time I open my mouth I put my foot in it." Rather than risk ridicule, they sit mute—and get more and more ignorant with each unasked question. They are immobilized by fear of exposure.

But ignorance is the only justification for taking any college course. If you know all about it, why sit there? How can a student get up the courage to ask all those burning questions?

To overcome fear of looking stupid, make ignorance your ally.

It has served you well all your life. Everything you now understand is a result of your not knowing anything about it initially. From the moment of birth you were a question-generating machine. You couldn't get enough of all that experience. What is more, it was exhilarating. Discovery was a wonderful stimulus, and over the years you accumulated billions of bits of information—all because of your infinite ignorance. Isn't that great?

If you want to have a marvelous time in college, luxuriate in your ignorance. All the great thinkers are running around ignorant as hell and asking all kinds of dumb questions. "Why does the toast taste different when I use the little toaster oven than when I use the regular toaster?" "I wonder if I could get the ants to go away if I just wrote them a note?" "Do things really stink, or is that just an arbitrary judgment?" "Why is Shakespeare terrific?" "Can anything *really* be known?"

Take advantage of the limitations of knowledge. If there is any wisdom to glean from all the millions of words in all the libraries of the world, it is that we know very little about this vast universe. The total of human knowledge is an infinitesimal speck. And not one bit of that knowledge is known with absolute certainty. No one knows why or how. So join the club.

We all know the same amount of stuff. There is roughly the same amount of data in your computer as in the mind of a Nobel laureate. Put another way, we are all equally ignorant about different things. The content of your head is different from that of mine. Education is the process of interfacing among minds. In that way, we gain additional viewpoints. Each viewpoint focuses the beam of attention on a fresh aspect of the universe painting. The process is called clarification, illumination, discovering a meaning of experience.

The more educated we become, the more we realize we do not know. We begin to appreciate the use of ignorance in our quest for clarity. Surprisingly, a world of questioned assumptions is far more exciting and vital than the smug world of certainty. K*nowledge shuts down the computer; ignorance turns it on.*

To get over the fear of appearing ignorant, realize how valuable it really is. Get used to asking dumb questions. You can't get educated any other way. A good learning environment does not ridicule questioning. Those who *don't* question are the problem, not those who do. If you should find yourself in a smug environment where others smile primly at your naive questions, go back and read the section in this chapter on accepting rejection.

If you want an education, grow a thick skin.

Take Down a Musical Instrument

Lighten up. If you can't get to 70 by a comfortable road, said Mark Twain, don't go. Life is too important to take seriously. Anxiety has no place in one's studies or anywhere else. Of course, it is useless to wish fear would go away or to pretend it isn't there, contaminating the thinking process and tainting whatever pleasure might be possible in or out of class. No one needs a third party on a date. But it can't be ignored. The only effective approach is to pay attention to it and resolve whatever conflict lies behind it. Fear is the symptom, not the disease.

The resolution lies in treating fear or anxiety like any other problem to be solved. Use *the mess-around theory of education.* Anxiety can be mastered as easily as taking tests or reading textbooks. That is, get into a playful mode, mess around until you pinpoint the real source of concern, fool with the problem until a strategy for dispatching it emerges, and then act on it. No doubt one of the tactics in this chapter or one of your own devices will do the job.

- First, calm down, using music and a relaxation ritual.
- Get into a sandbox mode and take a good look at the fear. If necessary, redefine it. Clarify what the problem is.
- Mess around until you discover a solution.

- Take necessary action.
- Get back to work.

We have to enjoy what we are doing, or we botch it. "When I wake, I take down a musical instrument," said the poet Rumi. That is another way of saying, "Tune up, tune in." Approach your work centered, in harmony. Play your musical instrument.

CHAPTER

7

Writing for First-Year English

Words are the windows of the soul.

In a nutshell:

- **Use the mess-around theory to get some words on paper.**
- **Add, delete, combine, rearrange.**
- **Read it out loud.**
- **Edit.**
- **Make a clean copy.**

What Do You Know About First-Year English?

Mark only the ideas you agree with. Then read the commentary that follows.

☐ **1.** A course in first-year English will help you write better.

☐ **2.** First-year English will help you write for other courses.

☐ **3.** Most English teachers are good writers.

☐ **4.** The best way to learn to write is to write for authentic needs.

☐ **5.** Professional writers recommend taking first-year English.

☐ **6.** It is best to take first-year English the first semester of college.

☐ **7.** First-year English will help you read better.

☐ **8.** First-year English will help you with your reading for other courses.

☐ **9.** First-year English will help you develop listening and speaking skills.

☐ **10.** First-year English is a liberal arts course, like music appreciation or a course in the humanities.

Commentary: What You Really Get from First-Year English

1. *A course in first-year English will help you write better?*

Heaven knows *what* first-year English will do for a student. There are 35,000 English teachers out there and about that many ideas of what ought to be going on in this course. But no matter what they say it is all about, most teachers of first-year English act as if they *must* teach people how to write.

There is no evidence whatever to show that such courses indeed help students write better. As you go through college, chances are good that you will become more comfortable getting your ideas onto paper in a more polished fashion. But what went on in first-year English has little to do with it. *In fact, many of the exercises and drills can actually interfere with normal growth in writing skill.*

So don't confuse learning to write with the goals of your course. The job is to discover what the teacher really wants and to find a way to produce it. If you want an A or B, keep your eye on the ball. The ball is the teacher. Interface with the teacher and your grade is assured.

So the task in first-year English is the same as for taking any course. The tactics for taking classes and doing assignments described in this book are the same.

> *Fiddle around until you are sure what needs to be done. You may find that the assignment needs to be reframed or redefined. Then, relaxed but alert, try out your plan, making changes as you go. Finally, go over what you did and make sure it all hangs together and looks good.*

This chapter presents some ideas for producing copy for English teachers.

2. *First-year English will help you write for other courses?*

Learning theory doesn't support such an assumption. Though many colleges offer first-year English as a service course for other disciplines, no one has been able to verify any connection with writing competence in other courses.

And no two teachers' demands are the same. The way a lab report must be written for one chemistry teacher will not do at all for another. Each history teacher has his or her own requirements. And so on. Furthermore, the amount of editing and polishing demanded is different for each teacher.

When English is taught as a service to others, the results are counterproductive and often confusing. Students become more awkward, self-conscious and doubtful. The writing tasks for each course are unique to that course and to that teacher. It is impossible to prepare for the myriad possibilities that may or may not occur.

> *In English, write for the English teacher; in Psychology, write for the Psychology teacher.*

Though there is no evidence that first-year English can help students get ideas onto paper for their other courses, reversing the sequence may help. That is, *taking other courses first could help you pass your English requirement.* Contrary to conventional wisdom, it can help to postpone first-year English. For many entering students this course is their most stressful experience. But after a semester or two, they know how to cope with most college problems. And course work, reading and conversation will familiarize them with the sort of discourse the college considers suitable. It is acquired lingo, a learning-to-ride-a-bicycle knack.

By just hanging around, you will become more skillful than you might expect. Meanwhile, you will have a chance to decide what sort of assistance you might need, and you can use the time to identify a compatible teacher—which can make all the difference. So ask around. Sit in, if possible. Find out how much work is required. Also examine A and B essays of your acquaintances. Read the teacher's comments. See what various teachers like.

Once you are enrolled in class, if you have problems not specifically related to composition, see the troubleshooting tips in Chapter 5. Minor tinkering may be all that is needed. Save drastic measures as a last resort.

3. *Most English teachers are good writers?*

Most English teachers are inexperienced beyond the writing they did for their course work. Most of that was in literature courses. A few may have done some creative writing, but hardly any have published more than occasional articles in academic journals and rarely anything beyond that protected environment. Furthermore, like teachers in other disciplines, they have little or no training in the teaching of their subject. How does one teach writing? What methods work? Indeed, how does one teach *anything?*

The upshot is that Literature majors end up teaching a subject they know very little about. They are reduced to trying to remember how it was done when they were first-year students and wishing it would all go away. If at all possible, they dump the distasteful job onto new teachers or teaching assistants. No wonder first-year English is a depressing experience for just about everyone involved.

4. *The best way to learn to write is to write for authentic needs?*

We learn what we do. The more writing you do in uncontrived situations, the more skilled you get at it. That is all there is to it. If what you put on paper is always an authentic communication for a genuine purpose, growth will be natural and timely.

Revising, editing and rewriting junk you never cared about in the first place is not only futile but counterproductive. The results are vacuous mechanical exercises or clumsy, awkward messes.

If you are asked to write mechanical essays, the only salvation is to write for yourself first. Then slap the results into a five-paragraph essay or whatever form is being pushed.

5. *Professional writers recommend taking first-year English?*

Most writers consider first-year English irrelevant. Whatever skills or art they have were learned on the job. Childhood influences for these people include passion for reading lots of good prose. Some wrote all the time but never took a writing course. Writing was just something one did: letters, diaries, journals, logs—but no school exercises, no corrections, no grade. Kurt Vonnegut's school in Indianapolis had a daily newspaper. A number of the students who worked on that paper later made their living writing.

Like other language skills, writing competence develops through ordinary social intercourse. If there is a need to communicate verbally in a visible form, then one gets out the writing instrument. If not interfered with, kids get better at it as they go along and self-correct as the need arises. If necessary, they learn to edit.

Like talking, writing is natural process.

6. *It is best to take first-year English the first semester in college?*

If you have been writing all along, you will be a capable writer by the time you reach college. If not, a writing course will not help.

Nonetheless, with or without the course, most students do become competent enough to meet the requirements of their college courses. Gradually, they collect a bag of tricks that get the job done, developing needed skills along the way. That is why *delaying first-year English could save lots of grief.* Once your head is on straight, you will be better positioned to get the class requirement out of the way. If possible, wait until you have the assurance and experience to dispatch it.

7. *First-Year English will help you read better?*

Most first-year courses include a reading list of "college-level" prose. Exercises are assigned to help students get at the content. Generally, it is a sweaty, joyless process. Studies show little or no lasting value from the effort. Reading a physics text or an anthology of literature is no easier after a course in reading than going in cold.

As one researcher in learning theory put it, "You don't read reading anymore than you write writing." You read a good story, enjoy it, talk with others about it—as you would a soccer game or a movie. Then you do it again, then again. If you like soccer or movies or short stories, you develop. You become better at it. Chapter 4 in this book tells you all about that.

8. *First-year English will help you with your reading for other courses?*

Forget it. To read a chapter in calculus, use the mess-around theory and BFAR. In other words, treat it as a problem-solving opportunity and use appropriate strategies. When motivated, you can read *anything*.

9. *First-year English will help you develop listening and speaking skills?*

Such skills provide a direct avenue to interfacing with other minds, and help make college stimulating and rewarding. Regular active listening and speaking in authentic dialogue are essential for normal development. But most classes are one-way monologues. A lecture class is more likely to impede these faculties. It takes exceptionally strong will power to resist falling into an hypnotic trance. Late-night bull sessions with intelligent peers are far more likely to hone these abilities.

10. *First-year English is a liberal arts course, like music appreciation or a course in the humanities?*

First-year English could be a wonderful course in the humanities. Somebody ought to try it sometime. Rather than serving ulterior ends, the subject could be an end in itself.

> *There is nothing more wonderful in the human mind than its language faculty.*

A semester-long excursion into the nature of language and its connection with everything human needs no other justification than the awareness it awakens in us of our own sweet selves. Such an exploration can be an immediate joy and can even engender a lifelong curiosity about what it means to be a language-using animal.

When language itself is the subject under investigation, reading, writing, listening and speaking become the means for the research. These abilities are natural components of the process and develop in an un-self-conscious way.

Coping with Writing Assignments

Since most English teachers like literature, they may be able to recognize an attractive finished product. But most have little background in persuading students to compose such a specimen. They are like native speakers of French who know when something sounds okay, but they may not be able to explain why. Once students understand this, they can use what English teachers do know to their advantage.

Most first-year English courses require students to produce two- or three-page essays every two weeks—nine or ten of these during the semester. If that is a big problem for you, there are lots of ways to manage the job without going crazy. A quiet mind and a few coping tactics will do the trick.

Getting Words on Paper

If you can talk, you can write. Once you have something tangible, something physical, you are in business. You can mess around, sticking things in, taking them out, moving them around, mixing them together.

Editing comes last. So forget all about "correctness" until you have a product that suits you.

Here are a few ways to get going:

Mess Around and Write It Out

Don't worry about "composing." That usually results in clumsy, self-conscious, artificial wording, not anything like you. *Ignore spelling, punctuation, definitions, felicitous wording. That comes later.*

1. **Get ready emotionally.**

   Use the music and relaxation exercise you like best. You want to be calm and alert, your mind on what you are doing—not giving yourself an anxiety attack.

2. **Fiddle around with your topic.**

   Jot down anything that comes to mind, any old way at all: fragments of ideas, details, facts. *Abbreviate.* If you feel like it, get down whole ideas, even some sentences. You can fit things together later. Get as much as you can out there physically, so that it can't slip out of memory.

   You should end up with a healthy pile of stuff. That should make you feel good. Most inexperienced writers fear they won't have enough material. This is one painless way to get plenty to work with.

   Sort the bits and pieces into bunches. Try for three or four clusters of things that seem to belong together. You may want to toss out some things or add some. Look it all over and see how it adds up in your mind.

3. **Write it all out straight through without stopping and without looking at your notes.** NO EDITING!

   Write as though you were telling it to your kid sister. You will know when she wouldn't understand. The idea is to get a clear and direct message with a good, rhythmic flow—the way you talk.

Don't stop writing until you get it all said. Keep that pen, pencil, or word processor going.

4. **Check your clusters to see if you left out anything important.**

   Insert details where they fit smoothly.

5. **Read your draft out loud and see how it sounds.**

   It should sound the way you normally talk. Straighten out any confusing sentences, and get rid of expressions that don't read the way you talk. If it came out the way you would say it out loud, you have a good working draft, ready for editing and polishing.

Talk It Out

Try telling your essay to someone. When you are really panicky, or if you can't think of anything at all, talking it through can keep you focused and on track. Let the other person ask questions as you go.

Either write out your conversation as you go along or use a tape recorder and copy it out later. The result is your first draft. Talking it out will yield a natural progression of thought and produce enough detail for something interesting and convincing. It is always a relief to have something physical to tinker with.

Use a Model

If you can *see* what the thing is supposed to look like, it is a lot easier to turn out something similar.

Instructions are hard to visualize, so work backwards. Get hold of a good finished product, and then put your own stuff into the same sort of package. Keep the sample in front of you as you work, and imitate it.

1. **Use as a model an essay from a previous class, written for the same teacher.**

   If no essay is available, find a magazine or newspaper article of about the length required for your class. The editorial or feature page of your newspaper is a good source. Choose something as close as possible to the way you would write.

2. **Decide on a topic.**

   If at all possible, write about something you know well. If you know it inside out, upside down and backwards, you will have an abundance of material to work with.

3. **Write out your first paragraph following the structure of your model.**

   That is, look at the first paragraph and see how it is put together. Do the same thing with your own essay. Imitate the model, sentence by sentence, varying the flow and rhythm, sentence length and pattern. Put your main sentence in roughly the same place as it is in the model, and provide the same amount of supporting commentary.

4. **Write your second paragraph in the same manner as that in the model. Do not edit or polish yet.**

   Continue the process until your paper is finished. The result will be an acceptable first draft.

Get Help

Use the feedback from the first graded paper handed back to you to develop a plan of attack. If you can understand your teacher's comments, use them when you do your next paper. If you don't have to work in the dark, the job will be much easier.

1. **If you don't understand the teacher's comments, ask for a conference.**

   This is no time to be timid. Students who get A's and B's make sure the teacher knows them and knows their names. And they make sure the teacher is aware of their commitment. If you are a terrible writer, it is even more important to get the teacher psychologically involved in your success.

   No teacher wants to flunk someone he or she has helped all semester. Even if you would be happy with a C grade, you have a much better chance of *at least* that grade if the teacher knows you. Hiding out is begging for a kick in the teeth.

2. **Work with a friend who is a good writer.**

   Don't have your friend write the paper but talk it out with him or her until you both are sure what you want the essay to say. Then write it together.

   During the process, watch the decisions your friend makes.

   Notice what is considered and dropped, what is added and why. When does he or she rephrase a sentence? Why? Get the feel of the composing process. Imitate it on your own. Let your friend help you rewrite.

Like any other skill, composing is a knack. It is not much different from talking. After three or four informed tries, you will begin to catch on.

Editing and Polishing

Edit and polish last. Wait till your essay sounds good when you read it out loud; then *edit.*

If your essay were intended to be heard and not read, you could skip the proofreading. The way you normally talk is the best medium for a listening audience. No one will see the spelling and punctuation. For written material, however, it is another story.

You will want the essay as tidy and as error-free as you can make it. You don't want the message judged on the way it looks rather than on what it has to say. Once the essay sounds good, proofread and polish until it is as error-free as you can make it.

Research shows that an unproofread, illegible paper can receive a letter-grade lower than the same paper cleaned up. Editing and polishing are an essential final step. If someone else is to read your paper, proofread it. *Always proofread and it will soon become a valuable habit.*

Sadly, most teachers are blinded by unconventional spelling and punctuation. They refuse to go beyond the surface features, and they ignore the squiggles on the paper as a *message.* Wonderful insights, poignant observations, refined sensibilities, are drowned in red ink. Teachers who missed their calling as copy editors never bother to see the communication first *from the writer's point of view,* and thus miss out on the deep joy English teaching can be.

Since editing is indeed what first-year English is all about, anyone playing the school game needs to address the task head on. So get good at editing.

Editing 1A

Despite all the talk about getting students to compose, teachers of first-year English *edit*. Name the course *Editing 1A* to start with, and it would clear things up for all concerned.

> "Look, this is a course in editing. We don't give a damn what you write about. Your grade will be based on how many editing skills you have acquired by the end of the semester."

That would be refreshingly forthright. Students could get to work immediately on the real goals of the course. Other departments and the school administration would be happy as clams. They yearn for prose with its hair combed and its face scrubbed.

Spelling

You don't have to be talented to get stuff spelled right. If you know you don't spell well, find a way to get around it. *After* your paper is composed the way you want it, make sure every word is spelled correctly.

1. **If you have the slightest doubt, get it right any way you can.**

   Good spelling comes from careful proofreading and close attention to the characteristics of each word. When you find the correct spelling, take a good look at it syllable by syllable. Is there a mnemonic (memory) device that will help? Write it out slowly and carefully, noticing silent letters, double letters, and so forth.

   The best spellers *see* the word. Be sure you are pronouncing the word properly (*perform* not *preform; tragedy*, not *tradegy*). Is there a problem with the vowel or a consonant?

   Separate the affixes and roots to see how they are formed. This will help you to keep from using too few or too many letters (*mis spell, public ly*). When you add a suffix, check to see if the final letter must be doubled (*plane, planing; plan, planning*).

   See, hear and write the word carefully and accurately.

   At first you will have to look up lots of words, but with experience you will develop a large vocabulary of words you do spell right automatically. Only words uncommon to your normal use will need to be checked.

2. **Use the spell-checker on your word processor.**

   Start a list of misspelled words. Each time you misspell it, put a check ✓ next to it. After three checks, ✓✓✓, you will probably start spelling it right.

3. **Use a pocket-sized spelling dictionary.**

   Use checks ✓ in the margin to keep track of what you looked up.

4. **Maintain a healthy distrust.**

   Don't expect miracles. You could take spelling courses and learn rules, but keeping track of your misspellings is all that you really need to do. At first you will use your dictionary heavily, but if you do pay attention, you will soon start spelling correctly the words you use all the time.

5. **Get a second opinion.**

   Until you know you can go it alone, get a good copy editor—someone you are *sure* is good at it—to check your work. Professional writers have no qualms about having a copy editor go over their work. It is easier for someone else to see mistakes.

   The writer sees what he or she intended, not what is there. In the publishing world, whole teams work together for a good product. Working all by yourself is not normal. So figure out your weaknesses and enlist competent help.

Punctuation

Most writers never formally study punctuation. They learn through observation. If you pay attention, your nonconscious mind will figure out the rules, just as it figures out how to drive or use a computer program. Observe the punctuation in material you read. You will catch on.

1. **Use punctuation to make your message clear.**

2. **Have a friend read your essay to you.**

   When a sentence doesn't sound like what you intended, see if you need to add or remove punctuation. If that doesn't work, use shorter sentences, move parts around, or add or remove things. When someone reads it back to you, it should make sense.

   Test your sentences by reading out loud.

3. **See how other people do it.**

   Examine newspapers, magazines, business letters—anything by experienced professionals—and see what they did and figure out why. Even as little as 15 minutes a day will soon give you the feel of it.

4. **Imitate examples in college English handbooks. Buy an English handbook.**

   If the explanations don't make sense, find an example that fits your problem and punctuate your own sentence the same way. Most of your questions will be about commas, so initially, just browse the comma rules. That will get you familiar with what is there. Later, when you have a specific problem; find an example that fits and imitate it.

   Sometimes you will have to look very carefully. Punctuate and format footnotes, for instance, *exactly* like the example. Don't get creative. Even the spaces between dots matter.

   Doing footnotes is like typing commands for computer operations. Every mark or space counts.

   Use the examples in your handbook for quotation marks (" "), em dashes (--), hyphens, and parentheses ( ). If semicolons (;) are too confusing for you, use shorter sentences or rearrange the sentence to eliminate the problem.

Every time you look up punctuation, put a check ✓ in the margin. Add you own examples in the appropriate section of the handbook. For future use, they will be where you need them.

5. **Use as little punctuation as possible.**

   Until you get used to the rules, you can avoid difficult problems by rearranging your sentences or by making them into two or three shorter ones. When your sentence could be misread otherwise, insert a comma.

School English

Cherish the variety of English you grew up using.

The way you talk contains your family history, your neighborhood, your roots. *If you are a native speaker of English, you use proper English.* Part of the fun of adventuring into the great world is meeting people who don't talk the way you do. *The more varieties you can understand, the more educated you are.*

Browse the Usage section of your English handbook. Get familiar with the sorts of things teachers notice. Don't even think about correctness. Forget the explanations. *Just look at the examples and practice doing it that way.*

Unless you grew up in a household in which everyone already talks like your teachers in school, you are in the process of learning another dialect, just as if you were learning another language. The only reason a turn of phrase is "correct" is that neighborhood folks say it that way. Make a list of your personal language differences—write down the way you normally would put it, and the way the teacher would. When you edit, go through your paper and *make your expressions match up with your teacher's.* Force yourself to check each sentence carefully, even if you have to lay a ruler under each line. If you have the least doubt, check it out.

Get a second opinion. Have a friend who is a good proofreader go over your paper for consistency with school English. Or ask another teacher. Get familiar with your English handbook.

Style

Only your own voice is durable.

The closer your utterances match your deepest self, the more elegant your style will be and the more unique. Style is the way you report your particular vantage point in the universe. So keep your own voice, but edit to make sure it comes out strong and clear.

Edit for style by adding, removing, replacing, rephrasing, rearranging or merging.

1. **Adding.** If it will make a sentence clearer, you can put in a word, a phrase, even a clause, wherever it works best and sounds best. Read it out loud to make sure.

2. **Removing.** Make every word count. Cut, cut, cut. The more severe the trimming, the more powerful the prose. Check it out.

3. **Replacing.** You know when a word isn't quite right. If you can, find the one that matches your inner vision. You will love the feeling. Play around until something clicks. Use a thesaurus. Your computer program may have a thesaurus installed. If not, buy a cheap paperback.

4. **Rephrasing.** If part of a sentence sounds dumb, try saying it another way.

5. **Rearranging.** You can move parts around, to the beginning, the middle, the end. See which way sounds best out loud. If a sentence gets out of hand, try breaking it into a couple of shorter ones.

6. **Merging.** You can bunch two or more sentences together by cutting out needless repetition the same subject for several verbs, for example, instead of monotonously repeating the subject. Use what illuminates your idea. Cut out everything else. Combine wherever possible.

Let It Steep

If you can, let the finished paper sit for a day or two. You will later see phrasing that could sound better. The more junk you can cut out the better.

Note: These editing techniques for improving style may be used not only for sentences but for paragraphs and whole essays, too.

Editing Example:

Below is a fifth or sixth revision of a page in *Get Your A Out of College.*

9. *Memorizing should be vigorous and aggressive, not relaxed and playful?*

When the conscious and non-conscious parts of the mind are not in harmony, the memorizing process slows or stops. We cannot italics bully our minds. There must be agreement among all the parts of the brain that the proposed behavior is desirable. Sitting up straight, frowning, and beating our breasts only interfere.

For example, a family-life teacher wondered why her quiet 8 A.M. section scored higher on tests than did her energetic 11 A.M. section of the same course. ~~A strong likelihood is that~~ It is likely the students in the early class were closer to their natural learning state than were the more intense students. When there is room enough and time for the mind to play ~~with data~~, we are in our optimum learning mode.

~~Thus, one thing we can do consciously and deliberately, when it is time to commit data to memory, is go through~~ Relaxation exercises will ~~to~~ reduce stress and renew self-trust and confidence. ~~Studying in such a state of mind has a dramatic effect on~~ The centered learning~~ing~~s and retains ~~retention~~. This chapter shows how to ~~gives suggestions for~~ the setting ~~setting~~ the stage. Not surprisingly, ~~the achieved conditions strongly~~ resembles ~~those of children in~~ a sandbox.

10. *Some subjects are harder than others to commit to memory?*

italics double indent

All knowledge involves placing information into ~~interconnecting~~ meaning networks. Every user ~~of~~ language ~~is already~~ thoroughly experienced in creating blueprints ~~at carrying on such activities and at the highest levels of complexity~~. Difficulty is a vacuum ~~simply lack~~ of familiarity. Getting the hang of chemistry is no different essentially from ~~getting the hang of~~ driving or becoming a cocktail server or a mail carrier. There are no difficult subjects, only areas of experience more distant from our daily involvement. If one plays around with a new subject as a child does with new experiences, in due time the code will be revealed, and the new field will be just as easy as anything else. The key is to know ~~this is~~ how the brain works ~~learning does take place~~ and to relax and allow it to do its job ~~happen~~.

Your Editing Library

Keep the following books on your shelf:

- A small spelling dictionary
- A college English handbook
- A collegiate dictionary
- A thesaurus

Editing Essay Tests

- **Leave time for editing.** Remember, the same essay, sloppy and unedited, can receive a full letter grade lower.
- **Use lots of paragraphs to make the writing look organized.** Insert roughly one new fact for each paragraph.
- **Replace repeated words or phrases with something else that means the same thing.** If possible, replace pronouns (words such as *I, we, he, she, it, they*) with nouns. The more variety of language, the more knowledgeable the essay will sound. So when you notice you have repeated an expression, substitute some other word or phrase.
- **Check spelling carefully.** If a spelling dictionary is not permitted in class, substitute a word you are sure of.
- **Leave plenty of space between paragraphs for later additions.**
- **Write neatly and legibly Do your corrections neatly, too. Leave space in the margins for inserts.**
- **Write straightforwardly. Keep your sentences relatively short.**

See also Chapter 3.

Visible Speech

In literate societies, reading and writing are part of every normal adult's verbal equipment. Acquisition of these skills comes almost as naturally as learning to talk. When everyone around uses graphic representation of speech, kids pick it up along the way. "There's the big *M* for MacDonald's." *A* stands for Andy: ME!" "Read me a story. I'll write you one."

If these reading and writing skills are part of regular communication, people get good at it. As they mature, they self-correct in real situations as needed. This is the way we learn. College students lucky enough to have had such nurturing are fully competent by the time they enter college. Enlightened teachers simply continue the process, using reading and writing as tools of meaningful activities: *little or no instruction in writing and reading, but lots of use of these skills.* Somebody ought to try it sometime.

But entering students have been *instructed* in writing year after year, and they have much to toss out. To cope with first-year English, you need to use good problem-solving skills. Once you clarify what is really going on, however, acing the course is a piece of cake:

1. Get a first draft. Mess around, make clusters, use a model, talk into a tape, work with someone else, whatever it takes.

2. Read it out loud for sound and sense.

3. Edit for spelling, punctuation, "community standards," style, smooth-flowing sentences.

4. Let it steep overnight. Read it out loud and fix it up as needed.

5. Save all your papers. You never know when you might want to dust off an earlier attempt and rewrite, expand or polish it for another assignment.

Meantime, observe how it is done in materials you read. Imitate models you like, but keep your own way of talking as much as possible.

APPENDICES

Appendix A: An Example of Using BFAR

Following is a guide through the BFAR process. Pages 208 contain the article to which these steps refer. The article first appeared in a professional journal, but it could easily be a chapter in a textbook.

To try out BFAR, do only what the first step suggests. Then turn back here for the next step, then the next, and so on.

Step 1

Give yourself no more than 10 seconds to find out what the article that begins on page 208 is all about. Don't read past the STOP sign until you complete this step.

STOP

You would not have to read further than the title to find out, right? It is about *barriers to communication* and *gateways to communication.*

If you are already familiar with communication theory or with psychotherapy, you may know what is likely to be discussed in the article. In that case your task would be to browse and see what is new for you. It could be only one new idea or none at all.

Step 2

Without looking at the article, how many main parts would you suppose there will be? (In your first 10 seconds, you could have had time to discover this.)

Now, in 10 seconds, check to see if you are right.

STOP

Right. There are two main sections. You would have had time to see what the author says the barrier is and what the gateway is. Each section has a centered, boldfaced heading. If you didn't notice, take 5 seconds now and find out what the barrier is and what the gateway is.

STOP

The barrier is *the tendency to evaluate.* The gateway is *listening with understanding.*

Step 3

Take no more than 20 seconds to see how long the article is and decide how long it would take you to master it.

STOP

Most students are shocked when I suggest they could probably get everything that is really important in this article in less than 5 minutes. But if you continue with this guided tour, you will see for yourself that it is quite possible.

The word *master* is ambiguous. You have to decide if you are reading just for yourself or just for the teacher or both. Clear that up. Your specific purpose will determine how long it will take. Most students notice there are a little over eight pages and decide it would take half an hour to an hour to be ready to be tested on the material. These are people who read everything at the same plodding pace and have not determined in advance what they would like to retain, if anything, from the reading.

Let's continue and see how much can be pulled out of the half dozen pages in 5 minutes. We have used up less than a minute so far.

Take 10 seconds and see how much space is devoted to the barrier and how much to the gateway.

STOP

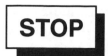

About 1 page for the barrier and about 5 for the gateway. That means about 6 pages of the 8+ are the essential part of the message. So if you did have less than 5 minutes, you could concentrate on the essential two-thirds.

An active reader would likely notice that only one-fifth of the message is devoted to the barrier. *And four-fifths are all about the gateway.* It *might* be possible to focus on only those pages out of the 8 or so and get the essence. That would certainly be wonderful, if you had less than 5 minutes. (Sooner or later, every student gets in a jam and simply has to make do with the limited time available.)

Just from the heading, we know *the barrier is the tendency to evaluate.* But we don't know what that means exactly, and we don't know why that would be a problem. However, it is more than likely, isn't it, that the author will absorb the barrier in his discussion of the gateway. He has to talk about it in order to provide a solution. So you could take a chance and just work on the gateway.

But is the *whole* section on the gateway really devoted to its *main* idea? Is there no break in that section? One page for the barrier and 5 for the gateway? That would be rather disproportionate, wouldn't it?

Step 5

Take 10 seconds and see how much the 5 pages on the gateway is really devoted to the main idea. What does the part that is not the main idea consist of?

STOP

Ah! No more than 2 pages are devoted to the main idea of the gateway—and indeed to the main idea of the whole article. That is, one-fourth of the article is the central concept. If you had to, then, you could spend your 5 minutes sloshing around in these two pages. This is not to say that you would be thoroughly versed in the entire article. But it is a safe bet that you will be more articulate and better able to discuss the concept intelligently than will students who spend an hour going about the task mechanically.

You will have noticed that most of the gateway section is really devoted to refinements, subpoints. How do we know this? By indented, italicized headings, beginning with "Need for Courage." The article is laid out so that we can *see* the structure.

So as not to feel too anxious about those subpoints, take a moment now and see *what* they are. Hint: Look at the sentence just above the first one, "Need for Courage."

STOP

Right. These subpoints are all *difficulties in listening with understanding,* the gateway. We will set these difficulties aside for now and take them up—*if we have time*—after we get a good grasp of *what* listening with understanding must mean.

Step 6

If you had to stop with only this much familiarity with the article, it is considerably more than zilch. Five or six passes through the material in less than a minute yield a clear view of the structure and even the first level of the content. You know what the article is about. You know there are two main parts and that the central idea has several subpoints. You know the barrier is the tendency to evaluate (whatever that means) and the way around that, the gateway, is listening with understanding. Not bad. How much do you usually understand in only 1 minute?

True, you don't know the article in depth, but you won't be totally at sea. If asked what the barrier is, you could say, "The tendency to evaluate." If asked what that means, you might chance a guess or respond, "That isn't quite clear to me. I was hoping we would talk about that." Something.

But we have 4 more minutes, so we can do much better than that. Let's see if we can skip the section on barriers and perhaps pick it up while exploring *listening with understanding* What *does* it mean to listen with understanding? We are likely to find an answer, aren't we, somewhere between the third and fifth page of the article. Even more likely, it will be in the first paragraph of that section—or at least a hint.

Take 30 seconds and find out what it means to listen with understanding and how it is accomplished.

STOP

This is our sixth or seventh pass through the article and it is the first time we have actually got down into the paragraphs. My question is answered several times in this section, so if you were browsing you might have discovered it anywhere.

Any approach at all that yields the meaning of a passage is legitimate.

If you notice *how* an author writes, it can help you understand him or her. This writer rephrases his idea repeatedly. So if you don't understand the idea in one place, you will find it explained in other words or in one or more examples. Also, this writer uses conversational language, for the most part, so you will probably not be overwhelmed by the style. That means you can go faster.

What does *listening with understanding* mean? One place where we find the answer is the last sentence of the first paragraph. And it is rephrased three times! It means, to see the idea (1) "from the other person's point of view," (2) "to sense how it feels to him." (3) "to achieve his frame of reference. . . ." Take your pick.

If that still doesn't make sense, look around for an example. Or even start with one. If, while browsing, you don't see a good illustration, you may have to get back up to the barrier section. But go only as far as you must in order to "get it."

By the way, if the gateway is seeing a message from the sender's point of view *first,* then the barrier—which we skipped for lack of time—must surely be something like seeing his or her statement *from our own point of view first.* So it is possible to deduce, at least in this article, a point that is embedded in another one. But to catch on, you do have to be on the ball.

Step 7

I would still like an example, something to hang on to, and I don't see it in this part. Just to see how this could work, take 20 to 30 seconds and check out the *other* section where an illustration might lurk, "Barrier," and find a more tactile example, something concrete.

STOP

For me, the words "That's a lie!" (at the end of the second paragraph in the Barrier section) jump right off the page and tell me everything. Someone says something; my response is immediate and spontaneous. I judge the statement from my point of view without any idea of what the other person may have meant by it. I don't pause to consider. Do I do that much? Yes, quite a lot. It's natural. Now I think I know what the article is all about:

> *Usually we evaluate a message before giving it much thought and usually from our own way of seeing. It would be better for me and all concerned to try to see the message first from the other person's perspective. But how?*

Step 8

Does the author give any ideas on *how* to listen with understanding before offering your response? After all, it is a hard habit to break.

Browse through the gateway section again. You may have noticed a rule in an earlier pass. If not, take 30 seconds to see if you can find it.

STOP

Did you find it? The rule is first stated in the quotation at the end of the fourth paragraph: "Each person can speak up for himself only *after* he has first stated it accurately and to that speaker's satisfaction." But the idea is rephrased in more than one way in the next paragraph, too. So you may have discovered it there first, or in the following paragraph, along with an example. This, of course, is the most important idea in the whole article, for it embodies the concept of listening with understanding, along with a specific procedure.

As you can see, the essentials of the article have been discovered in less than 2 minutes. To be sure, we have not absorbed the arguments supporting this concept, nor have we yet addressed difficulties. Nonetheless, an harassed student, under the pressure of time (and who ever has enough time?) would be well positioned to *listen with understanding* to a class discussion on the article. We have absorbed the structure, the organizational pattern, and have even delved some into the central topic.

Regardless of how much time you have or how thoroughly you intend to explore this article, the above procedure would be a necessary beginning. BFAR does indeed lead to *focusing, absorbing,* and *reinforcing.* But these are by-products of a series of passes through the material. In other words, *browse, browse, browse.* When you have accomplished your purpose, stop.

Now let's see how much more can be absorbed in the remaining three minutes of this experiment.

Step 9

Let's clean up some loose ends. You will recall that a couple of pages are devoted to difficulties in listening with understanding. In the next

10 seconds, find out how many difficulties are listed and what they are. Remember, the headings are indented and italicized.

STOP

There are four difficulties listed:

- Need for courage
- Heightened emotions
- Size of group
- Faith in social sciences

But why do we need courage, and what can we do about our heightened emotions? As for size of group, that may be something not relevant to your particular reason for reading the article. In that case, you could skip it. Right? And, if you are convinced that first restating the other person's idea to his or her satisfaction is a good idea, you don't need to worry about whether there is or is not confidence in the social sciences. So, depending on your purposes, you might be able to skip reading about the last two difficulties. Let's assume that is so. For now, we will deal only with need for courage and heightened emotions.

Step 10

Why do we need courage to see an idea from the speaker or writer's point of view? You may have noticed there are just two short paragraphs to browse in order to find out. So take no more than 15 seconds to find out why we need courage to do something so reasonable.

STOP

We risk being changed. The idea is reiterated and amplified throughout the two paragraphs, but it begins the second paragraph. It is hard to miss. If you "get it," you don't need to browse farther. If not, seek understanding in these paragraphs until the idea clicks.

What about the heightened emotions? Maybe from several passes through this article you already realize how our emotions can blind us to threatening ideas. You may already have tested that idea against your own experience. No one enjoys having his or her reality blanket threatened. At any rate, there are only three paragraphs to explore for amplification.

Step 11

Take 30 seconds to be sure why strong emotions impede communication. And find out what can be done about it. Does the author offer a solution?

STOP

Three paragraphs are allotted to heightened emotions, but the author gives a technique in the first: *Use* a *third party.* Someone with no vested interest first restates the speaker' message to his or her satisfaction before allowing a response. You may be familiar with this process from labor disputes or marriage counseling. If you do understand how the third party is used, you can stop. If not, browse until it is clear.

If your purpose in reading this article has been met at this point, all that is left to do is to go back and mark the article and reinforce. (At the time of the publication of this article, no data about large-group use of such techniques had been acquired. Furthermore, there was still widespread doubt about the validity of research in social sciences, so there was reluctance to try out the findings.)

Step 12

By now, there should be an image in your mind of the essence of this article. You will have browsed and focused on the central idea and begun to absorb what you wanted. At this stage, take a pencil—*not a pen*—and mark the text.

Marking is for your own use, so any system that works is fine. Following is a discussion of *one* way to mark. The article is about barriers to communication and about gateways. What is the barrier? Right, the tendency to evaluate. Find those words and underline them. Put the Roman numeral I in the margin.

STOP

I

Barrier: The Tendency to Evaluate

Even though the writer has already headlined the idea, you will want your own emphasis—for easy review later and for a neural bond. When you do something physical to the material, you take it over. You have taken a big step toward remembering it.

What does *the tendency to evaluate* mean? It means to see someone's idea from your own point of view first. In the Barrier section find and underline some words that say that, or mark an example that will remind you of what the idea is all about.

Always mark the fewest words possible. The less clutter the easier the review will be later on.

STOP

words, your primary reaction is to evaluate it from your own point of view, your own frame of reference.

There are several other places where this idea is rephrased. You could have marked any one of them. Just the following might work even better:

States." We rise as one person to say, "That's a lie!"

Step 13

What is the gateway? Listening with understanding. Find and underline it. Put a Roman numeral II in the margin.

STOP

II **Gateway: Listening with Understanding**

Step 14

Find and underline a few words that explain what listening with understanding means.

STOP

What does that mean? It means to see the expressed idea and attitude from the other person's point of view, to sense how it feels to him, to achieve his frame of reference in regard to the thing he is talking about.

There are many other places in this section that might do as well as or better than this one. How about the following:

Understand how it seems to him, if I can see its personal meaning for him, if I can sense the emotional flavor which it has for him, then I will be releasing potent forces of change in him.

Step 15

You will recall the author provides a specific technique for forcing oneself to listen with understanding. It has to do with stating the other person's ideas first and to his satisfaction before responding. Find it and underline the essential words.

STOP

and, for an experiment, institute this rule: "Each person can speak up for himself only after he has first stated the ideas and feelings of the previous speaker accurately and to that speaker's satisfaction.

Notice that only enough of the words of the sentence are underlined to get the essence. When you review, it will be refreshingly simple to locate the essentials and think about them. If you mark every single word, the page will look messy and confusing.

Step 16

You will recall there are four difficulties in listening with understanding. They are identified as "difficulties" in the sentence just above "need for Courage." So now underline that word and put the letter *A* in the margin. Then mark the difficulties 1, 2, 3, 4, and underline them. Add the word *No* to "Faith in the Social Sciences."

STOP

A *I will try to list the difficulties which keep it from being utilized.*

1 *Need for Courage.*

2 *Heightened Emotions.*

3 *Size of Group.*

4 No *Faith in Social Sciences.*

Step 17

You will recall we need courage because of the risk of being changed. And to manage heightened emotions, use a third party. Find those words and underline them.

STOP

This risk of being changed is one of the most frightening prospects many of us can face.

. . . insuperable obstacle in our experience in psychotherapy. A third party who is able to lay aside his own feelings and evaluations, can assist greatly by . . .

That completes the marking of this article. You will notice that going through and marking key ideas makes them stand out not only on the page but in the mind. An outline takes shape that you can see in your mind's eye.

When you review, erase anything you thought you couldn't live without but now see you can.

One more stage remains in the BFAR process. Without *reinforcing* you could easily forget overnight most of what you have understood and would be obliged to redo your work.

Step 18

From memory, jot down on scratch paper the essence of the article in the fewest possible words. Abbreviate. This is to make sure you do have it in your head as well as on paper.

STOP

Is your version something like this?

Bar: Tend eval
  Own pt vw 1st
  That's a lie!
Gate: Lit with und
  Othr. presn's pt vw 1st
  1st st to spkr's sat
Difs
  Nd cour

Rsk chng
Htnd emtns
3rd pty
Sz grp.
No faith

Jotting down the essentials is a self-test. If you can't recall something, you can turn to that part an refresh yourself.

> *Once you have the essentials in mind, you can copy them in the bottom margin of the last page of the article.*

Anytime you want to review, you will have everything all in one place. And if you find some part has faded from memory, you will be able to find it easily.

You will have noticed we have not been reverent. Because of our time limit for this experiment, we paid no attention to *who* wrote this article or to *when* it was written. We haven't explored to *whom* it was written or *why.* The by-line lists two writers. Carl Roger's work was and is a major cornerstone of modern psychotherapy. In 1952 this work was not widely understood outside the field. Readers of the *Harvard Business Review* needed some preparation. So noticing these sorts of things does indeed make a difference in how we read.

We also ignored the introduction and the summary. A summary or introduction *could* contain lots of useful information. We wanted to get right to the heart of the article, though, so we didn't risk precious time. If necessary, we could have jumped over to those parts anytime it seemed appropriate.

Nor did we dwell on tone or style. If you want a deep and sensitive understanding, as the article itself suggests, ah, yes, it helps to know where the writer is coming from to *see it from his or her point of view.*

Barriers and Gateways to Communication[1]

Carl R. Rogers and F. J. Roethlisberger

It may seem curious that a person like myself, whose whole professional effort is devoted to psychotherapy, should be interested in problems of communication. What relationship is there between obstacles to communication and providing therapeutic help to individuals with emotional maladjustments?

Actually the relationship is very close indeed. The whole task of psychotherapy is the task of dealing with a failure in communication. The emotionally maladjusted person, the "neurotic," is in difficulty, first, because communication within himself has broken down and, secondly, because as a result of this his communication with others has been damaged. To put it another way, the "neurotic" individual parts of himself which have been termed unconscious, or repressed, or denied to awareness, become blocked off so that they no longer communicated themselves to the conscious or managing part of himself; as long as this true, there are distortions in the way he communicates himself to others, and so he suffers both within himself and in his interpersonal relations.

The task of psychotherapy is to help the person achieve, through a special relationship with a therapist, a good communication within himself. Once this is achieved, he can communicate more freely and more effectively with others. We may say then that psychotherapy is good communication, within and between men. We may also turn this statement around and it will still be true. Good communication, free communication within or between men, is therapeutic.

It is, then, from a background of experience with communication in counseling and psychotherapy that I want to present two ideas: (1) I wish to state what I believe is one of the major factors in blocking or impeding communication, and then (2) I wish to present what in our experience has proved to be a very important way of improving or facilitating communication.

Barrier: The Tendency to Evaluate

I should like to propose, as a hypothesis for consideration, that the major barrier to mutual interpersonal communication is our very natural tendency to judge, to evaluate, to approve (or disapprove) the statement of the other person or the other group. Let me illustrate my meaning with some very simple examples. Suppose someone, commenting on this discussion, makes the statement, "I didn't like what that man said." What will you respond? Almost invariably you will respond by either approval or disapproval of the attitude expressed. Either you respond, "I didn't either; I though it was terrible," or else you tend to reply, "Oh, I thought it was really good." In other words, your primary reaction is to evaluate if from *your* point of view, your own frame of reference.

Or take another example. Suppose I say with some feeling, "I think the Republicans are behaving in ways that show a lot of good sound sense these days." What is the response that arises in your mind? The overwhelming likelihood is that it will be evaluative. In other words, you will find yourself agreeing, or disagreeing, or making some judgment about me such as "He must be a conservative," or "He seems solid in his thinking." Or let us take an illustration from the international scene [1952]. Russia says vehemently, "The treaty with Japan is a war plot on the part of the United States." We rise as one person to say, "That's a lie!"

This last illustration brings in another element connected with my hypothesis. Although the tendency to make evaluations is common in almost all interchange of language, it is very much heightened in those situations where feelings and emotions are deeply involved. So the stronger our feelings, the more likely it is that there will be no mutual element in the communication. There will be just two ideas, two feelings, two judgments, missing each other in psychological space.

I am sure you recognize this from your own experience. When you have not been emotionally involved yourself and have listened to a heated discussion, you often go away thinking, "Well, they actually weren't talking about the same thing." And they were not. Each was making a judgment, an evaluation, from his own frame of reference. There was really nothing which could be called communication in any genuine sense. This tendency to react to any emotionally meaningful statement by forming an evaluation of it from our own point of view is, I repeat, the major barrier to interpersonal communication.

Gateway: Listening with Understanding

Is there any way of solving this problem, of avoiding this barrier? I feel that we are making exciting progress toward this goal, and I should like to present it as simply as I can. Real communication occurs, and this evaluative tendency is avoided, when we listen with understanding. What does that mean? It means to see the expressed idea and attitude from the other person's point of view, to sense how it feels to him, to achieve his frame of reference in regard to the thing he is talking about.

Stated so briefly, this may sound absurdly simple, but it is not. It is an approach which we have found extremely potent in the field of psychotherapy. It is the most effective agent we know for altering the basic personality structure of an individual and for improving his relationships and his communications with others. If I can listen to what he can tell me, if I can understand how it seems to him, if I can see its personal meaning for him, if I can sense the emotional flavor which it has for him, then I will be releasing potent forces of change in him.

Again, if I can really understand how he hates his father, or hates the company, or hates Communism—if I can catch the flavor of his fear of insanity, or his fear of atom bombs, or of Russia—it will be of the greatest help to him in altering those hatreds and fears and in establishing realistic and harmonious relationships with the very people and situations toward which he has felt hatred and fear. We know from our research that such emphatic understanding—understanding *with* a person, not *about* him—is such an effective approach that it can bring about major changes in personality.

Some of you may be feeling that you listen well to people and yet you have never seen such results. The chances are great indeed that your listening has not been of the type I have described. Fortunately, I can suggest a little laboratory experiment which you can try to test the quality of your understanding. The next time you get into an argument with your wife, or your friend, or with a small group of friends, just stop the discussion for a moment and, for an experiment, institute this rule: "Each person can speak up for himself only *after* he has first stated the ideas and feelings of the previous speaker accurately and to that speaker's satisfaction."

You see what this would mean. It would simply mean that before presenting your own point of view, it would be necessary for you to achieve the other speaker's frame of reference—to understand his thoughts and feelings so well that you could summarize them for him. Sounds simple, doesn't it? But if you try it, you will discover that it is one of the most difficult things you have ever tried to do. However, once you have been able to see the other's point of view, your own comments will have to be drastically revised. You will also find the emotion going out of the discussion, the differences being reduced, and those differences which remain being of a rational and understandable sort.

Can you imagine what this kind of an approach would mean if it were projected into larger areas? What would happen to a labor-management dispute if it where conducted in such a way that labor, without necessarily agreeing, could accurately state management's point of view in a way that management could accept; and management, without approving labor's stand, could state labor's case in a way that labor agreed was accurate? It would mean that real communication was established, and one could practically guarantee that some reasonable solution would be reached.

If, then, this way of approach is an effective avenue to good communication and good relationships, as I am quite sure you will agree if you try the experiment I have mentioned, why is it not more widely tried and used? I will try to list the difficulties which keep it from being utilized.

Need for Courage. In the first place it takes courage, a quality which is not too widespread. I am indebted to Dr. S. I. Hayakawa, the semanticist, for pointing out that to carry on psychotherapy in this fashion is to take a very real risk, and that courage is required. If you really understand another person in this way, if you are willing to enter his private world and see the way life appears to him, without any attempt to make evaluative judgments, you run the risk of being changed yourself. You might see it his way; you might find yourself influenced in your attitudes or your personality.

This risk of being changed is one of the most frightening prospects many of us can face. If I enter, as fully as I am able, into the private world of a neurotic or psychotic individual, isn't there a risk that I might become lost in that world? Most of us are afraid to take that risk. Or if we were listening to a Russian Communist, or Senator Joe McCarthy, how many of us would dare to try to see the world from each of their points of view? The great majority of us could not *listen;* we would find ourselves compelled to *evaluate,* because listening would seem too dangerous. So the first requirement is courage, and we do not always have it.

Heightened Emotions. But there is a second obstacle. It is just when emotions are strongest that it is most difficult to achieve the frame of reference of the other person or group. Yet it is then the attitude is most needed if communication is to be established. We have not found this to be an insuperable obstacle in our experience in psychotherapy. A third party, who is able to lay aside his own feelings and evaluations, can assist greatly by listening with understanding to each person or group and clarifying the views and attitudes each holds.

We have found this effective in small groups in which contradictory or antagonistic attitudes exist. When the parties to a dispute realize that they are being understood, that someone sees how the situation seems to them, the statements grow less exaggerated and less defensive, and it is no longer necessary to maintain the attitude, "I am 100% right and you are 100% wrong." The influence of such an understanding catalyst in the group permits the members to come closer and closer to the objective truth involved in the relationship. In this way mutual communication is established, and some type of agreement becomes more possible.

So we may say that though heightened emotions make it much more difficult to understand *with* an opponent, our experience makes it clear that a neutral, understanding catalyst type of leader or therapist can overcome this obstacle in a small group.

Size of Group. That last phrase, however, suggests another obstacle to utilizing the approach I have described. Thus far all our experience has been with small face-to-face groups—groups exhibiting industrial tensions, religious tensions, racial tensions, and therapy groups in which many personal tensions are present. In these small groups our experience, confirmed by a limited amount of research, shows that this basic approach lead to improved communication, to greater acceptance of others by others, and to attitudes which are more positive and more problem-solving in nature. There is a decrease in defensiveness, in exaggerated statements, in evaluative and critical behavior.

But these findings are from small groups. What about trying to achieve understanding between larger groups that are geographically remote, or between face-to-face groups that are not speaking for themselves but simply as representatives of others? Frankly, we do not know the answers to these questions. I believe the situation might be put this way: As social scientists we have a tentative test-tube solution of the problem in the breakdown in communication. But to confirm the validity of this test-tube solution and to adapt it to the enormous problems of communication breakdown between classes, groups, and nations would involve additional funds, much more research, and creative thinking of a high order.

Yet with our present limited knowledge we can see some steps which might be taken even in large groups to increase the amount of listening *with* and decrease the amount of evaluation *about*. To be imaginative for a moment, let us suppose that a therapeutically oriented international group went to Russian leaders [during the cold war] and said, "We want to achieve a genuine understanding of your views and, even more important, of your attitudes and feelings toward the United States. We will summarize and resummarize these views and feelings if necessary until you agree that our description represents the situation as it seems to you."

Then suppose they did the same thing with the leaders in our own country. If they then gave the widest possible distribution to these two views, with the feelings clearly described but not expressed in name-calling, might not the effect be very great? It would not guarantee the type of understanding I have been describing, but it would make it much more possible. We can understand the feelings of a person who hates us much more readily when his attitudes are accurately described to us by a neutral third party than we can when he is shaking his fist at us.

Faith in Social Sciences. But even to describe such a first step is to suggest another obstacle to this approach of understanding. Our civilization does not yet have enough faith in the social sciences to utilize their findings. The opposite is true of the physical sciences. During the war [WWII] a test-tube solution was found to the problem of synthetic rubber, millions of dollars and an army of talent were turned loose on the problem of using that finding. If synthetic rubber could be made in milligrams, it could and would be made in the thousands of tons. And it was. But in the social science realm, if a way is found of facilitating communication and mutual understanding in small groups, there is no guarantee that the finding will be utilized. It may be a generation or more before the money and the brains will be turned loose to exploit that finding.

Summary

In closing, I should like to summarize this small-scale solution to the problem of barriers in communication, and to point out certain of its characteristics.

I have said that our research and experience to date would make it appear that breakdowns in communication, and the evaluative tendency which is the major barrier to communication, can be avoided. The solution is provided by creating a situation in which each of the different parties comes to understand the other from the *other's* point of view. This has been achieved, in practice, even when feelings run high, by the influence of a person who is willing to understand each point of view empathically, and who thus acts as a catalyst to precipitate further understand.

The procedure has important characteristics. It can be initiated by one party, without waiting for the other to be ready. It can be initiated by a neutral third person, provided he can gain a minimum of cooperation from one of the parties.

This procedure can deal with the insincerities, the defensive exaggerations, the lies, the "false fronts" which characterize almost every failure in communication. These defensive distortions drop away with astonishing speed as people find that the only intent is to understand, not to judge.

This approach leads steadily and rapidly toward the discovery of the truth, toward a realistic appraisal of the objective barriers to communication. The dropping of some defensiveness by one party leads to further dropping of defensiveness by the other party, and truth is thus approached.

This procedure gradually achieves mutual communication. Mutual communication tends to be pointed toward solving a problem rather than toward attacking a person or group. It leads to a situation in which I see how the problem appears to you as well as to me, and you see how it appears to me as well as to you. Thus accurately and realistically defined, the problem is almost certain to yield to intelligent attack, or if it is in part insoluble, it will be comfortably accepted as such.

This then appears to be a test-tube solution to the breakdown of communication as it occurs in small groups. Can we take this small-scale answer, investigate it further, refine it, develop it, and apply it to the tragic and well-nigh fatal failures of communication which threaten the very existence of our modern world? It seems to me that this a possibility and a challenge which we should explore.

---

[1] Reprinted by permission of Harvard Business Review. "Barriers and Gateways to Communication" by Carl C. Rogers and F. J. Roethlisberger (July–August 1952, November–December, 1991) Copyright © 1952, 1991 by the President and Fellows of Harvard College; all rights reserved.

Appendix B: Samples of Reading Problems and Solutions

Following are samples from various college reading assignments. First, do the "assignment" using whatever approach you think will work. Then look at the transcript of another student's response. Each transcript is an edited version of a student's out-loud attempt to figure out the passage. Is your approach more effective or less?

Naturally, there can be many approaches, depending on background and ingenuity, some shorter and some longer. Compare your approach with that in the transcript and see if any new possibilities emerge.

If the passage is easy for you, skip the transcript.

Sample One

Find the author's point. In other words, where *does* he live?

Where I Live

"Where do you live?" he asked. With a sudden shock I realized that this was a problem I had been confusedly thinking about for years. "Where do you live?" I handed him a card. But, needless to say, my address was not the answer to the riddle. . . .

It wasn't a question of streets or cities, not even of countries or continents; it was a question of universes. . . .

For what we are, what we know or think we know we are, determines where we live. Home, in a word, is homemade. Out of the raw material of given experience each of us constructs his own particular universe. . . .

For the great majority of animals, the most conspicuous features of every human universe are simply not there. Sun, moon, stars, the sea and the dry land, all the wealth of vegetation and the countless things that swim, crawl, fly and run—the worlds in which all but a very few species live, contain nothing that remotely resembles such objects. . . .

The nature of any island universe depends on the nature of the individual inhabiting it. . . .

All human worlds are more brightly colored than those inhabited by dogs. But not so deliciously smelly. All human worlds contain much greater extensions of space than does the world of the bees. To make up for this, the bees' world contains things which exist in no human world, such as two kinds of light, polarized and unpolarized, and objects whose color is ultraviolet. . . .

—Aldous Huxley, from "Where I Live," first published in *Esquire.*

Transcript of an Approach

Let's see. Six short paragraphs. It will likely take less than a minute to read, probably less then five or six to master. Browsing, I see from paragraph two he's not talking about addresses. Okay, what? I see this is an excerpt from a longer article. Starts in the middle. Browsing still, I see references to other animals and separate universes. I'm beginning to get the idea that he plans to change or extend what is meant by where one lives. Okay. So it's a new definition, then. I'll zip through now and see what he means. Okay. The first two paragraphs tell what he doesn't mean. He doesn't mean physical location on the earth. What, then?

Oh, here it is in paragraph three. Where we live (he's not just talking about himself but everyone) is where our consciousness says we do. We build "where we live" from our biological bodies and from our experiences.

That's not too clear. Oh, here in paragraph four he gives some examples. Humans, he says, by our physical nature, are able to experience other worlds, even though we might be in the same spot physically. It's getting clearer. I wish he'd give me something more definite. Okay, in the last paragraph he gives examples from dogs and bees, things humans experience and they can't, and vice versa.

All right, I think I have it now. I'll see if I can put it in my own words:

"In the broader sense, my feeling of "home" (or my world) is determined by what my body and mind are able to sense and organize. All species have different sensors, so all have different "worlds" or "homes." In fact, even in the same species no two individuals can experience the same "home."

Can I supply an example of my own? Well, a bird must experience an airiness I could never grasp, but a bird can't imagine what riding a bicycle is like (big deal). Each student in a class has an entirely different data bank (home) from every other one.

Now I'll go back and underline something that will serve as the gist for review. Okay, I underline It's a question of universes and the dog example. That should be plenty trigger recall later. Hmm, just the dog example would do it!

I'll read through quickly and see if it's really clear now. It is.

Notice that the reader has one problem to begin with: to get the author's point. But he redefines it as he gets familiar with the passage: to find a new meaning of "where I live." Then he reads fast for that one thing. When he thinks he has it, he puts it in his own words, marks the key idea and then verifies it by a quickly rereading. In print, the process takes about 450 words, but people don't think in complete sentences. The reading and analysis could easily be done in a minute or two.

Hmm, rereading, I got to thinking. "Why did he write this in the first place?" I think his real purpose was to celebrate or rejoice in the fact of unique worlds, the wonder of each creature being so different. He wants to share his enthusiasm about these universes. Since I "got the message," my island universe has a new dimension.

Notice that the reader goes one step further and wonders, So what? Most school assignments do not required this step. That is a pity; for in truth it is only at this stage that education begins. This is where the joy comes in: Getting the feel of other worlds and expanding and enriching one's own.

Sample Two

Find Aristotle's main idea.

For many readers, the problem in this passage is the style. Try getting it into your own language. Once you have it figured out, compare your approach with that of the transcript.

> We must be content, then, in speaking of such subjects and with such premises to indicate the truth roughly and in outline, and in speaking about things which are only for the most part true and with premises of the same kind to reach conclusions which are no better. In this spirit, therefore, should each type of statement be received; for it is the mark of an educated man to look for precision in each class of things just so far as the nature of the subject admits; it is evidently equally foolish to accept probable reasoning from a mathematician and to demand from a rhetorician scientific proofs.
>
> —Aristotle

Transcription

Browsing, I see it's very short. What are premises? What's a rhetorician? Browsing, I can see sentence style is my main problem. If this were my own way of saying things, I might be able to understand it. It's so short I think I'll read through it quickly.

That didn't help much. For one thing the first sentence is awfully long and it's general. There aren't any images for me to hang on to. Okay, I'll skip it for a moment. It looks like the second sentence is just another way of saying the first. All right, here at the end is a reference to mathematicians. I'll work on that. At least it's concrete. Cutting out the extra words. I get "It is . . . foolish to accept probable reasoning from a mathematician." All right, that I grasp. We expect the mathematician to be precise and exact. No guessing. Okay. He also says it's just as foolish, "equally" foolish, to expect a rhetorician to give scientific proofs. Swell. What's a rhetorician? Guess I'll have to deduce that to figure this thing out.

Probably he's something like the opposite of a mathematician, someone who doesn't pretend to deal in exact, precise, provable things. Maybe like a philosopher. Oh, I remember, rhetoric. I ran into that in English. Something to do with style, giving speeches. Ah: what you do to persuade people. You expect a speaker to get at the feel of an idea, not the precise proof of it. Now back to the sentence.

We should expect precise stuff from the mathematician and we should expect probable stuff from the orator. Okay. Now let's see what the rest of the sentence says. ". . . look for precision . . . just so far as the nature of the subject admits [allows]." If it's poetry, expect one kind of thinking; if it's statistics, expect another kind. Don't mix them. So an educated person won't expect more or less than the nature of the thing calls for.

Now let's go back to the first sentence. I see now that this is an excerpt and can only guess what the first part of the sentence refers to. What's a premise? Must be what comes before you get a conclusion, probably something like assumptions or arguments. Looks like the second half is another way of saying the first half. So, if something is mostly true, it doesn't mean it's always true. What's an example? Well, if I'm exposed to typhoid, you have to say I'll probably get sick. Now let's see if I can put it is my own words:

"For certain subjects I can only make general comments. I shouldn't draw more from the evidence than is justified. (I may not know enough.) Everything one hears should be checked in this manner. Educated people expect only as much precision as the original conditions make possible. It's foolish to expect a math teacher to talk like a speech teacher, and *vice versa.*"

The thinking transcribed above goes much quicker than it might appear, and steps are skipped if not needed. For most readers the idea itself isn't hard. Getting used to the style is. But once we play with it a while, it is rather charming. So fool around with it, grab on to something and work out from there. When the whole thing seems hopeless, get meaning from some simplified smaller part. Then move the more complicated whole.

Sample Three

What is the author's main point?

> The only subject presented to me for study is the content of my consciousness. You are able to communicate to me part of the content of your consciousness which thereby becomes accessible to my own. For reasons which are generally admitted, though I should not like to have to prove that they are conclusive, I grant your consciousness equal status with my own; and I use this second-hand part of my consciousness to "put myself in your place." Accordingly my subject of study becomes differentiated into the contents of many consciousness, each content constituting a view point. Then there arises the problem of combining the viewpoints. . . .
>
> —A. S. Eddington

Transcription (Abridged)

The sentences are clear and straightforward enough. And the vocabulary isn't too bad. I guess I just have to stop after each one, Let it sink in, and build to understanding that way.

I know right away what the main idea is. It's in the first sentence, but I don't yet understand it. Let's see. In my own words it's saying, "Things have to be in my head before I can think about them." Okay so far.

Next sentence translates: "Somehow part of what is in your head gets into mine, and I can think about that, too." Oh, I see. What I'm doing is rephrasing as I go along sort of writing my own understandable version.

Third sentence: "I have to act as though what is in your head is just as good as what is in mine. I'm willing accept that, but I'd hate to have to try to prove it. Anyway, once I accept it, I can think as you would in your place." (Walk a mile in your moccasins?) Gee, only two sentences to go.

Next to last: "All right. So I take what I get from you and also from all sorts of people. I have many consciousnesses in my head, then, to think about. Each one has a particular slant on things."

Last: How can I get them all fitted together? In my own words:

"The point is that I can only think about what is in my own head, but much of that comes from other people's legitimate views (somehow) and I have to fit them all together somehow."

The problem here, then, is to get the passage into the reader's own words. Once that is accomplished, it isn't hard to understand. The reader just thinks and rephrases as he goes along. As soon as he realizes what he needs to do, he goes about it purposefully.

Sample Four

How *do* you eat a giviak?

How to Eat a Giviak

Now it was winter, and Angutidluarssuk's giviak was frozen. He took his ax and started chopping up the icy stuff. Pink feathers and bird meat flew to all sides, while we watched in pious silence. At last the floor was completely covered with pieces of meat and blubber. Angutidluarssuk picked up a bite, tasted it, and threw it contemptuously away.

"Alas, as I told you: this is inedible. Possibly I have, through an oversight, filled the skin with dog's dung. Possible it is only my absolute ignorance about how to make a giviak that has caused this mistake! If you would show me this kindness, you would leave me now so that I could be alone with my shame!"

Upon this invitation, we started in. It tasted good the moment I got it in my mouth. But I had to be taught how to eat this remarkable dish. As long as it is frozen, you just chew away. You get feathers and bones in your mouth, of course, but you just spit them out. frozen meat always has an enticing taste, and as it dissolves in the mouth, you get the full aroma of the raw fermented bird. It is incredible how much you can down, unbelievable how hard it is to stop. If you happen to come across a fully developed egg inside a bird it tastes like a dream. Or the liver, which is like green cheese. Breast and drumsticks are cooling and refreshing. It was late before we were full, and there was then about half of the giviak left. This was put up on one of the bunks to thaw for later use.

When we had had some sleep, we started the second part of the feast. The giviak was now so much thawed that the little auks tasted entirely different, and it was possible to eat them in a new way. Whole birds could now be pried loose from the compressed mass, and when that is the case, great elegance can be demonstrated while enjoying them. A man with *savior-vivre* holds the bird by the legs with his teeth. Then he strokes it with both hands, thus brushing off the feathers that have already been loosened by the fermentation. He brushes his hands together to remove all feathers, whereupon he turns the bird and bites the skin loose around the beak. this can then be turned inside out and pulled free of the bird without letting go of the legs. The eater then sucks the whole skin into his mouth and pulls it out again, pressing his teeth slightly together. In this manner, he gets all the delicious fat sitting inside the skin. Taste is, as we know, an individual matter, but this one, I dare guarantee—can become a passion.

When the skin is free of fat, you bite it free around the bird's legs and swallow it in one piece. The breast is eaten by biting down on each side of the bone, and the bone can then be thrown away. This bares the innards, and you can enjoy the various parts one by one. The blood clot around the heart has coagulated and glues the teeth together, the liver and gall bladder have a spicy taste, while the bitter aroma of the intestines reminds one of lager beer. When these parts are consumed, the rest—wings, backbone, and pelvis—is taken into the mouth and thoroughly chewed.

Such delicacies were always served in Angutidluarssuck's house.

From *Peter Freuchen's Book of the Eskimos*

Snags

Some readers get sidetracked on what *giviak* means. The "assignment" is to find out how to eat one, not to say what one is. Some readers impose their own taste and decide the meal is gruesome. The author thinks it is delicious, but readers totally ignore that and don't give him a chance. The task is to find out how to eat it, not to pass judgment. To read accurately, first see it as the author sees it. (In *any* communication, first see the message from the *sender's* viewpoint.) Then go ahead and vomit if you still want to.

The real reading problem in "How to Eat a Giviak" is in *visualizing* the process. It is the same one for reading how to bake a cake or for how to install a CD-ROM drive. Zip through once to get an overview. Here, there are two major parts: when it is frozen and when it is thawed. Imagine going through each step. Try to "see" yourself doing it. You have understood the process when you can describe the steps in your own words. Of course, the best way to check your understanding is to install the drive, bake the cake, or eat the giviak.

This writer has never been able to visualize exactly what is done when the eater "bites the skin loose around the beak," and then turns it inside out and pulls it free without letting go of the legs. Thus, though he may know a great deal about how to eat a giviak, he can't say he knows how completely.

Incidentally, even though it is not part of the "assignment," it is possible to get a fairly good idea of *what* a giviak is from the context (the surrounding words). You can see that it is some kind of skin, filled not with dog's dung but with birds, feathers and all. The birds are small, are called auks, and are fermented. The kind of skin is not mentioned, but *blubber* suggests a seal skin, and indeed it is. The auks are caught in nets and killed by pressing the thumb against the rib cage, stopping the heart (hence, the blood clot around the heart). The skin is filled with auks and left to ferment in the shade during summer.

> "Now I can see what browsing does for you. It lets the mind open itself to receive data, get itself formatted, but in a comfortable, nonstressful way. It isn't overwhelming. Then, a

bit later when the mind has got itself used to the way the information is coming across, you can read through smoothly. You are primed for it."

—A student

Suggested Reading

Amabile, Teresa. *Growing Up Creative.* Crown Publishers, New York, 1989.

Bloom, Benjamin S. "Learning for Mastery," UCLA-CSEJP, *Evaluation Comment*, 1, number 2, 1968.

Brandt, Anthony. "The School Where Everyone Gets A's" *Family Circle.* March 17, 1981.

Encyclopedia of Education Research. Alkin, Marvin C., editor. Maxwell Macmillan, New York, 1992.

Glaser, Robert. "Ten Untenable Assumptions of College Instruction," *Educational Record.* Spring 1968.

Hilgard, Ernest R. "Learning Theory and Its Applications," *New Techniques Aids for the American Classroom.* Standord University, Institute for Communication Research, 1960.

Hoffmann, Banesh. *The Tyranny of Testing.* Collier, New York, 1962. Greenwood, New York, 1978.

Houts, Paul L., editor. *The Myth of Measurability.* Hart Publishing Company, New York, 1977.

Jennings, Wayne, and Joe Nathan. "Startling/Disturbing Research on School Program Effectiveness," *Phi Delta Kappan.* March 1977.

John Dewey on Education, Selected Writings. Archambault, Reginald D., ed. Random House, New York, 1964.

Owen, David. *None of the Above.* Houghton-Mifflin, Boston, 1985.

Selye, Hans, and Laurence Cherry. "Straight Talk About Stress," *Psychology Today.* March 1978.

Time-Use Chart			
	MONDAY	TUESDAY	WEDNEDAY
8:00			
9:00			
10:00			
11:00			
12:00			
1:00			
2:00			
3:00			
4:00			
5:00			
6:00			
7:00			
8:00			
9:00			
10:00			

Include book title or subject, number of pages read, amount of time, and where you studied. Abbreviate.

THURSDAY	FRIDAY	SATURDAY	SUNDAY

About the Author

Clark McKowen taught English at Diablo Valley College in Pleasant Hill, California, for more than 30 years. He is now a full-time writer of books and articles about teaching and learning.

Get Your A Out of College is one of five textbooks he has published: two freshman English books with Macmillan (*Image, Reflections on Language* and *Montage, Investigations in Language,* with William Sparke); a film book with Prentice-Hall (*It's Only a Movie,* with William Sparke); and *Thinking About Thinking* with William Kaufmann, Inc. A number of McKowen's articles about education have appeared in magazines and professional journals.

This revision of *Get Your A Out of College* benefits from more than 40 years of working with students from kindergarten through graduate school, from inner cities to Heidelberg. Mr. McKowen has been department chairman at the high-school and college levels and has lectured and conducted seminars and workshops on education at schools and colleges throughout the United States.

This book is completely updated. The concept is streamlined and a uniform approach is employed in every chapter. Every sentence is rewritten for a smoother, more conversational style. A new chapter has been added on how the brain processes information, and a demonstration of the BFAR reading method is included.